**IN PROCEEDINGS BEFORE
THE UNITED STATES SENATE**

TRIAL MEMORANDUM OF PRESIDENT DONALD J. TRUMP

Jay Alan Sekulow
Stuart Roth
Andrew Ekonomou
Jordan Sekulow
Mark Goldfeder
Benjamin Sisney

Counsel to President Donald J. Trump

Pat A. Cipollone
   Counsel to the President
Patrick F. Philbin
Michael M. Purpura
Devin A. DeBacker
Trent J. Benishek
Eric J. Hamilton

Office of White House Counsel

January 20, 2020

TABLE OF CONTENTS

EXECUTIVE SUMMARY

The Articles of Impeachment now before the Senate are an affront to the Constitution and to our democratic institutions. The Articles themselves—and the rigged process that brought them here—are a brazenly political act by House Democrats that must be rejected. They debase the grave power of impeachment and disdain the solemn responsibility that power entails. Anyone having the most basic respect for the sovereign will of the American people would shudder at the enormity of casting a vote to impeach a duly elected President. By contrast, upon tallying their votes, House Democrats jeered until they were scolded into silence by the Speaker. The process that brought the articles here violated every precedent and every principle of fairness followed in impeachment inquiries for more than 150 years. Even so, all that House Democrats have succeeded in proving is that the President did absolutely nothing wrong.

After focus-group testing various charges for weeks, House Democrats settled on two flimsy Articles of Impeachment that allege no crime or violation of law whatsoever—much less "high Crimes and Misdemeanors," as required by the Constitution. They do not remotely approach the constitutional threshold for removing a President from office. The diluted standard asserted here would permanently weaken the Presidency and forever alter the balance among the branches of government in a manner that offends the constitutional design established by the Founders. House Democrats jettisoned all precedent and principle because their impeachment inquisition was never really about discovering the truth or conducting a fair investigation. Instead, House Democrats were determined from the outset to find some way—any way—to corrupt the extraordinary power of impeachment for use as a political tool to overturn the result of the 2016 election and to interfere in the 2020 election. All of this is a dangerous perversion of the Constitution that the Senate should swiftly and roundly condemn.

I. The Articles Fail Because They Do Not Identify Any Impeachable Offense.

A. House Democrats' Theory of "Abuse of Power" Is Not an Impeachable Offense.

House Democrats' novel theory of "abuse of power" improperly supplants the standard of "high Crimes and Misdemeanors" with a made-up theory that would permanently weaken the Presidency by effectively permitting impeachments based merely on policy disagreements.

1.   By limiting impeachment to cases of "Treason, Bribery, or other high Crimes and Misdemeanors,"[1] the Framers restricted impeachment to specific offenses against "already known and established law."[2] That was a deliberate choice designed to constrain the impeachment power. In keeping with that restriction, every prior presidential impeachment in our history has been based on alleged violations of existing law—indeed, criminal law.[3] House Democrats' newly invented

---

[1]   U.S. Const. art. II, § 4.

[2]   4 William Blackstone, *Commentaries on the Laws of England* *256.

[3]   *See Impeachment Inquiry into President Donald J. Trump: Constitutional Grounds for Presidential Impeachment Before the H.R. Comm. on the Judiciary*, 116th Cong. (2019) (written statement of Professor Jonathan Turley, Geo. Wash. Univ. Law Sch., at 15, https://perma.cc/QU4H-FZC4); H.R. Res. 611, 106th Cong. (1998); H.R. Comm. on the Judiciary, *Impeachment of William Jefferson Clinton, President of the United States*, H.R. Rep. No. 105-830, 105th Cong. 143 (1998) (additional views of Rep. Bill McCollum); H.R. Comm. on the Judiciary, *Impeachment of Richard M. Nixon, President of the United States*, H.R. Rep. No. 93-1305, 93d Cong. 1–3 (1974).

"abuse of power" theory collapses at the threshold because it fails to allege any violation of law whatsoever.

2.   House Democrats' concocted theory that the President can be impeached for taking permissible actions if he does them for what they believe to be the ***wrong reasons*** would also expand the impeachment power beyond constitutional bounds. It would allow a hostile House to attack almost any presidential action by challenging a President's subjective motives. Worse, House Democrats' methods for identifying supposedly illicit motives ignore the constitutional structure of our government. As proof of improper motive, they claim that the President supposedly "disregarded United States foreign policy towards Ukraine,"[4] that he was "briefed on official policy"[5] but chose to ignore it, and that he "ignored, defied, and confounded every office and agency within the Executive Branch."[6] These assertions are preposterous and dangerous. They misunderstand the assignment of power under the Constitution and the very concept of democratic accountability. Article II states that "[t]he executive Power shall be vested in a President."[7] It is the President who defines foreign policy, not the unelected bureaucrats who are his subordinates. Any theory of an impeachable offense that turns on ferreting out supposedly "constitutionally improper"[8] motives by measuring the President's policy decisions against a purported interagency consensus[9] is both fundamentally anti-democratic and an absurdly impermissible inversion of the constitutional structure.

B.   House Democrats' Theory of "Obstruction of Congress" Is Not an Impeachable Offense.

House Democrats' "obstruction of Congress" claim is frivolous and dangerous. House Democrats propose removing the President from office because he asserted legal rights and privileges of the Executive Branch against defective subpoenas—based on advice from the Department of Justice. Accepting that theory would do lasting damage to the separation of powers.

1.   President Trump Properly Asserted Executive Branch Prerogatives.

Contrary to the mistaken charge that the President lacked "lawful cause or excuse" to resist House Democrats' subpoenas,[10] the President acted only after securing advice from the Department of Justice's Office of Legal Counsel (OLC) and based on established legal principles or immunities.

a.   Several Executive Branch officials refused to comply with subpoenas purportedly issued pursuant to an "impeachment inquiry" before the House had authorized any such inquiry, because, as OLC advised, the subpoenas were unauthorized and had no legal force.[11]

---

[4]   H.R. Comm. on the Judiciary, *Impeachment of Donald J. Trump, President of the United States*, H.R. Rep. No. 116-346, 116th Cong. 99 (2019) (HJC Report).

[5]   *Id.*

[6]   *Id.* at 103; *see also* Trial Mem. of the U.S. House of Representatives at 4.

[7]   U.S. Const. art. II, § 1.

[8]   HJC Report at 101.

[9]   *See id.* at 102.

[10]   H.R. Res. 755, 116th Cong. art. II (2019).

[11]   This advice was memorialized in a written opinion on January 19, 2020, which is attached as Appendix C. *See* Memorandum from Steven A. Engel, Assistant Attorney General, Office of Legal Counsel, to Pat A. Cipollone,

b.   The President directed three of his most senior advisers not to comply with subpoenas seeking their testimony because they are immune from compelled testimony before Congress. Through administrations of both political parties, OLC "has repeatedly provided for nearly five decades" that "Congress may not constitutionally compel the President's senior advisers to testify about their official duties."[12] In the Clinton administration, for example, Attorney General Janet Reno explained that "the immunity such [immediate] advisers enjoy from testimonial compulsion by a congressional committee *is absolute* and may not be overborne by competing congressional interests."[13]

c.   Under the President's supervision, Executive Branch officials were directed not to comply with subpoenas because the committees seeking their testimony refused to allow them to be accompanied by agency counsel. OLC concluded that the committees "may not bar agency counsel from assisting an executive branch witness without contravening the legitimate prerogatives of the Executive Branch," and that attempting to enforce a subpoena while barring agency counsel "would be unconstitutional."[14]

2.   Defending the Separation of Powers Is Not an Impeachable Offense.

Contrary to House Democrats' claims, asserting legal rights and constitutional privileges of the Executive Branch is not "obstruction."

a.   In a government of laws, asserting legal defenses cannot be treated as obstruction; it is a fundamental right. As the Supreme Court has instructed: "[F]or an agent of the State to pursue a course of action whose objective is to penalize a person's reliance on his legal rights is 'patently unconstitutional.'"[15] The same principles apply in impeachment. During the Clinton impeachment, Harvard Law Professor Laurence Tribe put it this way:

> The allegations that invoking privileges and otherwise using the judicial system to shield information . . . is an abuse of power that should lead to impeachment and removal from office is not only frivolous, but also dangerous.[16]

In 1998, now-Chairman Jerrold Nadler agreed that a president *cannot* be impeached for asserting a legal privilege: "[T]he use of a legal privilege is not illegal or impeachable by itself, a legal privilege, executive privilege."[17] And Chairman Adam Schiff has turned the law on its head with

---

Counsel to the President, *Re: House Committees' Authority to Investigate for Impeachment*, at 1 (Jan. 19, 2020) (*Impeachment Inquiry Authorization*).

[12]   *Testimonial Immunity Before Congress of the Former Counsel to the President*, 43 Op. O.L.C. __, *1 (May 20, 2019); *see also infra* note 296 (collecting prior opinions).

[13]   *See Assertion of Executive Privilege with Respect to Clemency Decision*, 23 Op. O.L.C. 1, 5 (1999) (emphasis added).

[14]   *Exclusion of Agency Counsel from Congressional Depositions in the Impeachment Context*, 43 Op. O.L.C. __, at *4 (Nov. 1, 2019).

[15]   *Bordenkircher v. Hayes*, 434 U.S. 357, 363 (1978) (citations omitted); *see also, e.g., United States v. Goodwin*, 357 U.S. 368, 372 (1982) ("For while an individual certainly may be penalized for violating the law, he just as certainly may not be punished for exercising a protected statutory or constitutional right.").

[16]   Harvey Berkman, *Top Profs: Not Enough to Impeach*, The National Law J. (Oct. 5, 1998) (quoting Professor Tribe), *reprinted in* 144 Cong. Rec. H10031 (1998).

[17]   H.R. Comm. on the Judiciary, 105th Cong., Ser. No. 18, Impeachment Inquiry: William Jefferson Clinton,

his unprecedented claim that it is "obstruction" for any official to assert rights that might prompt House committees even *"to consider* litigation" to establish the validity of their subpoenas in court.[18]

    b.   Where, as here, the principles the President invoked are critical for preserving Executive Branch prerogatives, treating the assertion of privileges as "obstruction" would do permanent damage to the separation of powers—among all three branches. House Democrats have essentially announced that they may treat any resistance to their demands as "obstruction" without taking *any* steps to resolve their dispute with the President. Accepting that unprecedented approach would fundamentally damage the separation of powers by making the House itself the sole judge of its authority. It would permit Congress to threaten *every* President with impeachment merely for protecting the prerogatives of the Presidency. As Professor Jonathan Turley testified before the House Judiciary Committee: "Basing impeachment on this obstruction theory would itself be an abuse of power . . . *by Congress*."[19]

    c.   At bottom, the "obstruction" charge asks the Senate to remove a duly elected President from office because he acted on the advice of the Department of Justice concerning his legal and constitutional rights as President. Stating that proposition exposes it as frivolous. The Framers restricted impeachment to reach only egregious conduct that endangers the Constitution. A difference of legal opinion over whether subpoenas are enforceable cannot be dressed up to approach that level. As Edmund Randolph explained in the Virginia ratifying convention, "No man ever thought of impeaching a man for an opinion."[20]

II.   The Impeachment Inquiry in the House Was Irredeemably Flawed.

A.   House Democrats' Inquiry Violated All Precedent and Due Process.

    1.   The process that resulted in these Articles of Impeachment was flawed from the start. Since the Founding of the Republic, the House has never launched an impeachment inquiry against a President without a vote of the full House authorizing it. And there is good reason for that. No committee can investigate pursuant to powers assigned by the Constitution to the House— including the "sole Power of Impeachment"[21]—unless the House has voted to delegate authority to the committee.[22] Here, it was emblematic of the lack of seriousness that characterized this whole process that House Democrats cast law and history aside and started their purported inquiry with nothing more than a press conference.[23] On that authority alone, they issued nearly two dozen

---

President of the United States, Consideration of Articles of Impeachment 398 (Comm. Print 1998).

[18]   *See* Transcript of Pelosi Weekly Press Conference Today (Oct. 2, 2019) (statement of Rep. Adam Schiff), https://perma.cc/RM2N-F2RC.

[19]   Turley Written Statement, *supra* note 3, at 42 (emphasis added) (ellipsis in original).

[20]   3 *The Debates in the Several State Conventions, on the Adoption of the Federal Constitution, as Recommended by the General Convention at Philadelphia, in 1787*, 401 (J. Elliot ed. 1836).

[21]   U.S. Const. art. I, § 2, cl. 5.

[22]   *Watkins v. United States*, 354 U.S. 178, 200–10 (1957); *see also United States v. Rumely*, 345 U.S. 41, 42–43 (1953); *Exxon Corp. v. FTC*, 589 F.2d 582, 592 (D.C. Cir. 1978) ("To issue a valid subpoena, . . . a committee or subcommittee must conform strictly to the resolution establishing its investigatory powers . . . ."); *Tobin v. United States*, 306 F.2d 270, 275 (D.C. Cir. 1962) ("[T]he first issue we must decide is whether Congress gave the Judiciary Committee . . . authority . . . to conduct the sweeping investigation undertaken in this case.").

[23]   Speaker Pelosi Announcement of Impeachment Inquiry, C-SPAN (Sept. 24, 2019), https://www.c-span.org/video/?464684-1/speaker-pelosi-announces-formal-impeachment-inquiry-president-trump.

subpoenas that OLC determined were unauthorized and invalid.[24] The full House did not vote to authorize the inquiry until five weeks later when it adopted House Resolution 660 on October 31, 2019. That belated action was a telling admission that the process was unauthorized.

2.   Next, House Democrats concocted an unheard of procedure that denied the President any semblance of fair process. The proceedings began with secret hearings in a basement bunker before three committees under the direction of Chairman Schiff of the House Permanent Select Committee on Intelligence (HPSCI). The President was denied any right to participate at all. He was denied the right to have counsel present, to cross examine witnesses, to call witnesses, and to see and present evidence. Meanwhile, House Democrats selectively leaked distorted versions of the secret testimony to compliant members of the press, who happily fed the public a false narrative about the President.

Then, House Democrats moved on to a true show trial as they brought their hand-picked witnesses, whose testimony had already been set in private, before the cameras to present pre-screened testimony to the public. There, before HPSCI, they continued to deny the President any rights. He could not be represented by counsel, could not present evidence or witnesses, and could not cross examine witnesses.

This process not only violated every precedent from the Nixon and Clinton impeachment inquiries, it violated every principle of justice and fairness known to our legal tradition. For more than 250 years, the common law system has regarded cross-examination as the "greatest legal engine ever invented for the discovery of truth."[25] House Democrats denied the President that right and every other right because they were not interested in the truth. Their only interest was securing an impeachment, and they knew that a fair process could not get them there.

When the impeachment stage-show moved on to the Judiciary Committee, House Democrats again denied the President his rights. The Committee had already decided to forego fact-finding and to adopt the one-sided record from HPSCI's *ex parte* hearings. Worse, Speaker Nancy Pelosi had already instructed the Committee to draft articles of impeachment. The only role for the Committee was to ram through the articles to secure a House vote by Christmas.[26] There could not have been a more blatant admission that evidence did not matter, the process was rigged, and impeachment was a pre-ordained result.

All of this reflected shameful hypocrisy from House Democrat leaders, who for decades had insisted on the importance of due process protections in an impeachment inquiry. Chairman Nadler himself has explained that a House impeachment inquiry "demands a rigorous level of due process."[27] Specifically, he explained that "due process mean[s] . . . the right to confront the

---

[24]   *See Impeachment Inquiry Authorization, infra* Appendix C, at 1–3.

[25]   *Perry v. Leeke*, 488 U.S. 272, 283 n.7 (1989) (quoting 5 J. Wigmore, *Evidence* § 1367 (J. Chadbourn ed. 1974)).

[26]   *See, e.g.*, Andrew Prokop, *Why Democrats Are Moving So Fast on Impeachment*, Vox (Dec. 5, 2019), https://perma.cc/H7BR-HNC4 ("House leaders have signaled they hope to wrap up proceedings in their chamber before Congress leaves for the December holidays. . . . 'Wouldn't that be a great Christmas gift for it to all wrap up by Christmas?' Rep. Val Demings (D-FL) asked."); Mary Clare Jalonick, *What's Next in Impeachment: A Busy December, and on to 2020*, AP News (Nov. 23, 2019), https://perma.cc/2HJH-QLMR ("Time is running short if the House is to vote on impeachment by Christmas, which Democrats privately say is the goal.").

[27]   *Examining the Allegations of Misconduct Against IRS Commissioner John Koskinen (Part II): Hearing Before the H.R. Comm. on the Judiciary*, 114th Cong. 3 (2016) (statement of Rep. Jerrold Nadler).

witnesses against you, to call your own witnesses, and to have the assistance of counsel."[28] Here, however, all due process rights were denied to the President.

3.   Chairman Schiff's hearings were fatally defective for another reason—Schiff himself was instrumental in helping to create the story behind them. This inquiry centered on the President's conversation on July 25, 2019, with the President of Ukraine. That call became a matter of public speculation after a so-called whistleblower relayed a distorted, second-hand version of the call to the Inspector General of the Intelligence Community (ICIG). Before laundering his distortions through the ICIG, the same person secretly shared his false account with Chairman Schiff's HPSCI staff and asked "for guidance."[29] After initially lying about it, Chairman Schiff was forced to admit that his staff had conferred with the so-called whistleblower before he filed his complaint. But the entirety of the role that Chairman Schiff and his staff played in orchestrating the complaint that launched this entire farce remains shrouded in secrecy to this day—Chairman Schiff himself shut down every effort to inquire into it.

4.   The denial of basic due process rights to the President is such a fundamental error infecting the House proceedings that the Senate could not possibly rely upon the corrupted House record to reach a verdict of conviction. Any such record is tainted, and any reliance on a record created through the wholesale denial of due process rights would be unconstitutional. Nor is it the Senate's role to remedy the House's errors by providing a "do-over" and developing the record itself.

B.   House Democrats' Goal Was Never to Ascertain the Truth.

House Democrats resorted to these unprecedented procedures because the goal was never to get to the truth. The goal was to impeach the President, no matter the facts.

House Democrats' impeachment crusade started *the day the President took office*. As Speaker Pelosi confirmed in December 2019, her party's quest to impeach the President had already been "going on for 22 months . . . [t]wo and a half years, actually."[30] The moment the President was sworn in, *The Washington Post* reported that partisans had launched a campaign to impeach him.[31] The current proceedings began with a complaint prepared with the assistance of a lawyer who declared in 2017 that he would use "impeachment" to effect a "coup."[32]

House Democrats originally pinned their impeachment hopes on the lie that the Trump Campaign had colluded with Russia during the 2016 election. That fixation brought the country the Mueller investigation. But after almost two years, $32 million, 2,800 subpoenas, and nearly 500 search warrants[33]—along with incalculable damage to the Nation—the Mueller investigation

---

[28] *Background and History of Impeachment: Hearing Before the Subcomm. on the Constitution of the H.R. Comm. on the Judiciary*, 105th Cong. 17 (1998) (statement of Rep. Jerrold Nadler).

[29] Alex Rogers, *Whistleblower Went to Intelligence Committee for Guidance Before Filing Complaint*, CNN (Oct. 2, 2019), https://perma.cc/5NVZ-W78H.

[30] Zack Stanton, *Pelosi: Unless We Impeach Trump, 'Say Hello to a President-King'*, Politico (Dec. 18, 2019), https://perma.cc/XLX5-XE7Z.

[31] Matea Gold, *The Campaign to Impeach President Trump Has Begun*, Wash. Post (Jan. 20, 2017), https://perma.cc/2376-PS6U.

[32] Mark S. Zaid (@MarkSZaidEsq), Twitter (Jan. 30, 2017 6:54 PM), https://perma.cc/BFV6-MKRE.

[33] Katelyn Polantz, *Mueller Investigation Cost $32 Million, Justice Department Says*, CNN (July 24, 2019),

thoroughly disproved Democrats' Russian collusion delusion. To make matters worse, we now know that the Mueller investigation (and its precursor, Crossfire Hurricane) also brought with it shocking abuses in the use of FISA orders to spy on American citizens and a major-party presidential campaign—including omissions and even outright lies to the Foreign Intelligence Surveillance Court and the fabrication of evidence by a committed partisan embedded in the FBI.

House Democrats could not tolerate the findings of the Mueller Report debunking the collusion myth. Instead, they launched hearings and issued subpoenas straining to find wrongdoing where Special Counsel Mueller and the Department of Justice had found none. And they launched new investigations, trying to rummage through the President's tax returns and pushing fishing expeditions everywhere in the hope that they might find something. No other President in history has been subjected to a comparable barrage of investigations, subpoenas, and lawsuits, all in service of an insatiable partisan desire to find some way to remove him from office.

When those proceedings went nowhere, House Democrats seized on the next vehicle that could be twisted to carry their impeachment dream: a perfectly appropriate telephone call between President Trump and the President of Ukraine. House Democrats have pursued their newly concocted charges for two reasons. First, they have been obsessed for years with overturning the 2016 election. Radical left Democrats have never been able to come to grips with losing the election, and impeachment provides them a way to nullify the judgment of the tens of millions of voters who rejected their candidate. Second, they want to use impeachment to interfere in the 2020 election. It is no accident that the Senate is being asked to consider a presidential impeachment during an election year. Put simply, Democrats have no response to the President's record of achievement in restoring prosperity to the American economy, rebuilding America's military, and confronting America's adversaries abroad. Instead, they are held hostage by a radical left wing that has foisted on their party an agenda of socialism at home and appeasement abroad that Democrat leaders know the American people will never accept. For the Democrats, impeachment became an electoral imperative. Congressman Al Green summarized that thinking best: "[I]f we don't impeach the [P]resident, he will get re-elected."[34] In their scorched-earth campaign against the President, House Democrats view impeachment merely as the continuation of politics by other means.

The result of House Democrats' pursuit of their obsessions—and their willingness to sacrifice every precedent and every principle standing in their way—is exactly what the Framers warned against: a wholly partisan impeachment. These articles were adopted without a single Republican vote. Indeed, there was bipartisan *opposition* to them.[35]

Democrats used to recognize that the momentous act of overturning a national election by impeaching a President should never be done on a partisan basis. As Chairman Nadler explained:

---

https://perma.cc/DX6K-58Y3; Special Counsel Robert S. Mueller, III, *Report on the Investigation into Russian Interference in the 2016 Presidential Election*, vol. I at 13 (Mar. 2019), https://perma.cc/EGB4-WA76.

[34] Rebecca Shabad and Alex Moe, *Impeachment Inquiry Ramps up as Judiciary Panel Adopts Procedural Guidelines*, NBC News (Sept. 12, 2019), https://perma.cc/4H7N-6ZPD.

[35] *See* Clerk, H.R., Final Vote Results for Roll Call 695 on Agreeing to Article I of the Resolution (Dec. 18, 2019), http://clerk.house.gov/evs/2019/roll695.xml; Clerk, H.R., Final Vote Results for Roll Call 696 on Agreeing to Article II of the Resolution (Dec. 18, 2019), http://clerk.house.gov/evs/2019/roll696.xml.

There must never be a narrowly voted impeachment or an impeachment supported by one of our major political parties and opposed by another. Such an impeachment will produce divisiveness and bitterness in our politics for years to come, and will call into question the very legitimacy of our political institutions.[36]

Senator Patrick Leahy agreed: "A partisan impeachment cannot command the respect of the American people. It is no more valid than a stolen election."[37] Chairman Nadler, again, acknowledged that merely "hav[ing] the votes" and "hav[ing] the muscle" in the House, without "the legitimacy of a national consensus," is just an attempted "partisan coup d'etat."[38] Just last year, even Speaker Pelosi acknowledged that an impeachment "would have to be so clearly bipartisan in terms of acceptance of it."[39] All of these prior invocations of principle have now been abandoned, adding to the wreckage littering the wake of House Democrats' impeach-at-all-costs strategy.

III. Article I Fails Because House Democrats Have No Evidence to Support Their Claims.

A. The Evidence Shows That the President Did Not Condition Security Assistance or a Presidential Meeting on Announcements of Any Investigations.

House Democrats have falsely charged that the President supposedly conditioned military aid or a presidential meeting on Ukraine's announcing a specific investigation. Yet despite running an entirely *ex parte*, one-sided process to gather evidence, House Democrats do not have a ***single witness*** who claims, based on direct knowledge, that the President ever actually imposed such a condition. Several undisputed, core facts make clear that House Democrats' charges are baseless.

1. In an unprecedented display of transparency, the President released the transcript of his July 25 call with President Volodymyr Zelenskyy, and it shows that the President did nothing wrong. The Department of Justice reviewed the transcript months ago and rejected the suggestion by the ICIG (based on the whistleblower's distorted account) that the call might have raised an election-law violation.[40]

2. President Zelenskyy, his Foreign Minister, and other Ukrainian officials have repeatedly said there was no quid pro quo and no pressure placed on them by anyone.

3. President Zelenskyy, his senior advisers, and House Democrats' own witnesses have all confirmed that Ukraine's senior leaders did not even know the aid was paused until after a *Politico* article was published on August 28, 2019—over a month after the July 25 call and barely two weeks before the aid was released on September 11.

---

[36] 144 Cong. Rec. H11786 (1998) (statement of Rep. Jerrold Nadler).

[37] 145 Cong. Rec. S1582 (1999) (statement of Sen. Patrick Leahy).

[38] 144 Cong. Rec. H11786 (1998) (statement of Rep. Jerrold Nadler).

[39] Nicole Gaudiano and Eliza Collins, *Exclusive: Nancy Pelosi Vows 'Different World' for Trump, No More 'Rubber Stamp' in New Congress*, USA Today (Jan. 3, 2019), https://perma.cc/55PK-3PZL.

[40] Tierney Sneed, *DOJ Declined to Act on Criminal Referral in Trump's Ukraine Smear Campaign*, Talking Points Memo (Sept. 25, 2019), https://perma.cc/HA3M-FBGU (quoting Statement of Kerri Kupec, Spokesperson for the Department of Justice).

4.   House Democrats' case rests almost entirely on: (i) statements from Ambassador to the European Union Gordon Sondland that he had come to *believe* (before talking to the President) that the aid and a meeting were "likely" linked to investigations; and (ii) hearsay and speculation from others echoing Sondland second- or third-hand. But Sondland admitted that he was only "presuming" a link.[41] He stated unequivocally that he has no evidence "[o]ther than [his] own presumption" that President Trump connected releasing the aid to investigations, and he agreed that "[n]o one on this planet told [him] that Donald Trump was tying aid to investigations."[42] Similarly, as for a link between a meeting and investigations, Sondland admitted that he was *speculating* about that as well, based on hearsay.[43] When asked if "the President ever [told him] personally about any preconditions for anything"—*i.e.*, for aid or a meeting—Sondland responded, "No."[44] And when Ambassador Kurt Volker, the special envoy who had actually been negotiating with the Ukrainians, was asked if the President ever withheld a meeting to pressure the Ukrainians, he said: "The answer to the question is no."[45] "[T]here was no linkage like that."[46]

The only two people with statements on record who spoke directly to the President on the matter—Sondland and Senator Ron Johnson—directly contradicted House Democrats' false allegations. Sondland testified that when he asked the President what he wanted, the President stated unequivocally: "I want nothing. I want no quid pro quo."[47] Similarly, Senator Johnson related that, when he asked the President if there was any linkage between investigations and the aid, the President responded: "(Expletive deleted) — No way. I would never do that."[48]

5.   The military aid flowed on September 11, 2019, and a presidential meeting was first scheduled for September 1 and then took place on September 25, 2019, all without the Ukrainian government having done anything about investigations.

6.   The undisputed reality is that U.S. support for Ukraine against Russia has *increased* under President Trump. President Trump provided Ukraine Javelin anti-tank missiles to use against Russia after President Obama refused to provide that assistance. President Trump also imposed heavy sanctions on Russia, for which President Zelenskyy thanked him.[49] A parade of State Department and National Security Council (NSC) career officials universally acknowledged that President Trump's policy was stronger in support of Ukraine against Russia than his predecessor's. Ambassador Yovanovitch testified that "our policy actually got stronger" under President Trump,[50] and Ambassador Taylor agreed that aid under President Trump was a

---

[41]   *Impeachment Inquiry: Ambassador Gordon Sondland Before the H.R. Permanent Select Comm. on Intelligence*, 116th Cong. 148–49 (Nov. 20, 2019) (Sondland Public Hearing).
[42]   *Id.* at 150–51.
[43]   G. Sondland Interview Tr. at 297:22–298:1 (Oct. 17, 2019).
[44]   Sondland Public Hearing, *supra* note 41, at 70.
[45]   K. Volker Interview Tr. at 36:1-9 (Oct. 3, 2019).
[46]   *Id.*
[47]   Sondland Public Hearing, *supra* note 41, at 40.
[48]   Letter from Sen. Ron Johnson to Jim Jordan, Ranking Member, H.R. Comm. on Oversight & Reform, and Devin Nunes, Ranking Member, H.R. Permanent Select Comm. on Intelligence, at 6 (Nov. 18, 2019).
[49]   Memorandum of Tel. Conversation with President Zelenskyy of Ukraine, at 2 (July 25, 2019) (July 25 Call Mem.). The transcript is attached as Appendix A.
[50]   M. Yovanovitch Dep. Tr. at 140:24–141:3 (Oct. 11, 2019); *see also Impeachment Inquiry: Ambassador Marie "Masha" Yovanovitch Before The H.R. Permanent Select Comm. on Intelligence*, 116th Cong. 76–77 (Nov. 15, 2019) (Yovanovitch Public Hearing).

"substantial improvement" over the previous administration, largely because "this administration provided Javelin anti-tank weapons," which "are serious weapons" that "will kill Russian tanks."[51]

The evidence shows that President Trump had legitimate concerns about corruption and burden-sharing with our allies—two consistent themes in his foreign policy. When his concerns had been addressed, the aid was released on September 11 without any action concerning investigations. Similarly, a bilateral meeting with President Zelenskyy was first scheduled for September 1 in Warsaw and, after rescheduling due to Hurricane Dorian, took place on September 25 in New York, again, all without the Ukrainians doing anything related to investigations.

As Professor Turley summed it up, this impeachment "stand[s] out among modern impeachments as the shortest proceeding, with the thinnest evidentiary record, and the narrowest grounds ever used to impeach a president."[52] It is a constitutional travesty.

B. House Democrats Rest on the False Premise that There Could Have Been No Legitimate Reason To Mention 2016 or the Biden-Burisma Affair.

The charges in Article I are further flawed because they rest on the mistaken premise that it would have been illegitimate for the President to mention to President Zelenskyy either (i) possible Ukrainian interference in the 2016 election; or (ii) an incident in which then-Vice President Biden had forced the dismissal of a Ukrainian prosecutor. House Democrats acknowledge that, even under their theory of "abuse of power," they must establish (in their words) that these matters were "bogus" or "sham investigations"[53]—that the *only* reason for raising them would have been "to obtain an improper personal political benefit."[54] But that is obviously false. Even if the President had raised those issues, there were legitimate reasons to do so.

1.   Uncovering potential foreign interference in U.S. elections is always a legitimate goal, whatever the source of the interference and whether or not it fits with Democrats' preferred narrative about 2016. House Democrats' assertion that asking historical questions about the *last* election somehow equates to securing "improper interference" in the *next* election is nonsensical. Asking about the past cannot be twisted into interference in a future election. Even if facts uncovered about conduct in the last election were to have some impact on the next election, uncovering historical facts is not improper interference. Nor can House Democrats self-servingly equate asking any questions about Ukraine with advocating that Ukraine, *instead of Russia*, interfered in 2016.[55] Actors in more than one country can interfere in an election at the same time, in different ways and for different purposes. And there has been plenty of public reporting to give reason to be suspicious about many Ukrainians' conduct in 2016. Even one of House Democrats' own star witnesses, Dr. Fiona Hill, acknowledged that Ukrainian officials "bet on Hillary Clinton winning the election," and that "they were trying to curry favor with the Clinton campaign" including by "trying to collect information . . . on Mr. Manafort and on other people as well."[56] All of that—and more—provides legitimate grounds for inquiry.

---

[51]   W. Taylor Dep. Tr. at 155:2–156:6 (Oct. 22, 2016).
[52]   Turley Written Statement, *supra* note 3, at 4.
[53]   Trial Mem. of the U.S. House of Representatives at 24; HJC Report at 4, 6.
[54]   H.R. Res. 755 art. I.
[55]   Trial Mem. of the U.S. House of Representatives at 2, 18; HJC Report at 10.
[56]   *Impeachment Inquiry: Dr. Fiona Hill and Mr. David Holmes Before the H.R. Permanent Select Comm. on*

2.   It also would have been legitimate to mention the Biden-Burisma affair. Public reports indicate that then-Vice President Biden threatened withholding U.S. loan guarantees to secure the dismissal of a Ukrainian prosecutor even though Biden was, at the time, operating under what appeared to be, at the very least, a serious conflict of interest. The prosecutor reportedly had been investigating Burisma—a Ukrainian energy company notorious for corruption—and Biden's son, Hunter, was sitting on Burisma's board.[57] Unless being son of the Vice President counted, Hunter had no apparent qualifications to merit that seat, or to merit being compensated (apparently) more richly than board members at Fortune 100 energy giants like ConocoPhillips.[58] In fact, numerous career State Department and NSC employees agreed that Hunter Biden's connection with Burisma created, at a minimum, the appearance of a conflict of interest,[59] and *The Washington Post* reported as early as 2014 that "[t]he appointment of the [V]ice [P]resident's son to a Ukrainian oil board looks nepotistic at best, nefarious at worst."[60] More than one official raised the issue with the Vice President's office at the time, but the Vice President took no action in response.[61]

On those facts, it would have been appropriate to raise this incident with President Zelenskyy. Ukraine cannot rid itself of corruption if its prosecutors are always stymied. Here, public reports suggested that Vice President Biden played a role in derailing a legitimate inquiry while under a monumental conflict of interest. If Biden were not running for President, House Democrats would not argue that merely raising the incident would have been improper. But former Vice President Biden did not immunize his past conduct (or his son's) from all scrutiny simply by declaring his candidacy for the presidency.

Importantly, even under House Democrats' theory, mentioning the matter to President Zelenskyy would have been entirely justified as long as there was a basis to think that would advance the public interest. To defend merely ***asking a question***, the President would not have to show that Vice President Biden (or his son) actually committed any wrongdoing. By contrast, under their own theory of the case, to show "abuse of power," the House Managers would have to

---

Intelligence, 116th Cong. 112:2-9 (Nov. 21, 2019) (Hill-Holmes Public Hearing).

[57]   Michael Kranish & David L. Stern, *As Vice President, Biden Said Ukraine Should Increase Gas Production. Then His Son Got a Job with a Ukrainian Gas Company*, Wash. Post (July 22, 2019), https://perma.cc/6JD2-KFCN ("In an email interview with The Post, Shokin [the fired prosecutor] said he believes his ouster was because of his interest in [Burisma]. . . . Had he remained in his post, Shokin said, he would have questioned Hunter Biden.").

[58]   *Compare* Tobias Hoonhout, *Hunter Biden Served as 'Ceremonial Figure' on Burisma Board for $80,000 Per Month*, National Rev. (Oct. 18, 2019), https://perma.cc/7WBU-XHCJ (reporting Hunter Biden's monthly compensation to be $83,333 monthly, or nearly $1 million per year), *with* 2019 Proxy Statement, ConocoPhillips, at 30 (Apr. 1, 2019), https://perma.cc/8HK2-XJTL (showing director compensation averaging approximately $302,000), *and* ConocoPhillips, Fortune 500, https://fortune.com/fortune500/2019/conocophillips/ (listing ConocoPhillips as #86).

[59]   *See, e.g.*, Hill-Holmes Public Hearing, *supra* note 56, at 89–90; *Impeachment Inquiry: Ms. Jennifer Williams & Lt. Col. Alexander Vindman*, 116th Cong. 129 (Nov. 19, 2019); Yovanovitch Public Hearing, *supra* note 50, at 135–36; Taylor Dep. Tr. at 90:3-5; G. Kent Interview Tr. at 227:3-8 (Oct. 15, 2019); *Impeachment Inquiry: Ambassador William B. Taylor & Mr. George Kent Before the H.R. Permanent Select Comm. on Intelligence*, 116th Cong. 148:23-25 (Nov. 13, 2019); *see also* Sondland Public Hearing, *supra* note 41, at 171.

[60]   Adam Taylor, *Hunter Biden's New Job at a Ukrainian Gas Company is a Problem for U.S. Soft Power*, Wash. Post (May 14, 2014), https://perma.cc/7DNH-GPF4.

[61]   Kent Interview Tr. at 227:1-23; Adam Entous, *Will Hunter Biden Jeopardize His Father's Campaign?*, The New Yorker (July 1, 2019), https://perma.cc/WB24-FTJG.

11

prove that the inquiry could have no public purpose whatsoever. They have no such evidence. The record shows it would have been legitimate to mention the Biden-Burisma affair.

IV.   The Articles Are Structurally Deficient and Can Only Result in Acquittal.

The articles are also defective because each charges multiple different acts as possible grounds for conviction. The problem with offering such a menu of options is that, for a valid conviction, the Constitution requires two-thirds of Senators present to agree *on the specific basis for conviction*. A vote on these articles, however, cannot ensure that a two-thirds majority agreed on a particular ground for conviction. Instead, such a vote could reflect an amalgamation of votes resting on several different theories, no single one of which would have garnered two-thirds support if it had been presented separately. This structural deficiency cannot be remedied by dividing the different allegations within each article for voting, because that is prohibited under Senate rules.[62] The only constitutional option is for the Senate to reject the articles as framed and acquit the President.

*   *   *

The Framers foresaw that the House might at times fall prey to tempestuous partisan tempers. Alexander Hamilton recognized that "the persecution of an intemperate or designing majority in the House of Representatives" was a real danger in impeachments,[63] and Jefferson acknowledged that impeachment provided "the most formidable weapon for the purposes of dominant faction that ever was contrived."[64] That is why the Framers entrusted the trial of impeachments to the Senate. As Justice Story explained, the Framers saw the Senate as a tribunal "removed from popular power and passions . . . and from the more dangerous influence of mere party spirit," and guided by "a deep responsibility to future times."[65] Now, perhaps as never before, it is essential for the Senate to fulfill the role Hamilton envisioned for it as a "guard[] against the danger of persecution, from the prevalency of a factious spirit" in the House.[66]

The Senate should speedily reject these deficient Articles of Impeachment and acquit the President. The only threat to the Constitution that House Democrats have brought to light is their own degradation of the impeachment process and trampling of the separation of powers. Their fixation on damaging the President has trivialized the momentous act of impeachment, debased the standards of impeachable conduct, and perverted the power of impeachment by turning it into a partisan, election-year political tool. The consequences of accepting House Democrats' diluted standards for impeachment would reverberate far beyond this election year and do lasting damage to our Republic. As Senator Lyman Trumbull, one of the seven Republican Senators who crossed the aisle to vote against wrongfully convicting President Andrew Johnson, explained: "Once [we] set the example of impeaching a President for what, when the excitement of the hour shall have subsided, will be regarded as insufficient causes . . . no future President will be safe . . . . [A]nd

---

[62]   Rules of Procedure and Practice in the Senate when Sitting on Impeachment Trials, Rule XXIII (1986), *in* Senate Manual Containing the Standing Rules, Orders, Laws and Resolutions Affecting the Business of the United States Senate, S. Doc. 113-1, 113th Cong. 228 (2014).

[63]   The Federalist No. 65, at 400 (Alexander Hamilton) (Clinton Rossiter ed., 1961).

[64]   Letter from Thomas Jefferson to James Madison (Feb. 15, 1798), *in* 3 *Memoir, Correspondence, and Miscellanies, from the Papers of Thomas Jefferson* 373 (Thomas Jefferson Randolph ed., 1830).

[65]   2 Joseph Story, *Commentaries on the Constitution* § 743 (1833).

[66]   The Federalist No. 66, at 402 (Alexander Hamilton) (Clinton Rossiter ed., 1961).

what then becomes of the checks and balances of the Constitution, so carefully devised and so vital to its perpetuity? They are all gone."[67] It is the solemn duty of this body to be the bulwark of the Constitution protecting against exactly this result.

Enough of the Nation's time and resources have been wasted on House Democrats' partisan obsessions. The Senate should bring a decisive end to these excesses so that Congress can get back to its real job: working together with the President to improve the lives of all Americans.

STANDARDS

The extraordinary process invoked by House Democrats under Article II, Section 4 of the Constitution is not the constitutionally preferred means to determine who should lead our country. It is a mechanism of last resort, reserved for exceptional circumstances—not present here—in which a President has engaged in unlawful conduct that strikes at the core of our constitutional system of government.

A.   The Senate Must Decide All Questions of Law and Fact.

The Constitution makes clear that an impeachment by the House of Representatives is nothing more than an accusation. The Articles of Impeachment approved by the House come to the Senate with no presumption of regularity in their favor. On each of the two prior occasions that the House adopted articles of impeachment against a President, the Senate refused to convict on them. Indeed, the Framers wisely forewarned that the House could impeach for the wrong reasons.[68] That is why the Constitution entrusts the Senate with the "sole Power to try all Impeachments."[69] Under that charge, it is the Senate's constitutional duty to decide for itself all matters of law and fact bearing upon this trial.[70] These decisions include whether the accusation presented by House Democrats even rises to the level of describing an impeachable offense, the standard of proof that House Democrats must meet to prove their case, and whether they have met this burden. As Rep. John Logan, a House manager in President Johnson's impeachment trial, explained "all questions of law or of fact are to be decided in these proceedings by the final vote"[71] of the Senate, and "in determining this general issue Senators must consider the sufficiency or insufficiency in law or in fact of every article of accusation."[72]

B.   An Impeachable Offense Requires a Violation of Established Law that Inflicts Sufficiently Egregious Harm on the Government that It Threatens to Subvert the Constitution.

The President of the United States occupies a unique position in the structure of our government. He is chosen directly by the People through a national election to be the head of an

---

[67]   *Trial of Andrew Johnson, President of the United States, Before the Senate of the United States on Impeachment by the House of Representatives for High Crimes and Misdemeanors*, 40th Cong., vol. III, at 328 (1868) (opinion of Sen. Lyman Trumbull).

[68]   The Federalist No. 65, at 400 (Alexander Hamilton) (Clinton Rossiter ed., 1961).

[69]   U.S. Const. art. I, § 3, cl. 6.

[70]   Michael J. Gerhardt, *The Lessons of Impeachment History*, 67 Geo. Wash. L. Rev. 603, 617 (1999) (noting that, "[g]iven the division of impeachment authority between the House and the Senate, the Senate has . . . the opportunity to review House decisions on what constitutes an impeachable offense" and has rejected House judgments in the past).

[71]   *Proceedings in the Trial of Andrew Johnson, President of the United States, Before the U.S. Senate on Articles of Impeachment*, 40th Cong. 524 (1868).

[72]   *Id.*

entire branch of government and Commander-in-Chief of the armed forces and is entrusted with enormous responsibilities for setting policies for the Nation. Whether Congress should supplant the will expressed by tens of millions of voters by removing the President from office is a question of breathtaking gravity. Approaching that question requires a clear understanding of the limits the Constitution places on what counts—and what does not count—as an impeachable offense.

1.   Text and Drafting History of the Impeachment Clause

Fearful that the power of impeachment might be abused, and recognizing that constitutional protections were required for the Executive, the Framers crafted a *limited* power of impeachment.[73] The Constitution restricts impeachment to enumerated offenses: "Treason, Bribery, or other high Crimes and Misdemeanors."[74] Treason and bribery are well defined offenses and are not at issue in this case. The operative text here is the more general phrase "other high Crimes and Misdemeanors." The structure and language of the clause—the use of the adjective "other" to describe "high Crimes and Misdemeanors" in a list immediately following the specific offenses "Treason" and "Bribery"—calls for applying the *ejusdem generis* canon of interpretation. This canon instructs that "'[w]here general words follow specific words in a statutory enumeration, the general words are construed to embrace only objects similar in nature to those objects enumerated by the preceding specific words."[75] Under that principle, "other high Crimes and Misdemeanors" must be understood to have the same qualities—in terms of seriousness and their effect on the functioning of government—as the crimes of "Treason" and "Bribery."[76]

Treason is defined specifically in the Constitution and "consist[s] only in levying War against [the United States], or in adhering to their Enemies, giving them Aid and Comfort."[77] This offense is "a crime against and undermining the very existence of the Government."[78] Bribery, like treason, is a serious offense against the government that subverts the proper functioning of the state. Blackstone, a "dominant source of authority" for the Framers,[79] called bribery an "offense against public justice."[80] Professor Akhil Amar describes bribery as "secretly bending laws to

---

[73]   *See, e.g.*, Raoul Berger, *Impeachment: The Constitutional Problems* 86 (1973).

[74]   U.S. Const. art. II, § 4.

[75]   *Circuit City Stores v. Adams*, 532 U.S. 105, 114–15 (2001) (quoting 2A N. Singer, *Sutherland on Statutes and Statutory Construction* § 47.17 (1991)).

[76]   *Background and History of Impeachment: Hearing Before the Subcomm. on the Constitution of the H.R. Comm. on the Judiciary*, 105th Cong. 69 (1998) (*Clinton Judiciary Comm. Hearing on Background of Impeachment*) (statement of Professor Matthew Holden, Jr., Univ. of Va., Dept. of Gov't and Foreign Affairs) ("[I]t seems that this late-added provision refers to such '*other* high Crimes and Misdemeanors,' as would be comparable in their significance to 'treason' and 'bribery.'"); Arthur M. Schlesinger, Jr., *Reflections on Impeachment*, 67 Geo. Wash. L. Rev. 693, 693 (1999) ("According to the legal rule of construction *ejusdem generis*, the other high crimes and misdemeanors must be on the same level and of the same quality as treason and bribery.").

[77]   U.S. Const. art. III, § 3, cl. 1. This definition is repeated in the United States criminal code: "Whoever, owing allegiance to the United States, levies war against them or adheres to their enemies, giving them aid and comfort within the United States or elsewhere, is guilty of treason . . . ." 18 U.S.C. § 2381 (2018).

[78]   *Proceedings of the U.S. Senate in the Impeachment Trial of President William Jefferson Clinton, Vol. IV: Statements of Senators Regarding the Impeachment Trial of William Jefferson Clinton*, S. Doc. 106–4 at 2861 (1999) (*Clinton Senate Trial*) (statement of Sen. Patrick J. Leahy).

[79]   *See Clinton Judiciary Comm. Hearing on Background of Impeachment*, *supra* note 76, at 40 (statement of Gary L. McDowell, Director, Inst. for U.S. Studies, Univ. of London) ("[T]he most dominant source of authority on the common law for those who wrote and ratified the Constitution was Sir William Blackstone and his justly celebrated *Commentaries on the Laws of England* (1765–69). That was a work that was described by Madison in the Virginia ratifying convention as nothing less than 'a book which is in every man's hand.'").

[80]   4 William Blackstone, *Commentaries on the Laws of England* *139.

favor the rich and powerful" and contends that in this context it "involves official corruption of a highly malignant sort, threatening the very soul of a democracy committed to equality under the law."[81] According to Professor Philip Bobbitt, "[l]ike treason, the impeachable offense of bribery . . . must be an act that actually threatens the constitutional stability and security of the State."[82] The text of the Constitution thus indicates that the "other" crimes and misdemeanors that qualify as impeachable offenses must be sufficiently egregious that, like treason and bribery, they involve a fundamental betrayal that threatens to subvert the constitutional order of government.

Treason and bribery are also, of course, offenses defined by law. Each of the seven other references in the Constitution to impeachment also supports the conclusion that impeachments must be evaluated in terms of offenses against settled law: The Constitution refers to "Conviction" for impeachable offenses twice[83] and "*Judgment* in Cases of Impeachment."[84] It directs the Senate to "*try* all Impeachments"[85] and requires the Chief Justice's participation when the President is "tried."[86] And it implies impeachable offenses are "Crimes" and "Offenses" in the Jury Trial Clause and the Pardon Clause, respectively.[87] These are all words that indicate violations of established law.

The use of the term "high" in the Impeachment Clause is also significant, and was clearly deliberate. Under English common law, "high" indicated crimes against the state; Blackstone defined "high treason" to include only offenses against "the supreme executive power, or the king and his government," calling it the "highest civil crime."[88]

In addition, "high Crimes and Misdemeanors" had a technical meaning in English law,[89] and there is evidence that the Framers were aware of this "limited," "technical meaning."[90] In England, "high Crimes and Misdemeanors" referred to offenses that could be the subject of impeachment in parliament. No less an authority than Blackstone, however, made clear that "an impeachment before the lords by the commons of Great Britain, in parliament, is *a prosecution of the already known and established law*."[91] As a result, nothing in the Constitution's use of the term "other high Crimes and Misdemeanors" suggests that impeachment under the Constitution

---

81 Akhil Reed Amar, *On Impeaching Presidents*, 28 Hofstra L. Rev. 291, 302 (1999).

82 Charles L. Black, Jr. & Philip Bobbitt, *Impeachment: A Handbook* 110 (2018). Gouverneur Morris's comments at the Constitutional Convention indicate the paradigm of bribery that the Framers had in mind as he cited King Louis XIV of France's bribe of England's King Charles II and argued, "no one would say that we ought to expose ourselves to the danger of seeing the first Magistrate in foreign pay without being able to guard [against] it by displacing him." 2 *The Records of the Federal Convention of 1787*, at 68–69 (Max Farrand ed., 1911).

83 U.S. Const. art. I, § 3, cl. 6; art. II, § 4.

84 U.S. Const. art. I, § 3, cl. 7 (emphasis added).

85 U.S. Const. art. I, § 3, cl. 6 (emphasis added).

86 *Id.*

87 U.S. Const. art. III, § 2, cl. 3 ("The Trial of all Crimes, except in Cases of Impeachment, shall be by Jury . . . ."); U.S. Const. art. II, § 2, cl. 1 ("[H]e shall have Power to grant Reprieves and Pardons for Offenses against the United States, except in Cases of Impeachment.").

88 *See* 4 Blackstone, *Commentaries* *74–75.

89 *See* Berger, *supra* note 73, at 71.

90 *Id.* at 86–87. Shortly before the Convention agreed to the "high Crimes and Misdemeanors" standard, delegates rejected the use of "high misdemeanor" in the Extradition Clause because "high misdemeanor" was thought to have "a technical meaning too limited." 2 *Records of the Federal Convention*, *supra* note 82, at 443; *see also* Berger, *supra* note 73, at 74.

91 4 Blackstone, *Commentaries* *256 (emphasis added). Blackstone, in fact, listed numerous "high misdemeanors" that might subject an official to impeachment, including "maladministration." *Id.* at *121.

could reach anything other than a known offense defined in existing law.

Significantly, the records of the Constitutional Convention also make clear that, in important respects, the Framers intended the scope of impeachable offenses under the Constitution to be much **narrower** than under English practice. When the draft Constitution had limited the grounds for impeachment to "Treason, or bribery,"[92] George Mason argued that the provision was too narrow because "[a]ttempts to subvert the Constitution may not be Treason" and that the clause "will not reach many great and dangerous offenses."[93] He proposed the addition of "maladministration,"[94] which had been a ground for impeachment in English practice. Madison opposed that change on the ground that "[s]o vague a term" would make the President subject to "a tenure during [the] pleasure of the Senate,"[95] and the Convention agreed on adding "other high crimes & misdemeanors" instead.[96]

By rejecting "maladministration," the Framers significantly narrowed impeachment under the Constitution and made clear that mere differences of opinion, unpopular policy decisions, or perceived misjudgments cannot constitutionally be used as the basis for impeachment. Indeed, at various earlier points during the Convention, drafts of the Constitution had included as grounds for impeachment "malpractice or neglect of duty"[97] and "neglect of duty [and] malversation,"[98] but the Framers rejected all of these formulations. The ratification debates confirmed the point that differences of opinion or differences over policy could not justify impeachment. James Iredell warned delegates to North Carolina's ratifying convention that "[a] mere difference of opinion might be interpreted, by the malignity of party, into a deliberate, wicked action,"[99] and thus should not provide the basis for impeachment. And Edmund Randolph pointed out in the Virginia ratifying convention that "[n]o man ever thought of impeaching a man for an opinion."[100]

Taken together, the text, drafting history, and debates surrounding the Constitution make several points clear. First, the debates "make quite plain that the Framers, far from proposing to confer illimitable power to impeach and convict, intended to confer a **limited** power."[101] As Senator Leahy has put it, "[t]he Framers purposely restrained the Congress and carefully circumscribed [its] power to remove the head of the co-equal Executive Branch."[102]

Second, the terminology of "high Crimes and Misdemeanors" makes clear that an impeachable offense must be a violation of established law. The Impeachment Clause did not

---

[92] 2 *Records of the Federal Convention, supra* note 82, at 499.

[93] *Id.* at 550.

[94] *Id.*

[95] *Id.*

[96] *Id.* "The conscious and deliberate character of [the Framers'] rejection [of 'maladministration'] is accentuated by the fact that a good many state constitutions of the time did have 'maladministration' as an impeachment ground." Black & Bobbitt, *supra* note 82, at 27.

[97] 2 *Records of the Federal Convention, supra* note 82, at 64.

[98] *Id.* at 337.

[99] 4 *The Debates in the Several State Conventions on the Adoption of the Federal Constitution*, at 127 (Jonathan Elliot 2nd ed. 1987).

[100] 3 *The Debates in the Several State Conventions on the Adoption of the Federal Constitution*, at 401 (Jonathan Elliot 2nd ed. 1987).

[101] Berger, *supra* note 73, at 86.

[102] *Clinton Senate Trial, supra* note 78, vol. IV at 2842 (statement of Sen. Patrick J. Leahy); *see also id.* at 2883 (statement of Sen. James M. Jeffords) ("The framers intentionally set this standard at an extremely high level to ensure that only the most serious offenses would justify overturning a popular election.").

confer upon Congress a roving license to make up new standards of conduct for government officials and to permit removal from office merely on a conclusion that conduct was "bad" if there was not an existing law that it violated.

Third, by establishing that "other" impeachable offenses must fall in the same class as the specific offenses of "treason" and "bribery," the Framers intended to establish a requirement of particularly egregious conduct threatening the constitutional order to justify impeachment. Justice Story recognized impeachment was "intended for occasional and extraordinary cases" only.[103] For Professor Bobbitt, "[a]n impeachable offense is one that puts the Constitution in jeopardy."[104] Removal of the freely elected President of the United States based on any lesser standard would violate the plan of the Founders, who built our government on the principle it would "deriv[e] [its] just powers from the consent of the governed."[105]

2.   The President's Unique Role in Our Constitutional Structure

For at least two reasons, the President's unique role in our constitutional structure buttresses the conclusion that offenses warranting presidential impeachment must involve especially egregious conduct that threatens to subvert the constitutional order of government.

First, conviction of a President raises particularly profound issues under our constitutional structure because it means overturning the democratically expressed will of the people in the only national election in which all eligible citizens participate. The impeachment power permits the possibility that "the legislative branch [will] essentially cancel[] the results of the most solemn collective act of which we as a constitutional democracy are capable: the national election of a President."[106]

As even the House Managers have acknowledged, "the issue" in a presidential impeachment trial "is whether to overturn the results of a national election, the free expression of the popular will of the American people."[107] That step can be justified only by an offense crossing an exceptional threshold. As Chairman Nadler has put it, "[w]e must not overturn an election and remove a President from office except to defend our system of government or our constitutional liberties against a dire threat . . . ."[108] Especially where the American people are already starting the process of voting for candidates for the next presidential election, removing a President from office and taking that decision away from the people requires meeting an extraordinarily high standard. As then-Senator Biden confirmed during President Clinton's trial, "to remove a duly elected president will unavoidably harm our constitutional structure" and "[r]emoving the President from office without compelling evidence would be historically anti-democratic."[109]

Any lesser standard would be inconsistent with the unique importance of the President's

---

[103] 2 Joseph Story, *Commentaries on the Constitution* § 749 (1833); *see also* 1 James Bryce, *The American Commonwealth* 283 (1888) ("Impeachment . . . is the heaviest piece of artillery in the congressional arsenal, but because it is so heavy it is unfit for ordinary use. It is like a hundred-ton gun which needs complex machinery to bring it into position, an enormous charge of powder to fire it, and a large mark to aim at.").

[104] Black & Bobbitt, *supra* note 82, at 111.

[105] The Declaration of Independence para. 2 (U.S. 1776).

[106] Laurence H. Tribe, *Defining "High Crimes and Misdemeanors": Basic Principles*, 67 Geo. Wash. L. Rev. 712, 723 (1999).

[107] 144 Cong. Rec. H10018 (1998) (statement of Rep. Jerrold Nadler).

[108] *Id.* at H11786 (statement of Rep. Jerrold Nadler).

[109] *Clinton Senate Trial*, *supra* note 78, vol. IV at 2578, 2580 (statement of Sen. Joseph R. Biden, Jr.).

role in the structure of the government, the profound disruption and danger of uncertainty that attend to removing a president from office, and the grave implications of negating the will of the people expressed in a national election.

Second, because the President himself is vested with the authority of an entire branch of the federal government, his removal would cause extraordinary disruption to the Nation. Article II, Section 1 declares in no uncertain terms that "[t]he executive Power shall be vested in a President of the United States of America."[110] As Justice Breyer has explained, "Article II makes a single President responsible for the actions of the Executive Branch in much the same way that the entire Congress is responsible for the actions of the Legislative Branch, or the entire Judiciary for those of the Judicial Branch."[111] As a result, "the application of the Impeachment Clause to the President of the United States involves the uniquely solemn act of having one branch essentially overthrow another."[112] It also carries the risk of profound disruption for the operation of the federal government.

As "the chief constitutional officer of the Executive branch," the President is "entrusted with supervisory and policy responsibilities of utmost discretion and sensitivity."[113] Because he is assigned responsibility to "take Care that the Laws be faithfully executed,"[114] all federal law enforcement depends, ultimately, on the direction of the President. In addition, he is the Commander-in-Chief of the armed forces[115] and "the sole organ of the federal government in the field of international relations."[116] The foreign policy of the Nation is determined primarily by the President. His removal would necessarily create uncertainty and pose unique risks for U.S. interests around the globe. As OLC put it, removal of the President would be "politically and constitutionally a traumatic event,"[117] and Senator Bob Graham rightly called it "one of the most disruptive acts imaginable in a democracy" during President Clinton's trial.[118]

3.   Practice Under the Impeachment Clause

The practical application of the Impeachment Clause by Congress supports the conclusion that an impeachable offense requires especially egregious conduct that threatens the constitutional order and, specifically, that it requires a violation of established law. The extraordinary threshold required for impeachment is evidenced by the fact that, in over two centuries under our Constitution, the House has impeached a President only twice. In each case, moreover, the Senate found the charges brought by the House insufficient to warrant removal from office.

In addition, until now, even in the articles of impeachment that the Senate found insufficient, the House has ***never*** impeached a President on charges that did not include a violation

---

[110]   U.S. Const. art. II, § 1.
[111]   *See Clinton v. Jones*, 520 U.S. 681, 712 (1997) (Breyer, J., concurring in the judgment).
[112]   Tribe, *supra* note 106, at 723. The unique importance of a presidential impeachment is reflected in the text of the Constitution as it requires, in contrast to all other cases of impeachment, that the Chief Justice of the United States preside over any Senate trial of a President. U.S. Const. art. I, § 3, cl. 6.
[113]   *Nixon v. Fitzgerald*, 457 U.S. 731, 750 (1982).
[114]   U.S. Const. art. II, § 3.
[115]   U.S. Const. art. II, § 2, cl. 1.
[116]   *United States v. Curtiss-Wright Export Corp.*, 299 U.S. 304, 320 (1936).
[117]   Memorandum from Robert G. Dixon, Jr., Assistant Attorney General, Office of Legal Counsel, *Re: Amenability of the President, Vice President and other Civil Officers to Federal Criminal Prosecution While in Office*, at 32 (Sept. 24, 1973).
[118]   *Clinton Senate Trial*, *supra* note 78, vol. IV at 2793 (statement of Sen. Bob Graham).

of established law. President Clinton was impeached on charges that included perjury and obstruction of justice, both felonies under federal law.[119] Similarly, in the near-impeachment of President Nixon, the articles of impeachment approved by the House Judiciary Committee included multiple violations of law.[120] Article I alleged obstruction of justice.[121] And Article II asserted numerous legal breaches.[122]

The impeachment of Andrew Johnson proves the same point. In 1867, the House Judiciary Committee recommended articles of impeachment against President Johnson. The articles, however, did not allege any violation of law. Largely as a result of that fact, the Committee could not secure approval for them from a majority of the House. The minority report from the Committee arguing *against* adoption of the articles of impeachment explained that "[t]he House of Representatives may impeach a civil officer, but it must be done according to law. It must be *for some offence known to the law*, and not created by the fancy of the members of the House."[123] Rep. James F. Wilson argued the position of the minority report on the House floor, explaining that "no civil officer of the United States can be lawfully impeached except for a crime or misdemeanor known to the law."[124] As one historian has explained, "[t]he House had refused to impeach Andrew Johnson . . . at least in part because many representatives did not believe he had committed a specific violation of law."[125] It was only after President Johnson violated the Tenure of Office Act, a law passed by Congress, that he was successfully impeached.[126]

Even if *judicial* impeachments have been based on charges that do not involve a criminal offense or violation of statute,[127] that would provide no sound basis for diluting the standards for *presidential* impeachment. Textually, the Constitution's Good Behavior Clause alters the standard for the impeachment of judges.[128] In addition, for all the reasons outlined above, the President's

---

[119] H.R. Res. 611, 105th Cong. (1998); H.R. Comm. on the Judiciary, *Impeachment of William Jefferson Clinton, President of the United States*, H.R. Rep. No. 105-830, 105th Cong. 143 (1998) (additional views of Rep. Bill McCollum) ("President Clinton actively sought to thwart the due administration of justice by repeatedly committing the felony crimes of perjury, witness tampering, and obstruction of justice.").

[120] H.R. Comm. on the Judiciary, *Impeachment of Richard M. Nixon, President of the United States*, H.R. Rep. No. 93-1305, 93d Cong. 1–4 (1974); *see also id.* at 3 (alleging that Nixon "violat[ed] the constitutional rights of citizens" and "contravene[ed] the laws governing agencies of the executive branch.").

[121] *Id.* at 34 (asserting that Nixon "caused action. . . to cover up the Watergate break-in. This concealment required perjury, destruction of evidence, obstruction of justice—all of which are crimes").

[122] Article II claimed that President Nixon "violat[ed] the rights of citizens," "contraven[ed] the laws governing agencies of the executive branch," and "authorized and permitted to be maintained a secret investigative unit within the Office of the President . . . [that] engaged in covert and unlawful activities." *Id.* at 3. Although the House Judiciary Committee's report described Article II generally as involving "abuse of the powers of the office of President," *id.* at 139, that was not the actual *charge* included in the articles of impeachment. The actual charges in the recommended article of impeachment included specific violations of laws.

[123] H.R. Rep. Com. No. 7, 40th Cong. 60 (1867) (emphasis added).

[124] Cong. Globe, 40th Cong., 2d Sess. app. 63 (1867).

[125] Michael Les Benedict, *The Impeachment and Trial of Andrew Johnson* 102 (1973).

[126] Cong. Globe, 40th Cong., 2d Sess., 1616–18, 1638–42 (1868).

[127] *See, e.g.*, Berger, *supra* note 73, at 56–57. Some scholars dispute the characterization that many judicial impeachments do not involve charges that amount to violations of law. *See, e.g.*, Frank Thompson, Jr., & Daniel H. Pollitt, *Impeachment of Federal Judges: An Historical Overview*, 49 N.C. L. Rev. 87, 118 (1970) ("Except for a few abberations [sic] in the early-1800[s] period of unprecedented political upheaval, Congress has refused to impeach a judge for lack of 'good behaviour' unless the behavior was both job-related and criminal.").

[128] U.S. Const. art. III, § 1; *see also* John R. Labovitz, *Presidential Impeachment* 92-93 (1978) (The Good Behavior Clause "could be interpreted as a separate standard for the impeachment of judges or it could be interpreted as an aid in applying the term 'high crimes and misdemeanors' to judges. Whichever interpretation was adopted, it was clear

unique role in the constitutional structure sets him apart and warrants more rigorous standards for impeachment. "When Senators remove one of a thousand federal judges (or even one of nine justices), they are not transforming an entire branch of government. But that is exactly what happens when they oust America's one and only President, in whom all executive power is vested by the first sentence of Article II."[129] Unlike a presidential impeachment inquiry, impeachment of a federal judge "does not paralyze the Nation" or cast doubt on the direction of the country's domestic and foreign policy.[130] Similarly, "[t]he grounds for the expulsion of the one person elected by the entire nation to preside over the executive cannot be the same as those for one member of the almost four-thousand-member federal judiciary."[131] Thus, as then-Senator Biden recognized: "The constitutional scholarship overwhelmingly recognizes that the fundamental structural commitment to a separation of powers requires [the Senate] to view the President as different than a Federal judge."[132] Indeed, "our history establishes that, as applied, the constitutional standard for impeaching the President has been distinctive, and properly so."[133]

C. The Senate Cannot Convict Unless It Finds that the House Managers Have Proved an Impeachable Offense Beyond a Reasonable Doubt.

Given the profound implications of removing a duly elected president from office, an exceptionally demanding standard of proof must apply in a presidential impeachment trial.[134] Senators should convict on articles of impeachment against a President only if they find that the House Managers have carried their burden of proving that the President committed an impeachable offense beyond a reasonable doubt.

As Senator Russ Feingold recognized in the Clinton impeachment, "[i]n making a decision of this magnitude, it is best not to err at all. If we must err, however, we should err on the side of . . . respecting the will of the people."[135] Democrat and Republican Senators alike applied the beyond a reasonable doubt standard during President Clinton's impeachment trial.[136] As Senator

---

that the clause made a difference in judicial impeachments, confounding the application of these cases to presidential impeachment."); *Clinton Senate Trial*, *supra* note 78, vol. IV at 2692 (statement of Sen. Max Cleland) (citing the "Good Behaviour" clause and explaining "that there is indeed a different legal standard for impeachment of Presidents and Federal judges").

[129] Amar, *supra* note 81, at 304.

[130] *See* Cass R. Sunstein, *Impeaching the President*, 147 U. Pa. L. Rev. 279, 304 (1998).

[131] Black & Bobbitt, *supra* note 82, at 119.

[132] *Clinton Senate Trial*, *supra* note 78, vol. IV at 2575 (statement of Sen. Joseph R. Biden, Jr.). Numerous other Senators distinguished the lower standard for judicial impeachments. *See, e.g.*, *id.* at 2692 (statement of Sen. Max Cleland) ("After review of the record, historical precedents, and consideration of the different roles of Presidents and Federal judges, I have concluded that there is indeed a different legal standard for impeachment of Presidents and Federal judges."); *id.* at 2811 (statement of Sen. Edward M. Kennedy) ("Removal of the President of the United States and removal of a Federal judge are vastly different.").

[133] Sunstein, *supra* note 130, at 300; *see also Clinton Judiciary Comm. Hearing on Background of Impeachment*, *supra* note 76, at 350 (statement of Professors Frank O. Bowman, III, Stephen L. Sepinuck, Gonzaga University School of Law) ("[C]omparative analysis suggests that Congress has applied a discernibly different standard to the removal of judges.").

[134] To the extent that the Senate voted in the impeachment trial of Judge Claiborne not to require all Senators to apply the beyond-a-reasonable-doubt standard, *see* 132 Cong. Rec. 29,153 (1986), that decision in a ***judicial*** impeachment has little relevance here.

[135] *Clinton Senate Trial*, *supra* note 78, vol. IV at 3052 (statement of Sen. Russell D. Feingold); *see also id.* at 2563 (statement of Sen. Patty Murray) ("If we are to remove a President for the first time in our Nation's history, none of us should have any doubts.").

[136] *See, e.g.*, *Proceedings of the U.S. Senate in the Impeachment Trial of President William Jefferson Clinton, Volume*

Barbara Mikulski put it then: "The U.S. Senate must not make the decision to remove a President based on a hunch that the charges may be true. The strength of our Constitution and the strength of our Nation dictate that [the Senate] be sure—beyond a reasonable doubt."[137]

D. The Senate May Not Consider Allegations Not Charged in the Articles of Impeachment.

Under the Constitution, the House is given the "sole Power of Impeachment" and the Senate is given the "sole Power to try all Impeachments."[138] An impeachment is literally a "charge" of particular wrongdoing.[139] Thus, under the division of responsibility in the Constitution, the Senate can conduct a trial solely on the charges specified in articles of impeachment approved by a vote of the House and presented to the Senate. The Senate cannot expand the scope of a trial to consider mere assertions appearing in House reports that the House did not include in the articles of impeachment submitted to a vote. Similarly, House Managers trying the case in the Senate must be confined to the specific conduct alleged in the Articles approved by the House.

These restrictions follow both from the plain terms of the Constitution limiting the Senate to trying an "impeachment" framed by the House and from elementary principles of due process. "[T]he senator's role is solely one of acting on the accusations (Articles of Impeachment) voted by the House of Representatives. The Senate cannot lawfully find the president guilty of something not charged by the House, any more than a trial jury can find a defendant guilty of something not charged in the indictment."[140] "No principle of procedural due process is more clearly established than that *notice of the specific charge*, and a chance to be heard in *a trial of the issues raised by that charge*, if desired, are among the constitutional rights of every accused."[141] As the Supreme Court has explained, it has been the rule for over 130 years that "a court cannot permit a defendant to be tried on charges that are not made in the indictment against him."[142] Doing so is "fatal error."[143]

Under the same principles of due process, the Senate must similarly refuse to consider any uncharged allegations as a basis for conviction.

PROCEDURAL HISTORY

House Democrats have focused these proceedings on a telephone conversation between President Trump and President Zelenskyy of Ukraine on July 25, 2019.[144] At some unknown time shortly after that call, a staffer in the Intelligence Community (IC)—who had no first-hand knowledge of the call—approached the staff of Chairman Adam Schiff on the House Permanent

---

II: Floor Trial Proceedings, S. Doc. 106–4 at 1876 (1999) (statement of Sen. Chris Dodd); *Clinton Senate Trial, supra* note 78, vol. IV at 2548 (statement of Sen. Kay Bailey Hutchison); *id.* at 2559 (statement of Sen. Kent Conrad); *id.* at 2562 (statement of Sen. Tim Hutchinson); *id.* at 2642 (statement of Sen. George V. Voinovich).

[137] *Id.* at 2623 (statement of Sen. Barbara A. Mikulski).

[138] U.S. Const. art. I, § 2, cl. 5; *id.* at § 3, cl. 6.

[139] 1 John Ash, *New and Complete Dictionary of the English Language* (1775) (definition of "impeachment": "[a] public charge of something criminal, an accusation").

[140] Black & Bobbitt, *supra* note 82, at 14.

[141] *Cole v. Arkansas*, 333 U.S. 196, 201 (1948) (emphases added).

[142] *Stirone v. United States*, 361 U.S. 212, 217 (1960).

[143] *Id.*

[144] July 25 Call Mem., *infra* Appendix A.

Select Committee on Intelligence (HPSCI) raising complaints about the call.[145] Although it is known that Chairman Schiff's staff provided the IC staffer some "guidance,"[146] the extent of the so-called whistleblower's coordination with Chairman Schiff's staff remains unknown to this day.

The IC staffer retained counsel, including an attorney who had announced just days after President Trump took office that he supported a "coup" and "rebellion" to remove the President from office.[147]

On August 12, 2019, the IC staffer filed a complaint about the July 25 telephone call with the Inspector General of the IC.[148] The Inspector General found that there was "some indicia of an arguable political bias on the part of [the so-called whistleblower] in favor of a rival political candidate."[149]

On September 24, 2019, Speaker Nancy Pelosi unilaterally announced at a press conference that "the House of Representatives is moving forward with an official impeachment inquiry"[150] based on the anonymous complaint about the July 25 telephone call. There was no vote by the House to authorize such an inquiry.

On September 25, pursuant to a previous announcement,[151] the President declassified and released the complete record of the July 25 call.[152]

On September 26, HPSCI held its first hearing regarding the so-called whistleblower complaint.[153] And just one week later, on October 3, Chairman Schiff began a series of secret, closed-door hearings regarding the complaint.[154] The President and his counsel were not permitted to participate in any of these proceedings.

On October 31, after five weeks of hearings, House Democrats finally authorized an impeachment inquiry when the full House voted to approve House Resolution 660.[155] By its terms, the Resolution did not purport to retroactively authorize investigative efforts before October 31.[156]

---

[145] Julian Barns et al., *Schiff Got Early Account of Accusations as Whistle-Blower's Concerns Grew*, N.Y. Times (Oct. 2, 2019), https://perma.cc/5KWF-U7ZS.

[146] Ellen Nakashima, *Whistleblower Sought Informal Guidance from Schiff's Committee Before Filing Complaint Against Trump*, Wash. Post (Oct. 2, 2019), https://perma.cc/23UT-BGJL.

[147] Mark S. Zaid (@MarkSZaidEsq), Twitter (Jan. 30, 2017, 6:54 PM), https://perma.cc/Z9LS-TDM2 ("#coup has started. First of many steps. #rebellion. #impeachment will follow ultimately. #lawyers.").

[148] Letter from IC Staffer to Richard Burr, Chairman, S. Comm. on Intelligence, and Adam Schiff, Chairman, H.R. Permanent Select Comm. on Intelligence (Aug. 12, 2019), https://perma.cc/MT4D-634A.

[149] Letter from Michael K. Atkinson, Inspector General of the Intelligence Community, to Joseph Maguire, Acting Director of National Intelligence, at 5 (Aug. 26, 2019), https://perma.cc/2SV7-BUP5.

[150] Speaker Pelosi Announcement of Impeachment Inquiry, C-SPAN (Sept. 24, 2019), https://www.c-span.org/video/?464684-1/speaker-pelosi-announces-formal-impeachment-inquiry-president-trump.

[151] Donald J. Trump (@realDonaldTrump), Twitter (Sept. 24, 2019, 11:12 AM), https://perma.cc/UZ4E-D3ST ("I am currently at the United Nations representing our Country, but have authorized the release tomorrow of the complete, fully declassified and unredacted transcript of my phone conversation with President Zelensky of Ukraine.").

[152] July 25 Call Mem., *infra* Appendix A.

[153] *Whistleblower Disclosure: Hearing Before the H.R. Permanent Select Comm. on Intelligence*, 116th Cong. (Sept. 26, 2019).

[154] K. Volker Interview Tr. (Oct. 3, 2019).

[155] H.R. Res. 660, 116th Cong. (2019).

[156] *Id.*

On November 13, HPSCI held the first of seven public hearings featuring some of the witnesses who had already testified in secret. At this stage, too, the President and his counsel were denied any opportunity to participate. HPSCI released a report on December 3, 2019.[157]

On December 4, the House Judiciary Committee held its first hearing, which featured four law professors, three of whom were selected by Democrats.[158]

The next day, December 5, Speaker Pelosi announced the outcome of the Judiciary Committee's proceedings and directed Chairman Jerrold Nadler to draft articles of impeachment.[159]

On December 9, four days after Speaker Pelosi announced that articles of impeachment would be drafted, the Judiciary Committee held its second and last hearing, which featured presentations solely from staff members from HPSCI and the Judiciary Committee.[160] The House Judiciary Committee did not hear from any fact witnesses at any time.

On December 10, Chairman Jerrold Nadler offered two articles of impeachment for the Judiciary Committee's consideration,[161] and the Committee approved the articles on December 13 on a party-line vote.[162]

On December 18, a mere 85 days after the press conference purportedly launching the inquiry, House Democrats completed the fastest presidential impeachment inquiry in history and adopted the Articles of Impeachment over bipartisan opposition.[163]

House Democrats justified their unseemly haste by claiming they had to move forward "without delay" because the President would allegedly "continue to threaten the Nation's security, democracy, and constitutional system if he is allowed to remain in office."[164] In a remarkable reversal, however, as soon as they had voted, they decided that there was no urgency at all. House Democrats took a leisurely *four weeks* to complete the ministerial act of transmitting the articles to the Senate—more than three times longer than the entire length of proceedings before the House Judiciary Committee.

The Senate now has the "sole Power to try" the Articles of Impeachment transmitted by

---

[157] Press Release, H.R. Permanent Select Comm. on Intelligence, *House Intelligence Committee Releases Draft Report as Part of Impeachment Inquiry* (Dec. 3, 2019), https://perma.cc/B23P-7NBD.

[158] *The Impeachment Inquiry into President Donald J. Trump: Constitutional Grounds for Presidential Impeachment: Hearing Before the H.R. Comm. on Judiciary*, 116th Cong. (Dec. 4, 2019).

[159] Nicholas Fandos, *Pelosi Says House Will Draft Impeachment Charges Against Trump*, N.Y. Times (Dec. 5, 2019), https://perma.cc/T7SC-W2VX.

[160] *The Impeachment Inquiry into President Donald J. Trump: Presentations from the House Permanent Select Comm. on Intelligence and House Judiciary Comm.: Hearing Before the H.R. Comm. on Judiciary*, 116th Cong. (Dec. 9, 2019).

[161] Press Release, H.R. Comm. on Judiciary, *Chairman Nadler Announces the Introduction of Articles of Impeachment Against President Donald J. Trump* (Dec. 10, 2019), https://perma.cc/9ERV-9PZX.

[162] *House Judiciary Passes Articles of Impeachment Against President Trump*, C-SPAN (Dec. 13, 2019), https://www.c-span.org/video/?467395-1/house-judiciary-committee-approves-articles-impeachment-23-17.

[163] H.R. Res. 755, 116th Cong. (2019); Clerk, H.R., Final Vote Results for Roll Call 695 on Agreeing to Article I of the Resolution (Dec. 18, 2019), http://clerk house.gov/evs/2019/roll695.xml; Clerk, H.R., Final Vote Results for Roll Call 696 on Agreeing to Article II of the Resolution (Dec. 18, 2019), http://clerk house.gov/evs/2019/roll696.xml.

[164] HJC Report at 129–30.

the House.[165]

THE ARTICLES SHOULD BE REJECTED AND
THE PRESIDENT SHOULD IMMEDIATELY BE ACQUITTED.

I.   The Articles Fail to State Impeachable Offenses as a Matter Of Law.

A.   House Democrats' Novel Theory of "Abuse of Power" Does Not State an Impeachable Offense and Would Do Lasting Damage to the Separation of Powers.

House Democrats' novel conception of "abuse of power" as a supposedly impeachable offense is constitutionally defective. It supplants the Framers' standard of "high Crimes and Misdemeanors"[166] with a made-up theory that the President can be impeached and removed from office under an amorphous and undefined standard of "abuse of power." The Framers adopted a standard that requires a violation of established law to state an impeachable offense. By contrast, in their Articles of Impeachment, House Democrats have not even attempted to identify any law that was violated. Moreover, House Democrats' theory in this case rests on the radical assertion that the President could be impeached and removed from office entirely for his *subjective motives*—that is, for undertaking permissible actions for supposedly "forbidden reasons."[167] That unprecedented test is so flexible it would vastly expand the impeachment power beyond constitutional limits and would permanently weaken the Presidency by effectively permitting impeachments based on policy disagreements.

House Democrats cannot salvage their unprecedented "abuse of power" standard with fuzzy claims that the Framers particularly intended impeachment to address "foreign entanglements" and "corruption of elections."[168] Those assertions are makeweights that distort history and add no legitimacy to the radical theory of impeachment based on subjective motive alone.

Under the Constitution, impeachable offenses must be defined under established law. And they must be based on objective wrongdoing, not supposed subjective motives dreamt up by a hostile faction in the House and superimposed onto a President's entirely lawful conduct.

1.   House Democrats' Novel Theory of "Abuse of Power" as an Impeachable Offense Subverts Constitutional Standards and Would Permanently Weaken the Presidency.

House Democrats' theory that the President can be impeached and removed from office under a vaguely defined concept of "abuse of power" would vastly expand the impeachment power beyond the limits set by the Constitution and should be rejected by the Senate.

---

[165]   U.S. Const. art. I, § 3, cl. 6.
[166]   U.S. Const. art. II, § 4.
[167]   HJC Report at 44.
[168]   *See id.* at 48–53; Trial Mem. of U.S. House of Representatives at 10–11.

(a) House Democrats' Made-Up "Abuse of Power" Standard Fails To State an Impeachable Offense Because It Does Not Rest on Violation of an Established Law.

House Democrats' claim that the Senate can remove a President from office for running afoul of some ill-defined conception of "abuse of power" finds no support in the text or history of the Impeachment Clause. As explained above,[169] by limiting impeachment to cases of "Treason, Bribery, or other high Crimes and Misdemeanors,"[170] the Framers restricted impeachment to specific offenses against "already *known and established law*."[171] That was a deliberate choice designed to constrain the power of impeachment.[172] Restricting impeachment to offenses established by law provided a crucial protection for the independence of the Executive from what James Madison called the "impetuous vortex" of legislative power.[173] As many constitutional scholars have recognized, "the Framers were far more concerned with protecting the presidency from the encroachments of Congress . . . than they were with the potential abuse of executive power."[174] The impeachment power necessarily implicated that concern. If the power were too expansive, the Framers feared that the Legislative Branch may "hold [impeachments] as a rod over the Executive and by that means effectually destroy his independence."[175] One key voice at the Constitutional Convention, Gouverneur Morris, warned that, as they crafted a mechanism to make the President "amenable to Justice," the Framers "should take care to provide some mode that will not make him dependent on the Legislature."[176] To limit the impeachment power, Morris argued that only "few" "offences . . . ought to be impeachable," and the "cases ought to be enumerated & defined."[177]

Indeed, the debates over the text of the Impeachment Clause particularly reveal the Framers' concern that ill-defined standards could give free rein to Congress to utilize impeachment to undermine the Executive. As explained above,[178] when "maladministration" was proposed as a ground for impeachment, it was rejected based on Madison's concern that "[s]o vague a term will

---

[169] *See supra* Standards Part B.1.

[170] U.S. Const. art. II, § 4.

[171] 4 William Blackstone, *Commentaries on the Laws of England* *256 (emphasis added).

[172] *Background and History of Impeachment: Hearing Before the Subcomm. on the Constitution of the H.R. Comm. on the Judiciary*, 105th Cong. 48 (1998) ("Of these distinctive features, the one of greatest contemporary concern is the founders' choice of the words—'treason, bribery, and other high crimes and misdemeanors'—for the purpose of narrowing the scope of the federal impeachment process.") (statement of Professor Michael Gerhardt) (*Clinton Judiciary Comm. Hearing on Background of Impeachment*).

[173] The Federalist No. 48, at 309 (James Madison) (Clinton Rossiter ed., 1961).

[174] Jack N. Rakove, *Statement on the Background and History of Impeachment*, 67 Geo. Wash. L. Rev. 682, 688 (1999). The Framers' "predominant fear" was "oppression at the hands of Congress." Raoul Berger, *Impeachment: The Constitutional Problems* 4 (1973); *see also Consumer Energy Council of Am. v. Fed. Energy Regulatory Comm'n*, 673 F.2d 425, 464 (D.C. Cir. 1982) ("Perhaps the greatest fear of the Framers was that in a representative democracy the Legislature would be capable of using its plenary lawmaking power to swallow up the other departments of the Government."); Ronald C. Kahn, *Process and Rights Principles in Modern Constitutional Theory: The Supreme Court and Constitutional Democracy*, 37 Stan. L. Rev. 253, 260 (1984) ("[T]he Framers' greatest fear was the unlawful use of legislative power."). The ratification debates also reflected fear of Congress. Berger, *supra*, at 119.

[175] 2 *The Records of the Federal Convention of 1787*, at 66 (Max Farrand ed., 1911) (*Records of the Federal Convention*) (Charles Pinckney).

[176] *Id.* at 69 (Gouverneur Morris).

[177] *Id.* at 65.

[178] *See supra* notes 92–100 and accompanying text.

be equivalent to a tenure during [the] pleasure of the Senate."[179] Madison rightly feared that a nebulous standard could allow Congress to use impeachment against a President based merely on policy differences, making it function like a parliamentary no-confidence vote. That would cripple the independent Executive the Framers had crafted and recreate the Parliamentary system they had expressly rejected. Circumscribing the impeachment power to reach only existing, defined offenses guarded against such misuse of the authority.[180]

As Luther Martin, who had been a delegate at the Constitutional Convention, summarized the point at the impeachment trial of Justice Samuel Chase in 1804, "[a]dmit that the House of Representatives have a right to impeach for acts which are not contrary to law, and that thereon the Senate may convict and the officer be removed, you leave your judges and all your other officers at the mercy of the prevailing party."[181] The Framers prevented that dangerous result by limiting impeachment to defined offenses under the law.

House Democrats cannot reconcile their amorphous "abuse of power" standard with the constitutional text simply by asserting that, "[t]o the founding generation, abuse of power was a specific, well-defined offense."[182] In fact, they conspicuously fail to provide any citation for that assertion. Nowhere have they identified any contemporaneous definition delimiting this purportedly "well-defined" offense.

Nor can House Democrats shore up their theory by invoking English practice.[183] According to House Democrats, 400 years of parliamentary history suggests that the particular offenses charged in English impeachments can be abstracted into several categories of offenses, including one involving abuse of power.[184] From there, they jump to the conclusion that "abuse of power" itself can be treated as an offense and that any fact pattern that could be described as showing abuse of power can be treated as an impeachable offense. But that entire methodology is antithetical to the approach the Framers took in defining the impeachment power. The Framers sought to confine impeachable offenses within known bounds to protect the Executive from

---

[179]   2 *Records of the Federal Convention*, *supra* note 175, at 550 (James Madison).

[180]   Alexander Hamilton's description in Federalist No. 65 does not support House Democrats' theory of a vague abuse-of-power offense. In an often-cited passage, Hamilton observed that the subjects of impeachment are "offenses which proceed from the misconduct of public men, or, in other words, from the abuse or violation of some public trust." The Federalist No. 65, at 396 (Alexander Hamilton) (Clinton Rossiter ed., 1961). Hamilton was merely noting fundamental ***characteristics*** common to impeachable offenses—that they involve (or "proceed from") misconduct in public office or abuse of public trust. He was no more saying that "abuse or violation of some public trust" provided, in itself, the ***definition*** of a chargeable offense than he was saying that "misconduct of public men" provided such a definition.

[181]   III Hinds' Precedents § 2361, at 763 (1907) (Hinds' Precedents). Justice Chase was acquitted by the Senate. *Id.* at § 2363, at 770–71. He had been charged with purported offenses that turned largely on claims that he had misapplied the law in his rulings while sitting as a circuit justice. *See* William H. Rehnquist, *Grand Inquests* 76–77, 114 (1992). His acquittal has been credited with having "a profound effect on the American judiciary," because the Senate's rejection of the charges was widely viewed as "safeguard[ing] the independence" of federal judges. *Id.* at 114.

[182]   HJC Report at 5.

[183]   *See, e.g., id.* at 38–40.

[184]   *Id.* at 39. House Democrats rely on several secondary sources, each of which extracts general categories of impeachment cases from specific prosecutions. *See, e.g.*, Berger, *supra* note 174, at 70 (asserting that impeachment cases are "reducible to intelligible categories" including those involving "abuse of official power"); Staff of H.R. Comm. on the Judiciary, 93d Cong., *Constitutional Grounds for Presidential Impeachment* 7 (Comm. Print 1974) (arguing that "particular allegations of misconduct" in English cases suggest several general types of damage to the state, including "abuse of official power").

arbitrary exercises of power by Congress. Indeed, the Framers expressly rejected vague standards such as "maladministration" that had been used in England in order to constrain the impeachment power within defined limits. Deriving general categories from ancient English cases and using those categories as the labels for new, more nebulously defined purported "offenses" is precisely counter to the Framers' approach. As the Republican minority on the House Judiciary Committee in the Nixon impeachment inquiry explained, "[t]he whole tenor of the Framers' discussions, the whole purpose of their many careful departures from English impeachment practice, was in the direction of limits and of standards."[185]

House Democrats' theory also has no grounding in the history of presidential impeachments. Until now, the House of Representatives has *never* impeached a President of the United States without alleging a violation of law—indeed, a crime. The articles of impeachment against President Clinton specified charges of perjury and obstruction of justice, both felonies under federal law.[186] In the Nixon impeachment inquiry, the articles approved by the House Judiciary Committee accused the President of obstructing justice, among multiple other violations of the law.[187] And as explained above,[188] the impeachment of President Johnson provides the clearest evidence that a presidential impeachment requires alleged violations of existing law. When the House Judiciary Committee recommended impeaching Johnson in 1867 based on allegations that included no violations of law, the House rejected the recommendation.[189] A majority in the House was persuaded by the arguments of the minority on the Judiciary Committee, who argued that "[t]he House of Representatives may impeach a civil officer, but it must be done according to law. It must be *for some offence known to the law*, and not created by the fancy of the members of the House."[190] Congress did not impeach President Johnson until the following year, when he was impeached for violating the Tenure of Office Act.[191] The history of presidential impeachments provides no support for House Democrats' vague "abuse of power" charge.

> **(b)   House Democrats' Unprecedented Theory of Impeachable Offenses Defined by Subjective Intent Alone Would Permanently Weaken the Presidency.**

House Democrats' conception of "abuse of power" is especially dangerous because it rests on the even more radical claim that a President can be impeached and removed from office solely for doing something he is allowed to do, if he did it for the "wrong" *subjective* reasons. Under

---

[185]   H.R. Comm. on the Judiciary, *Impeachment of Richard M. Nixon, President of the United States*, H.R. Rep. No. 93-1305, 93d Cong. 371 (1974) (Minority Views of Messrs. Hutchinson, Smith, Sandman et al.).

[186]   *See H.R. Comm. on the Judiciary, Impeachment of William Jefferson Clinton, President of the United States,* H.R. Res. 611, 105th Cong. (1998); *see also* H.R. Rep. No. 105-830, 105th Cong. 143 (1998) (additional views of Rep. Bill McCollum) ("President Clinton actively sought to thwart the due administration of justice by repeatedly committing the felony crimes of perjury, witness tampering, and obstruction of justice.").

[187]   H.R. Rep. No. 93-1305, at 1–3; *see also id.* at 10 (alleging that Nixon "violated the constitutional rights of citizens" and "contravened the laws governing agencies of the executive branch").

[188]   *See supra* notes 123–126 and accompanying text.

[189]   *See* III Hinds' Precedents § 2407, at 843.

[190]   H.R. Rep. Com. No. 7, 40th Cong. 60 (1867) (Minority Views) (emphasis added); *see also* Michael Les Benedict, *The Impeachment and Trial of Andrew Johnson* 102 (1973).

[191]   Cong. Globe, 40th Cong., 2d Sess., 1616–18, 1638–42 (1868); *see also* Charles L. Black & Philip Bobbitt, *Impeachment: A Handbook, New Edition* 114 (2018); HJC Report at 48 ("Rather than directly target President Johnson's faithless execution of the laws, and his illegitimate motives in wielding power, the House resorted to charges based on the Tenure of Office Act.").

this view, impeachment can turn entirely on "whether the President's **real reasons**, the ones actually in his mind at the time, were legitimate."[192] That standard is so malleable that it would permit a partisan House—like this one—to attack virtually any presidential decision by questioning a President's motives. By eliminating any requirement for wrongful conduct, House Democrats have tried to make thinking the wrong thoughts an impeachable offense.

House Democrats' theory of impeachment based on subjective motive alone is unworkable and constitutionally impermissible.

First, by making impeachment turn on nearly impossible inquiries into the subjective intent behind entirely lawful conduct, House Democrats' standard would open virtually every presidential decision to partisan attack based on questioning a President's motives. As courts have repeatedly observed, "[i]nquiry into the motives of elected officials can be both difficult and undesirable, and such inquiry should be avoided when possible."[193] Thus, for example, courts will not invalidate laws within Congress's constitutional authority based on allegations about legislators' motives.[194] As constitutional historian Raoul Berger has observed, this principle "is equally applicable to executive action within statutory or constitutional limits."[195] Even House Democrats' own expert, Professor Michael Gerhardt, has previously explained (in defending the Obama Administration against charges of abuse of power) that "the President has the ability to . . . strongly push back against any inquiry into either the motivations or support for his actions."[196]

The Framers did not intend to expand the impeachment power infinitely by allowing Congress to attack objectively lawful presidential conduct based solely on unwieldy inquiries into subjective intent. Under the Framers' plan, impeachment was intended to apply to **objective** wrongdoing as identified by offenses defined under existing law. As noted above, the Framers rejected maladministration as a ground for impeachment precisely because it was "[s]o vague a term."[197] Instead, they settled on "high Crimes and Misdemeanors,"[198] as a term with a "limited and technical meaning."[199] "[H]igh Crimes and Misdemeanors," as well as "Treason" and "Bribery,"[200] all denote **objectively** wrongful conduct as defined by existing law. Each of the seven other references in the Constitution to impeachment also supports the conclusion that impeachments must be evaluated in terms of offenses against settled law: The Constitution refers to "Conviction" for impeachable offenses twice[201] and "**Judgment** in Cases of Impeachment."[202] It directs the Senate to "**try** all Impeachments"[203] and requires the Chief Justice's participation when the President is "tried."[204] And it implies impeachable offenses are "Crimes" and "Offenses"

---

[192] HJC Report at 33 (emphasis in original).

[193] *United States v. Marengo Cty. Comm'n*, 731 F.2d 1546, 1558 (11th Cir. 1984).

[194] *See* Berger, *supra* note 174, at 294–95.

[195] *Id.* at 295.

[196] *Obama Administration's Abuse of Power: Hearing Before the H.R. Comm. on the Judiciary*, 112th Cong. 20 (2012) (written statement of Professor Michael J. Gerhardt).

[197] 2 *Records of the Federal Convention*, *supra* note 175, at 550.

[198] U.S. Const. art. II, § 4.

[199] Berger, *supra* note 174, at 118 (internal quotation marks omitted).

[200] U.S. Const. art. II, § 4.

[201] U.S. Const. art. I, § 3, cl. 6; art. II, § 4.

[202] U.S. Const. art. I, § 3, cl. 7 (emphasis added).

[203] U.S. Const. art. I, § 3, cl. 6 (emphasis added).

[204] *Id.*

in the Jury Trial Clause and the Pardon Clause, respectively.[205] These are all words that indicate violations of established law. The Framers' words limited the impeachment power and, in particular, sought to ensure that impeachment could not be used to attack a President based on mere policy differences.

Given their apprehensions about misuse of the impeachment power, it is inconceivable that the Framers crafted a purely intent-based impeachment standard. Such a standard would be so vague and malleable that entirely permissible actions could lead to impeachment of a President (and potentially removal from office) based solely on a hostile Congress's assessment of the President's subjective motives. If that were the rule, any President's political opponents could take virtually any of his actions, mischaracterize his motives after the fact, and misuse impeachment as a tool for political opposition instead of as a safeguard against egregious presidential misconduct.[206] As Republicans on the House Judiciary Committee during the Nixon impeachment inquiry rightly explained, "[a]n impeachment power exercised without extrinsic and objective standards would be tantamount to the use of bills of attainder and *ex post facto* laws, which are expressly forbidden by the Constitution and are contrary to the American spirit of justice."[207]

House Democrats justify their focus on subjective motives based largely on a cherry-picked snippet from a statement James Iredell made in the North Carolina ratification debates.[208] Iredell observed that "the President would be liable to impeachment [if] . . . he had acted from some corrupt motive or other."[209] But nothing in that general statement suggests that Iredell—let alone the Framers or the hundreds of delegates who ratified the Constitution in the states—subscribed to House Democrats' current theory treating impeachment as a roving license for Congress to attack a President's lawful actions based on subjective motive alone. To the contrary, in the very same speech, Iredell himself warned against the dangers of allowing impeachment based on assessments of subjective motive. He explained that there would often be divisions between political parties and that, due to a lack of "charity," each might often "attribute every opposition" to its own views "to an ill motive."[210] In that environment, he warned, "[a] mere difference of opinion might be interpreted, by the malignity of party, into a deliberate, wicked action."[211] That, he argued, should ***not*** be a basis for impeachment.[212]

House Democrats' assertions that past presidential impeachments provide support for their

---

[205] U.S. Const. art. III, § 2, cl. 3 ("The Trial of all Crimes, except in Cases of Impeachment, shall be by Jury . . . ."); U.S. Const. art. II, § 2, cl. 1 ("[H]e shall have Power to grant Reprieves and Pardons for Offenses against the United States, except in Cases of Impeachment.").

[206] The offense of bribery, of course, involves an ***element*** of intent, and thus requires some evaluation of the accused's motivations and state of mind. *See* 4 Blackstone, *Commentaries* *139 ("BRIBERY . . . is when a judge, or other person concerned in the administration of justice, takes any undue reward to influence his behavior in his office."). There is a wide gulf, however, between proving a specific offense such as bribery that involves wrongful conduct along with the requisite intent and House Democrats' radical theory that ***any*** lawful action may be treated as an impeachable offense based on a characterization of subjective intent alone.

[207] H.R. Rep. No. 93-1305, at 371 (Minority Views of Messrs. Hutchinson, Smith, Sandman et al.).

[208] Trial Mem. of U.S. House of Representatives at 9; HJC Report at 31, 46, 70, 78.

[209] 4 Elliot, Debates in the Several State Conventions on the Adoption of the Federal Constitution 126 (2d ed. 1888).

[210] *Id.* at 127.

[211] *Id.*

[212] *Id.*

made-up impeachment-based-on-subjective-motives-alone theory are also wrong.[213] Contrary to their claims, neither the Nixon impeachment inquiry nor the impeachment of President Johnson supports their assertions.

In the Nixon impeachment inquiry, none of the articles recommended by the House Judiciary Committee was labeled "abuse of power" or framed the charge in those terms. And it is simply wrong to say that the theory underlying the proposed articles was that President Nixon had taken permissible actions with the wrong subjective motives. Article I alleged President Nixon obstructed justice, a clear violation of law.[214] And Article II asserted numerous breaches of the law. It claimed that President Nixon "violat[ed] the constitutional rights of citizens," "contraven[ed] the laws governing agencies of the executive branch," and "authorized and permitted to be maintained a secret investigative unit within the office of the President . . . which unlawfully utilized the resources of the Central Intelligence Agency, [and] engaged in covert and unlawful activities."[215] Those allegations did not turn on describing permissible conduct that had simply been done with the wrong subjective motives.[216] Instead, they charged *unlawful* conduct.[217]

House Democrats' reliance on the Johnson impeachment fares no better. According to House Democrats, the Johnson impeachment supports their concocted impeachment-based-on-subjective-motives theory under the following tortured logic: The articles of impeachment actually adopted by the House charged the violation of the Tenure of Office Act.[218] But that was not the "real" reason the House sought to remove President Johnson. The real reason was that he had undermined Reconstruction. And, in House Democrats' view, his improper desire to thwart Reconstruction was actually a *better* reason to impeach him.[219] For support, House Democrats cite a recent book co-authored by one of their own staffers (Joshua Matz) and Laurence Tribe.[220] This is nonsense. Nothing in the Johnson impeachment involved charging the President with taking objectively permissible action for the wrong subjective reasons. Johnson was impeached for violating a law passed by Congress.[221] Moreover, President Johnson was acquitted, despite whatever subjective motives he might have had. House Democrats cannot conjure a precedent out of thin air by simply imagining that the Johnson impeachment articles said something other than

---

[213] *See* HJC Report at 45–48.

[214] H.R. Rep. No. 93-1305, at 1–2. "This report . . . contains clear and convincing evidence that the President caused action—not only by his own subordinates but by agencies of the United States . . .—to cover up the Watergate break-in. This concealment required perjury, destruction of evidence, obstruction of justice—all of which are crimes." *Id.* at 33–34.

[215] *Id.* at 3. While the House Judiciary Committee's report described Article II generally as involving "abuse of the powers of the office of President," *id.* at 139, it is significant that the actual *charge* the Judiciary Committee specified in the recommended article of impeachment was not framed in terms of that amorphous concept. To the contrary, the article of impeachment itself charged unlawful actions and dropped the vague terminology of "abuse of power."

[216] The third recommended article charged President Nixon with defying congressional subpoenas "without lawful cause or excuse" and asserted that the President had violated the assignment of the "sole power of impeachment" to the House by resisting subpoenas. *Id.* at 4. It also provides no precedent for House Democrats' abuse-of-power theory.

[217] *See, e.g., Debate on Articles of Impeachment: Hearings Before the H.R. Comm. on the Judiciary*, 93d Cong. 412 (1974) (statement of Rep. Don Edwards) ("[A]rticle II charges President Nixon with intentional violations of the Constitution, chiefly amendments one, four, five, and six.").

[218] HJC Report at 45.

[219] *Id.* at 47–48.

[220] *Id.* at 48 n.244.

[221] Cong. Globe, 40th Cong., 2d Sess., 1616–18, 1638–42 (1868).

what they said.[222]

If the Johnson impeachment established any precedent relevant here, it is that the House refused to impeach the President until he clearly violated the letter of the law. As one historian has explained, despite widespread anger among Republicans about President Johnson's actions undermining Reconstruction, until Johnson violated the Tenure of Office Act, "[t]he House had refused to impeach [him] . . . at least in part because many representatives did not believe he had committed a specific violation of law."[223]

Second, House Democrats' theory raises particular dangers because it makes "personal political benefit" one of the "forbidden reasons" for taking government action.[224] Under that standard, a President could potentially be impeached and removed from office for taking any action with his political interests in view. In a representative democracy, however, elected officials almost *always* consider the effect that their conduct might have on the next election. And there is nothing wrong with that.

By making "personal political gain" an illicit motive for official action, House Democrats' radical theory of impeachment would permit a partisan Congress to remove virtually *any* President by questioning the extent to which his or her action was motivated by electoral considerations rather than the "right" policy motivation. None of this has any basis in the constitutional text, which specifies particular offenses as impeachable conduct. Just as importantly, under such a rule, impeachments would turn on unanswerable questions that ultimately reduce to policy disputes— exactly what the Framers saw as an impermissible basis for impeachment. For example, if it is impeachable conduct to act with *too much* of a view toward electoral results, how much of a focus on electoral results is too much, even assuming that Congress could accurately disaggregate a President's actual motives? And how does one measure presidential motives against some unknowable standard of the "right" policy result uninfluenced by considerations of political gain? That question, of course, quickly boils down to nothing more than a dispute about the "right" policy in the first place. None of this provides any permissible basis for impeaching a President.

Third, aptly demonstrating why all of this leads to unconstitutional results, House Democrats have invented standards for identifying supposedly illicit presidential motives that turn the Constitution upside down. According to House Democrats, they can show that President Trump acted with illicit motives because, in their view, the President supposedly "disregarded

---

[222] Even the source they cite undermines House Democrats' theories. Tribe and Matz explain that one of the most important lessons from Johnson's impeachment is "it really does matter which acts are identified in articles of impeachment" and that impeachment proceedings are "technical and legalistic." Laurence Tribe & Joshua Matz, *To End a Presidency: The Power of Impeachment* 54 (2018).

[223] Benedict, *supra* note 190, at 102. Even if President Johnson's impeachment did support House Democrats' novel theory—which it does not—it does not provide a model to be emulated. As House Democrats' hand-picked expert, Professor Michael Gerhardt, has explained, the Johnson impeachment is a "dubious precedent" because it is "widely regarded as perhaps the most intensely partisan impeachment rendered by the House"—at least until now. Michael J. Gerhardt, *The Federal Impeachment Process* 179 (3d ed. 2019); *see also* Berger, *supra* note 174, at 295 ("The impeachment and trial of Andrew Johnson, to my mind, represent a gross abuse of the impeachment process . . . ."); Jonathan Turley, *Democrats Repeat Failed History with Mad Dash to Impeach Donald Trump*, The Hill (Dec. 17, 2019), https://perma.cc/4Y3X-FCBW ("The Johnson case has long been widely regarded as the very prototype of an abusive impeachment. . . . Some critics have actually cited Johnson as precedent to show that impeachment can be done on purely political grounds. In other words, the very reason the Johnson impeachment is condemned by history is now being used today as a justification to dispense with standards and definitions of impeachable acts.").

[224] HJC Report at 44.

United States foreign policy towards Ukraine,"[225] ignored the "official policy"[226] that he had been briefed on, and "ignored, defied, and confounded every agency within the Executive Branch" with his decisions on Ukraine.[227] These assertions are preposterous and dangerous. They fundamentally misunderstand the assignment of power under the Constitution.

Article II of the Constitution states that "the executive Power shall be vested in a President"—not Executive Branch staff.[228] The vesting of the Executive Power in the President makes him "the sole organ of the nation in its external relations, and its sole representative with foreign nations."[229] He sets foreign policy for the Nation, and in "this vast external realm," the "President alone has the power to speak . . . as a representative of the nation."[230] The Constitution assigns him control over foreign policy precisely to ensure that the Nation speaks with one voice.[231] His decisions are authoritative regardless of the judgments of the unelected bureaucrats participating in an inter-agency process that exists solely to facilitate his decisions, not to make decisions for him. Any theory of an impeachable offense that turns on ferreting out supposedly "constitutionally improper" motives by measuring the President's policy decisions against a purported "interagency consensus" formed by unelected staff is a transparent and impermissible inversion of the constitutional structure.

It requires no leap of imagination to see the absurd consequences that would follow from House Democrats' theory. Imagine a President who, in an election year, determined to withdraw troops from an overseas deployment to have them home by Christmas. Should hostile lawmakers be able to seek impeachment and claim proof of "illicit motive" because an alleged "interagency consensus" showed that the "real" national security interests of the United States required keeping those troops in place? Manufacturing an impeachment out of such an assertion ought to be dismissed out of hand.

House Democrats' abuse-of-power theory is also profoundly anti-democratic. In assigning the Executive Power to the President, the Constitution ensures that power is exercised by a person who is democratically responsible to the people through a quadrennial election.[232] This ensures that the people themselves will regularly and frequently have a say in the direction of the Nation's policy, including foreign policy. As a result, removing a President on the ground that his foreign policy decisions were allegedly based on "illicit motives"—because they failed to conform to a purported "consensus" of career bureaucrats—would fundamentally subvert the democratic principles at the core of our Constitution.

This very impeachment shows how anti-democratic House Democrats' theory really is.

---

[225] *Id.* at 99.

[226] *Id.*

[227] *Id.* at 103.

[228] U.S. Const. art. II, § 1.

[229] *United States v. Curtiss-Wright Exp. Corp.*, 299 U.S. 304, 319 (1936) (citation omitted).

[230] *Id.*

[231] *See Zivotofsky ex rel. Zivotofsky v. Kerry*, 135 S. Ct. 2076, 2086 (2015).

[232] U.S. Const. art. II, § 1; *cf.* Joseph Story, *Commentaries on the Constitution* § 1450 (1833) ("One motive, which induced a change of the choice of the president from the national legislature, unquestionably was, to have the sense of the people operate in the choice of the person, to whom so important a trust was confided."); *Hamdi v. Rumsfeld*, 542 U.S. 507, 531 (2004) (plurality opinion) (emphasizing that "our Constitution recognizes that core strategic matters of warmaking belong in the hands of those who are best positioned and most politically accountable for making them").

Millions of Americans voted for President Trump precisely because he promised to disrupt the foreign policy status quo. He promised a new, "America First" foreign policy that many in the Washington establishment derided. And the President has delivered, bringing fresh and successful approaches to foreign policy in a host of areas, including relations with NATO, China, Israel, and North Korea. In particular, with respect to Ukraine and elsewhere, his foreign policy has focused on ensuring that America does not shoulder a disproportionate burden for various international missions, that other countries do their fair share, and that taxpayer dollars are not squandered. House Democrats' theory that a purported inter-agency "consensus" among career bureaucrats can be used to show improper motive is an affront to the tens of millions of American citizens who voted for President Trump's foreign policy and not a continuation of the Washington establishment's policy preferences.

2. **House Democrats' Assertions that the Framers Particularly Intended Impeachment to Guard Against "Foreign Entanglements" and "Corruption" of Elections Are Makeweights that Distort History.**

House Democrats try to shore up their made-up theory of abuse of power by pretending that anything related to what they call "foreign entanglements" or elections strikes at the core of impeachment.[233] This novel accounting of the concerns animating the impeachment power conveniently allows House Democrats to claim that their allegations just happen to raise the perfect storm of impeachable conduct, as if their accusations show that "President Trump has realized the Framers' worst nightmare."[234] That is preposterous on its face. The Framers were concerned about the possibility of treason and the danger that foreign princes with vast treasuries at their disposal might actually buy off the Chief Executive of a fledgling, debt-ridden republic situated on the seaboard of a vast wilderness continent—most of which was still claimed by European powers eager to advance their imperial interests. Their worst nightmare was not the President of the United States-as-superpower having an innocuous conversation with the leader of a comparatively small European republic and disclosing the conversation for all Americans to see.

To peddle their distortion of history, House Democrats cobble together snippets from the Framers' discussions on various different subjects and try to portray them as if they define the contours of impeachable offenses. As explained above, the Framers intended a limited impeachment power. But when House Democrats find the Framers raising concerns about any risks to the new government, they leap to the conclusion that those concerns must identify impeachable offenses. Such transparently results-driven historical analysis is baseless and provides no support for House Democrats' drive to remove the President.

First, House Democrats mangle history in offering "foreign entanglements" as a type of impeachable offense. Their approach confuses two different concepts—entangling the country in alliances and fears of foreign governments buying influence—to create a false impression that there is something insidious about anything involving a foreign connection that should make it a particularly ripe ground for impeachment.

When the Framers spoke about foreign "entanglements" they had a particular danger in mind. That was the danger of the young country becoming ensnared in alliances that would draw

---

[233] HJC Report at 48–53, 79–81.

[234] *Id.* at 131; *see also id.* at 31 (pretending that House Democrats' have presented "the strongest possible case for impeachment and removal from office").

it into conflicts between European powers. When President Washington asserted that "history and experience prove that foreign influence is one of the most baneful foes of republican government," he was not warning about Chief Executives meriting removal from office.[235] He was advocating for neutrality in American foreign policy, and in particular, with respect to Europe.[236] One of President Washington's most controversial decisions was establishing American neutrality in the escalating war between Great Britain and revolutionary France.[237] He then used his Farewell Address to argue against "entangl[ing] [American] peace and prosperity in the toils of European ambition, rivalship, interest, humor [and] caprice."[238] Again, he was warning about the United States being drawn into foreign alliances that would trap the young country in disputes between European powers. House Democrats' false allegations here have nothing to do with the danger of a foreign entanglement as the Founders understood that term, and the admonitions from the Founding era they cite are irrelevant.[239]

The Framers were also concerned about the distinct problem of foreign attempts to *interfere* in the governance of the United States.[240] But on that score, they identified particular concerns based on historical examples and addressed them specifically. They were concerned about officials being bought off by foreign powers. Gouverneur Morris articulated this concern: "Our Executive . . . may be bribed by a greater interest to betray his trust; and no one would say that we ought to expose ourselves to the danger of seeing the first Magistrate in foreign pay without being able to guard [against] it by displacing him."[241] He specifically mentioned the bribe King Louis XIV of France had paid to King Charles II of England to influence English policy.[242] This is why "Bribery" and "Treason" were made impeachable offenses. The Framers also addressed the danger of foreign inducements directed at the President by barring his acceptance of "any present, Emolument, Office, or Title" in the Foreign Emoluments Clause.[243] House Democrats' Articles of Impeachment make no allegations under any of these specific offenses identified in the Constitution.

In the end, House Democrats' ahistorical arguments rest on a non sequitur. They essentially argue that because the Framers showed concern about the Nation being betrayed in these specific provisions, any accusations that relate to foreign influence must equally amount to impeachable conduct. That simply does not follow. To the contrary, since the Framers made specific provisions for the types of foreign interference they feared, there is no reason to think that the Impeachment Clause must be stretched and contorted to reach *other* conduct simply because it has to do with something foreign. The Framers' approach to treason, in particular, suggests that House Democrats' logic is wrong. The Framers defined treason in the Constitution to *limit* it.[244]

---

[235]   Trial Mem. of U.S. House of Representatives at 10–11 (quoting George Washington Farewell Address (1796), https://perma.cc/6FSA-8HBN (Washington Farewell Address)); HJC Report at 31 (quoting Washington Farewell Address).

[236]   Washington Farewell Address, *supra* note 235.

[237]   William R. Casto, *Foreign Affairs and the Constitution in the Age of the Fighting Sail*, 19–34, 59–82 (2006).

[238]   Washington Farewell Address, *supra* note 235.

[239]   If anything, the concerns of the Founding generation would suggest here that the U.S. should not be giving aid to Ukraine to halt Russian aggression because *that* is a foreign entanglement. The foreign policy needs of the Nation have obviously changed.

[240]   *See* HJC Report at 49–50.

[241]   2 *Records of the Federal Convention*, *supra* note 175, at 68.

[242]   *Id.* at 69–70.

[243]   U.S. Const. art. I, § 9, cl. 8; 2 *Records of the Federal Convention*, *supra* note 175, at 389.

[244]   Benjamin Franklin explained the Framers adopted a narrow definition of treason because "prosecutions for

Nothing about their concern for *limiting* treason suggests that a general concern about foreign betrayal should be used as a ratchet to *expand* the scope of the Impeachment Clause and make it infinitely malleable so that all charges cast in the vague language of "foreign entanglements" should automatically state impeachable conduct.

Second, House Democrats point to the Founders' concerns that a President might bribe electors to stay in office.[245] But that specific concern does not mean, as they claim, that anything to do with an election was a central concern of impeachment and that impeachment is the tool the Framers created to deal with it. The historical evidence shows the Framers had a specific concern with presidential candidates bribing members of the Electoral College.[246] That concern was addressed by the clear terms of the Constitution, which made "Bribery" a basis for impeachment.[247] Nothing in House Democrats' sources suggests that simply because one grave form of corruption related to elections became a basis for impeachment, then any accusations of any sort related to elections necessarily must fall within the ambit of impeachable conduct. That is simply an invention of the House Democrats.

> **B.** **House Democrats' Charge of "Obstruction" Fails Because Invoking Constitutionally Based Privileges and Immunities to Protect the Separation of Powers Is Not an Impeachable Offense.**

House Democrats' charge of "obstruction" is both frivolous and dangerous. At the outset, the very suggestion that President Trump has somehow "obstructed" Congress is preposterous. The President has been extraordinarily transparent about his interactions with President Zelenskyy. Immediately after questions arose, President Trump took the unprecedented step of declassifying and releasing the full record of his July 25 telephone call, and he later released the transcript of an April 21, 2019 call as well. It is well settled that the President has a virtually absolute right to maintain the confidentiality of his diplomatic communications with foreign leaders.[248] And keeping such communications confidential is essential for the effective conduct of diplomacy, because it ensures that foreign leaders will be willing to talk candidly with the President. Nevertheless, after weighing such concerns, the President determined that complete transparency was important in this case, and he released both call records so that the American people could judge for themselves exactly what he said to the President of Ukraine. That should have put an end to this inquiry before it began. The President was not "obstructing" when he freely released

---

treason were generally virulent; and perjury too easily made use of against innocence." 2 *Records of the Federal Convention, supra* note 175, at 348. Article III, Section 3 not only defines treason in specific terms but it establishes a high standard of proof, requiring the testimony of two witnesses or a confession.

[245] HJC Report at 52, 80.

[246] 2 *Records of the Federal Convention, supra* note 175, at 65 (George Mason) ("One objection agst. Electors was the danger of their being corrupted by the Candidates: & this furnished a peculiar reason in favor of impeachments whilst in office."); *id.* at 69 (Gouverneur Morris) ("The Executive ought therefore to be impeachable for . . . Corrupting his electors.").

[247] U.S. Const. art. II, § 4.

[248] *United States v. Nixon*, 418 U.S. 683, 710–11 (1974) (explaining that "courts have traditionally shown the utmost deference to Presidential responsibilities" for foreign policy and national security and emphasizing that claims of privilege in this area would receive a higher degree of deference than invocations of "a President's generalized interest in confidentiality"); *Assertion of Executive Privilege for Documents Concerning Conduct of Foreign Affairs with Respect to Haiti*, 20 Op. O.L.C. 6, 6 (1996) (citing *Nixon*, 418 U.S. at 705–13); *see also Department of the Navy v. Egan*, 484 U.S. 518, 529 (1988) ("The Court also has recognized the generally accepted view that foreign policy was the province and responsibility of the Executive.") (internal quotation marks and citation omitted).

the central piece of evidence in this case.

The President also was not "obstructing" when he rightly decided to defend established Executive Branch confidentiality interests, rooted in the separation of powers, against unauthorized efforts to rummage through Executive Branch files and to demand testimony from some of the President's closest advisers. As the Supreme Court has explained, the privilege protecting the confidentiality of presidential communications "is fundamental to the operation of Government and inextricably rooted in the separation of powers under the Constitution."[249] For future occupants of the Office of President, it was essential for the President, like past occupants of the Office, to protect Executive Branch confidentiality against House Democrats' overreaching intrusions.

The President's proper concern for requiring the House to proceed by lawful measures and for protecting long-settled Executive Branch confidentiality interests cannot be twisted into an impeachable offense. To the contrary, House Democrats' charge of "obstruction" comes nowhere close to the constitutional standard. It does not charge any violation of established law. More important, it is based on the fundamentally mistaken premise that the President can be removed from office for invoking established legal defenses and immunities against defective subpoenas from House committees.

The President does not commit "obstruction" by asserting legal rights and privileges.[250] And House Democrats turn the law on its head with their unprecedented claim that it is "obstruction" for anyone to assert rights that might require the House to try to establish the validity of its subpoenas in court.[251] House Democrats' radical theories are especially misplaced where, as here, the legal principles invoked by the President and other Administration officials are critical for preserving the separation of powers—and based on advice from the Department of Justice's Office of Legal Counsel.

Treating a disagreement regarding constitutional limits on the House's authority to compel documents or testimony as an impeachable offense would do permanent damage to the Constitution's separation of powers and our structure of government. It would allow the House of Representatives to declare itself supreme and turn *any* disagreement with the Executive over informational demands into a purported basis for removing the President from office. As Professor Turley has explained, "Basing impeachment on this obstruction theory would itself be an abuse of power . . . *by Congress*."[252]

---

[249] *Nixon*, 418 U.S. at 708.

[250] *See Prosecution for Contempt of Congress of an Executive Branch Official Who Has Asserted a Claim of Executive Privilege*, 8 Op. O.L.C. 101, 140 (1984) ("[T]he Constitution does not permit Congress to make it a crime for an official to assist the President in asserting a constitutional privilege that is an integral part of the President's responsibilities under the Constitution.").

[251] Press Release, Transcript of Pelosi Weekly Press Conference Today (Oct. 2, 2019), https://perma.cc/YPM4-WCNX (Rep. Adam Schiff, Chairman of the House Intelligence Committee, stating that "any action like that, that forces us to litigate or have to consider litigation, will be considered further evidence of obstruction of justice").

[252] *Impeachment Inquiry into President Donald J. Trump: Constitutional Grounds for Presidential Impeachment Before the H.R. Comm. on the Judiciary*, 116th Cong. (Dec. 4, 2019) (written statement of Professor Jonathan Turley, George Washington Univ. Law School, at 42, https://perma.cc/QU4H-FZC4) (emphasis added).

1. **President Trump Acted Properly—and upon Advice from the Department of Justice—by Asserting Established Legal Defenses and Immunities to Resist Legally Defective Demands for Information from House Committees.**

House Democrats' purported "obstruction" charge is based on three actions by the President or Executive Branch officials acting under his authority, each of which was entirely proper and taken only after securing advice from OLC.

(a) **Administration Officials Properly Refused to Comply with Subpoenas that Lacked Authorization from the House.**

It was entirely proper for Administration officials to decline to comply with subpoenas issued pursuant to a purported "impeachment inquiry" before the House of Representatives had authorized any such inquiry. No House committee can issue subpoenas pursuant to the House's impeachment power without authorization from the House itself. On precisely that basis, OLC determined that all subpoenas issued before the adoption of House Resolution 660 on October 31, 2019, purportedly to advance an "impeachment inquiry," were unauthorized and invalid.[253] Numerous witness subpoenas and *all* of the document subpoenas cited in Article II are invalid for this reason alone. These invalid subpoenas imposed no legal obligation on the recipients, and it was entirely lawful for the recipients not to comply with them.[254] The belated adoption of House Resolution 660 on October 31 to authorize the inquiry essentially conceded that a vote was required and did nothing to remedy the inquiry's invalid beginnings.

(i) **A Delegation of Authority from the House Is Required Before Any Committee Can Investigate Pursuant to the Impeachment Power.**

No committee can exercise authority assigned by the Constitution to the House absent a clear delegation of authority from the House itself.[255] The Constitution assigns the "sole Power of Impeachment"[256] to the House as a chamber—not to individual Members or subordinate units. Assessing the validity of a committee's inquiry and subpoenas thus requires "constru[ing] the scope of the authority which the House of Representatives gave to" the committee.[257] Where a committee cannot demonstrate that its inquiries have been authorized by an affirmative vote of the House assigning the committee authority, the committee's actions are *ultra vires*, and its subpoenas

---

[253] Memorandum from Steven A. Engel, Assistant Attorney General, Office of Legal Counsel, to Pat A. Cipollone, Counsel to the President, *Re: House Committees' Authority to Investigate for Impeachment*, at 1–3 (Jan. 19, 2020) (*Impeachment Inquiry Authorization*), *infra* Appendix C.

[254] *See Watkins v. United States*, 354 U.S. 178, 206, 215 (1957) (holding that congressional subpoenas were invalid where they exceeded "the mission[] delegated to" a committee by the House); *United States v. Rumely*, 345 U.S. 41, 44 (1953) (holding that the congressional committee was without power to compel the production of certain information because the requests exceeded the scope of the authorizing resolution); *Tobin v. United States*, 306 F.2d 270, 276 (D.C. Cir. 1962) (reversing a contempt conviction on the basis that the subpoena requested documents outside the scope of the Subcommittee's authority to investigate).

[255] *Watkins*, 354 U.S. at 200–10.

[256] U.S. Const. art. I, § 2, cl. 5.

[257] *Rumely*, 345 U.S. at 42–44; *see also Trump v. Mazars USA, LLP*, 940 F.3d 710, 722 (D.C. Cir. 2019); *Exxon Corp. v. FTC*, 589 F.2d 582, 592 (D.C. Cir. 1978); *Tobin*, 306 F.2d at 275.

have no force.[258]

To pursue an "impeachment inquiry," and to compel testimony and the production of documents for such an inquiry, the committee must be authorized to conduct an inquiry pursuant to the House's impeachment power. That power is distinct from the power to legislate assigned to Congress in Article I, Section 1. Congress's power to investigate in support of its power to legislate is limited to inquiring into topics "on which legislation could be had."[259] An impeachment inquiry is not subject to the same constraint. An impeachment inquiry does not aid Congress in considering legislation, but instead requires reconstructing past events to examine the conduct of specific persons. That differs from the forward-looking nature of any legislative investigation.[260] Given these differences, a committee seeking to investigate pursuant to the impeachment power must show that the House has actually authorized the committee to use that specific power.

The Speaker of the House cannot treat the House's constitutional power as her own to distribute to committees based on nothing more than her own say-so. That would exacerbate the danger of a minority faction invoking the power of impeachment to launch disruptive inquiries without any constitutional legitimacy from a majority vote in the House. It would also permit a minority to seize the House's formidable investigative powers to pursue divisive investigations for partisan purposes that a House majority might not be willing to authorize. House Democrats have not identified any credible support for their theory of authorization by press conference.[261]

---

[258] *E.g.*, *Watkins*, 354 U.S. at 207 ("[C]ommittees are restricted to the missions delegated to them . . . ."); *Tobin*, 306 F.2d at 276; Alissa M. Dolan et al., Cong. Research Serv., RL30240, *Congressional Oversight Manual* 24 (2014).

[259] *McGrain v. Daugherty*, 273 U.S. 135, 177 (1927).

[260] *Senate Select Comm. on Presidential Campaign Activities v. Nixon*, 498 F.2d 725, 732 (D.C. Cir. 1974).

[261] Nothing in the recent decision in *In re Application of Committee on the Judiciary* establishes that a committee can pursue an investigation pursuant to the impeachment power without authorization by a vote from the House. *See* __ F. Supp. 3d __, 2019 WL 5485221, at *26–28 (D.D.C. Oct. 25, 2019). Any such discussion was dicta. The question before the court was whether a particular Judiciary Committee inquiry was being conducted "preliminarily to" an impeachment trial in the Senate, a question that the court viewed as depending on the inquiry's "purpose" and whether it could lead to such a trial—"not the source of authority Congress acts under." *Id.* at *28 n.37. In any event, the court's analysis was flawed.

First, the court, like the Committees, misread a House annotation to Jefferson's Manual. *See, e.g.*, Letter from Elijah E. Cummings, Chairman, House Oversight Committee, et al., to John Michael Mulvaney, Acting White House Chief of Staff, at 2 (Oct. 4, 2019). The language quoted by the court states that "various events have been credited with setting an impeachment in motion." H. Doc. 114-192, 114th Cong. § 603 (2017). But that does not mean that any of these "various events" automatically confers authority on a committee to begin an impeachment inquiry. It merely acknowledges the historical fact that there is more than one way the House may *receive information* that may prompt the House to *then* authorize a committee to pursue an impeachment investigation.

Second, the court misread III Hinds' Precedents § 2400 as showing that "a resolution 'authoriz[ing]' HJC 'to inquire into the official conduct of Andrew Johnson' was passed *after* HJC 'was already considering the subject.'" *Id.* at *27. That section discusses *two* House votes on *two* separate resolutions that occurred weeks apart. The House first voted to authorize the Johnson inquiry (which the court missed), and it then voted to refer a second matter (the resolution cited by the court), which touched upon President Johnson's impeachment, "to the Committee on the Judiciary, which was already considering the subject." III Hinds' Precedents § 2400. The court also misread the Nixon precedent as involving an "investigation well before the House passed a resolution authorizing an impeachment inquiry." *In re Application of the Comm. on the Judiciary*, 2019 WL 5485221, at *27. But that pre-resolution work did not involve any exercise of the House's impeachment power and was instead limited to preliminary, self-organizing work conducting "research into the constitutional issue of defining the grounds for impeachment" and "collecting and sifting the evidence available in the public domain." Staff of H.R. Comm. on the Judiciary, *Constitutional Grounds for Presidential Impeachment*, 93d Cong. 1–3 (Comm. Print 1974). The Chairman of the Committee himself acknowledged that, to actually launch an inquiry, a House resolution "is a necessary step." 120 Cong. Rec. 2351 (Feb. 6, 1974 statement of Rep. Rodino).

(ii) Nothing in Existing House Rules Authorized Any Committee to Pursue an Impeachment Inquiry.

Nothing in the House Rules adopted at the beginning of this Congress delegated authority to pursue an impeachment inquiry to any committee. In particular, Rule X, which defines each committee's jurisdiction, makes clear that it addresses only committees' *legislative jurisdiction*—not impeachment.[262] Rule X does not assign any committee any authority whatsoever with respect to impeachment. It does not even mention impeachment. And that silence is not accidental. Rule X devotes more than 2,000 words to describing the committees' areas of jurisdiction in detail. The six committees that Speaker Pelosi instructed to take part in the purported impeachment inquiry here have their jurisdiction defined down to the most obscure legislative issues, ranging from the Judiciary Committee's jurisdiction over "[s]tate and territorial boundary lines"[263] to the Oversight Committee's responsibility for "[h]olidays and celebrations."[264] But Rule X does not assign any committee authority regarding impeachment. Neither does Rule XI's grant of specific investigative powers, such as the power to hold hearings and to issue subpoenas. Each committee's specific investigative powers under Rule XI are restricted to Rule X's jurisdictional limits[265]—which do not include impeachment.[266]

Rule X's history confirms that the absence of any reference to "impeachment" was deliberate. When the House considered a number of proposals between 1973 and 1974 to transfer power from the House to committees and to remake committee jurisdiction, the House specifically rejected an initial proposal that would have added "impeachments" to the Judiciary Committee's jurisdiction.[267] Instead, the House amended the rules to provide standing authorization for

---

Third, the court misread House Resolution 430, which was adopted on June 11, 2019. The court plucked out language from the resolution granting the Judiciary Committee "any and all necessary authority under Article I of the Constitution," as if to suggest that the Judiciary Committee could, under that grant, initiate an impeachment inquiry. *In re Application of Comm. on Judiciary*, 2019 WL 5485221, at *29 (quoting H.R. Res. 430, 116th Cong. (2019)). But House Resolution 430 is actually much more narrow. After providing certain authorizations for filing lawsuits, the resolution simply gave committees authority to pursue litigation effectively by providing that, "*in connection with any judicial proceeding brought under the first or second resolving clauses*, the chair of any standing or permanent select committee exercising authority thereunder has any and all necessary authority under Article I of the Constitution." H.R Res. 430 (emphasis added). Simply by providing authority to pursue lawsuits, House Resolution 430 did not authorize any committee to initiate an impeachment investigation.

[262] Clerk, House of Representatives, *Rules of the House of Representatives*, 116th Cong. (2019) (H.R. Rule).

[263] H.R. Rule X.1(l)(18).

[264] H.R. Rule X.1(n)(5).

[265] H.R. Rule XI.1(b)(1) (limiting the power to conduct "investigations and studies" to those "necessary or appropriate in the exercise of its responsibilities under rule X"); H.R. Rule XI.2(m)(1) (limiting the power to hold hearings and issue subpoenas to "the purpose of carrying out any of [the committee's] functions and duties under this rule and rule X (including any matters referred to it under clause 2 of rule XII)").

[266] The mere referral of an impeachment resolution by itself could not authorize a committee to begin an impeachment inquiry. The "Speaker's referral authority under Rule XII is . . . limited to matters within a committee's Rule X legislative jurisdiction" and "may not expand the jurisdiction of a committee by referring a bill or resolution falling outside the committee's Rule X legislative authority." *Impeachment Inquiry Authorization*, *infra* Appendix C, at 30; *see* H.R. Rule XII.2(a); 18 Deschler's Precedents of the House of Representatives, app. at 578 (1994) (Deschler's Precedents). If a mere referral could authorize an impeachment inquiry, then a single House member could trigger the delegation of the House's "sole Power of Impeachment" to a committee and thus, for the House's most serious investigations, end-run Rule XI.1(b)(1)'s limitation of committee investigations to the committees' jurisdiction under Rule X.

[267] H.R. Res. 988, 93d Cong. 1, 13 (1974), *reprinted in* H.R. Select Comm. on Comms., *Committee Reform Amendments of 1974*, H.R. Rep. No. 93-916, 93d Cong. 367, 379 (1974); *see also* 120 Cong. Rec. 32,962 (1974).

committees to use investigatory powers only pursuant to their *legislative* jurisdiction[268] (previously, for example, a separate House vote was required to delegate subpoena authority to a particular committee for a particular topic).[269] Thus, after these amended rules were adopted, committees were able to begin investigations within their legislative jurisdiction and issue subpoenas without securing House approval, but that resolution did not authorize self-initiated impeachment inquiries. Indeed, it was precisely because "impeachment was not specifically included within the jurisdiction of the House Judiciary Committee" that then-Chairman Peter Rodino announced that the "Committee on the Judiciary will have to seek subpoena power from the House" for the Nixon impeachment inquiry.[270] The House majority, minority, and Parliamentarian, as well as the Department of Justice, all agreed on this point.[271]

(iii) More Than 200 Years of Precedent Confirm that the House Must Vote to Begin an Impeachment Inquiry.

Historical practice confirms the need for a House vote to launch an impeachment inquiry. Since the Founding of the Republic, the House has *never* undertaken the solemn responsibility of a presidential impeachment inquiry without first authorizing a particular committee to begin the inquiry. That has also been the House's nearly unbroken practice for every judicial impeachment for two hundred years.

In every prior presidential impeachment inquiry, the House adopted a resolution explicitly authorizing the committee to conduct the investigation before any compulsory process was used.[272] In President Clinton's impeachment, the House Judiciary Committee explained that the resolution was a constitutional requirement "[b]ecause impeachment is delegated solely to the House of Representatives by the Constitution" and thus "the full House of Representatives should be involved in critical decision making regarding various stages of impeachment."[273] As the Judiciary Committee Chairman explained during President Nixon's impeachment, an "authoriz[ation] . . . resolution has always been passed by the House" for an impeachment inquiry and "is a *necessary* step."[274] Thus, he recognized that, without authorization from the House, "the committee's subpoena power [did] not now extend to impeachment."[275] Indeed, with respect to impeachments

---

That language was stripped from the resolution by an amendment, *see* 120 Cong. Rec. 32,968–72 (1974), the amended resolution was adopted, *id.* at 34,469–70, and impeachment has remained outside the scope of any standing committee's jurisdiction ever since. *Cf. Barenblatt v. United States*, 360 U.S. 109, 117–18 (1959) (disapproving of "read[ing] [a House rule] in isolation from its long history" and ignoring the "persuasive gloss of legislative history").

[268] H.R. Res. 988, 93d Cong. (Oct. 8, 1974); Staff of the Select Comm. on Comms., *Committee Reform Amendments of 1974*, 93d Cong. 117 (Comm. Print 1974).

[269] Certain committees, not relevant here, had authority to issue subpoenas. Rules of the House of Representatives of the United States, H.R. Doc. No. 114-192, at 584 (2017).

[270] Congressional Quarterly, *Impeachment and the U.S. Congress* 20 (Robert A. Diamond ed., 1974).

[271] 3 Deschler's Precedents ch. 14, § 15.2, at 2171 (statements of Rep. Peter Rodino and Rep. Hutchinson); *id.* at 2172 (Parliamentarian's Note); *see also* Dep't of Justice, Office of Legal Counsel, *Legal Aspects of Impeachment: An Overview*, at 42 n.21 (1974), https://perma.cc/X4HU-WVWS.

[272] H.R. Res. 581, 105th Cong. (1998) (Clinton); H.R. Res. 803, 93d Cong. (1974) (Nixon); Cong. Globe, 40th Cong., 2d Sess. 784–85, 1087 (1868) (Johnson); Cong. Globe, 39th Cong., 2d Sess. 320–21 (1867) (Johnson); *see also* III Hinds' Precedents of the House of Representatives § 2408, at 845 (1907) (Hinds' Precedents) (Johnson); *id.* § 2400, at 823–24 (Johnson).

[273] H.R. Comm. on the Judiciary, *Investigatory Powers of the Comm. on the Judiciary with Respect to its Impeachment Inquiry*, H.R. Rep. No. 105-795, 105th Cong. 24 (1998).

[274] 3 Deschler's Precedents ch. 14, § 15.2, at 2171 (statement of Rep. Rodino) (emphasis added); *see also, e.g.*, 120 Cong. Rec. 2356 (1974) (statement of Rep. Jordan).

[275] Richard L. Lyons, *GOP Picks Jenner as Counsel*, Wash. Post (Jan. 8, 1974), at A1, A6.

of judges or lesser officers in the Executive Branch, the requirement that the full House pass a resolution authorizing an impeachment inquiry traces back to the first impeachments under the Constitution.[276]

That historical practice has continued into the modern era, in which there have been only three impeachments that did not begin with a House resolution authorizing an inquiry. Each of those three outliers involved impeachment of a lower court judge during a short interlude in the 1980s.[277] Those outliers provide no precedent for a presidential impeachment. To paraphrase the Supreme Court, "when considered against 200 years of settled practice, we regard these few scattered examples as anomalies."[278] In addition, as explained above,[279] "[t]he impeachment of a federal judge does not provide the same weighty considerations as the impeachment of a president."[280] Setting aside these three outliers, precedent shows that a House vote is required to initiate an impeachment inquiry for judges and subordinate executive officials. At least the same level of process must be used to begin the far more serious process of inquiring into impeachment of the President.

> (iv)   **The Subpoenas Issued Before House Resolution 660 Were Invalid and Remain Invalid Because the Resolution Did Not Ratify Them.**

The impeachment inquiry was unauthorized and all the subpoenas issued by House committees in pursuit of the inquiry were therefore invalid. OLC reached the same conclusion.[281]

---

[276] In 1796, the Attorney General advised the House that, to proceed with impeachment of a territorial judge, "a committee of the House of Representatives" must "be appointed for [the] purpose" of examining evidence. III Hinds' Precedents § 2486, at 982. The House accepted and ratified this advice in its first impeachment the next year and in each of the next twelve impeachments of judges and subordinate executive officers. III Hinds' Precedents §§ 2297, 2300, 2321, 2323, 2342, 2364, 2385, 2444–2445, 2447–2448, 2469, 2504; VI Cannon's Precedents of the House of Representatives §§ 498, 513, 544 (1936) (Cannon's Precedents); 3 Deschler's Precedents ch. 14, § 18.1. In some cases before 1870, such as the impeachment of Judge Pickering, the House relied on information presented directly to the House to impeach an official before conducting an inquiry, and then authorized a committee to draft specific articles of impeachment and exercise investigatory powers. III Hinds' Precedents § 2321. Those few cases adhere to the rule that a vote of the full House is necessary to authorize any committee to investigate for impeachment purposes.

[277] H.R. Comm. on the Judiciary, *Impeachment of Walter L. Nixon, Jr.*, H.R. Rep. No. 101-36, 101st Cong. 12–13 (1989) (Judge Nixon Jr.); H.R. Comm. on the Judiciary, *Impeachment of Judge Alcee L. Hastings*, H.R. Rep. No. 100-810, 100th Cong. 7–8, 29–31, 38–39 (1988) (Judge Hastings); H.R. Comm. on the Judiciary, *Impeachment of Judge Harry E. Claiborne*, H.R. Rep. No. 99-688, 99th Cong. 18–20 (1986) (Judge Claiborne). These aberrations are still distinguishable because the House adopted resolutions authorizing subpoenas for depositions during the impeachment investigations of Judges Nixon and Hastings, *see* H.R. Res. 562, 100th Cong. (1988); H.R. Res. 320, 100th Cong. (1987), and the Judiciary Committee apparently did not issue any subpoenas in Judge Claiborne's impeachment inquiry.

[278] *NLRB v. Noel Canning*, 573 U.S. 513, 538 (2014); *see also Impeachment Inquiry Authorization, infra* Appendix C, at 27.

[279] *See supra* Standards Part B.3.

[280] H.R. Rep. No. 105-830, at 265 (Minority Views).

[281] *See Impeachment Inquiry Authorization, infra* Appendix C, at 1–3. Although the committees also referred to their oversight and legislative jurisdiction in issuing these subpoenas, the committees cannot "leverage their oversight jurisdiction to require the production of documents and testimony that the committees avowedly intended to use for an unauthorized impeachment inquiry." *Id.* at 32–33. These "assertion[s] of dual authorities" were merely "token invocations of 'oversight and legislative jurisdiction,'" without "any apparent legislative purpose." *Id.* The committees transmitted the subpoenas "[p]ursuant to the House['s] impeachment inquiry," admitted that documents would "be collected as part of the House's impeachment inquiry," and confirmed that they would be "shared among the Committees, as well as with the Committee on the Judiciary as appropriate"—all to be used in the impeachment

The vast bulk of the proceedings in the House were thus founded on the use of unlawful process to compel testimony. Until now, House Democrats have consistently agreed that a vote by the House is required to authorize an impeachment inquiry. In 2016, House Democrats on the Judiciary Committee agreed that "[i]n the modern era, the impeachment process begins in the House of Representatives *only* after the House has voted to authorize the Judiciary Committee to investigate whether charges are warranted."[282] As current Judiciary Committee member Rep. Hank Johnson said in 2016, "[t]he impeachment process *cannot begin* until the 435 Members of the House of Representatives adopt a resolution authorizing the House Judiciary Committee to conduct an independent investigation."[283] As Chairman Nadler put it, an impeachment inquiry without a House vote is "an obvious sham" and a "fake impeachment,"[284] or as House Manager Rep. Hakeem Jeffries explained, it is "a political charade," "a sham," and "a Hollywood-style production."[285]

These invalid subpoenas remain invalid today. House Resolution 660 merely directed the six investigating committees to "continue their ongoing investigations"[286] and did not even purport to ratify retroactively the nearly two dozen invalid subpoenas issued before it was adopted,[287] as OLC has explained.[288] The House knows how to use language effectuating ratification when it wants to—indeed, it used such language less than six months ago in a resolution that "ratifie[d] . . . all subpoenas previously issued" by a committee.[289] The omission of anything similar from House Resolution 660 means that subpoenas issued before House Resolution 660 remain invalid, and the entire fact-gathering process pursuant to those subpoenas was *ultra vires*.

*   *   *

Contrary to false claims from House Democrats, the President did not "declare[] himself above impeachment," reject "any efforts at accommodation or compromise," or declare "himself and his entire branch of government exempt from subpoenas issued by the House."[290] The White House simply made clear that Administration officials should not participate in House Democrats' inquiry "under these circumstances"—meaning a process that was unauthorized under the House's own rules and suffered from the other serious defects.[291] The President's counsel also made it clear that, if the investigating committees sought to proceed under their oversight authorities, the White House stood "ready to engage in that process as [it] ha[s] in the past, in a manner consistent

---

inquiry. *E.g.*, Letter from Elijah E. Cummings, Chairman, H.R. Comm. on Oversight & Reform, et al., to John M. Mulvaney, Acting White House Chief of Staff, at 1 (Oct. 4, 2019).

[282] Press Release, Democratic Staff of the H.R. Comm. on the Judiciary, Fact Sheet: GOP Attacks on IRS Commissioner are Not Impeachment Proceedings (Sept. 21, 2016) (emphasis in original), https://perma.cc/6W8E-7KV8.

[283] *Impeachment Articles Referred on John Koskinen (Part III): Hearing Before the H.R. Comm. on the Judiciary*, 114th Cong. 30 (2016) (*Koskinen Impeachment Hearing: Part III*) (statement of Rep. Johnson) (emphasis added).

[284] *Id.* at 16 (statement of Rep. Nadler); Jerry Nadler (@RepJerryNadler), Twitter (Sept. 21, 2016, 7:01 AM), https://perma.cc/A4VY-TFGM.

[285] *Koskinen Impeachment Hearing: Part III*, *supra* note 283, at 54 (statement of Rep. Jeffries).

[286] H.R. Res. 660, 116th Cong. (2019).

[287] *See infra* Appendix B.

[288] *Impeachment Inquiry Authorization*, *infra* Appendix C, at 37.

[289] H.R. Res. 507, 116th Cong. (2019) (expressly "ratif[ying] and affirm[ing] all current and future investigations, as well as *all subpoenas previously issued* or to be issued in the future") (emphasis added).

[290] HJC Report at 134, 137, 157.

[291] *See supra* Part I.B.1(a); *infra* Part II; Letter from Pat A. Cipollone, Counsel to the President, to Nancy Pelosi, Speaker, House of Representatives, et al., at 7 (Oct. 8, 2019).

with well-established bipartisan constitutional protections."[292] It was Chairman Schiff and his colleagues who refused to engage in any accommodation process with the White House.

(b) The President Properly Asserted Immunity of His Senior Advisers from Compelled Congressional Testimony.

The President also properly directed his senior advisers not to testify in response to subpoenas.[293] Those subpoenas suffered from a separate infirmity: they were unenforceable because the President's senior advisers are immune from compelled testimony before Congress.[294] Consistent with the longstanding position of the Executive Branch, OLC advised the Counsel to the President that those senior advisers (the Acting Chief of Staff, the Legal Advisor to the National Security Council, and the Deputy National Security Advisor) were immune from the subpoenas issued to them.[295]

Across administrations of both political parties, OLC "has repeatedly provided for nearly five decades" that "Congress may not constitutionally compel the President's senior advisers to testify about their official duties."[296] For example, President Obama asserted the same immunity for a senior adviser in 2014.[297] Similarly, during the Clinton administration, Attorney General Janet Reno opined that "immediate advisers" to the President are immune from being compelled to testify before Congress, and that the "the immunity such advisers enjoy from testimonial compulsion by a congressional committee *is absolute* and may not be overborne by competing congressional interests."[298] She explained that "compelling one of the President's immediate advisers to testify on a matter of executive decision-making would . . . raise serious constitutional

---

[292] Oct. 8, 2019 Letter from Pat. A Cipollone, *supra* note 291, at 8.

[293] *See* Letter from Pat A. Cipollone, Counsel to the President, to William Pittard, Counsel for Mick Mulvaney (Nov. 8, 2019); Letter from Pat A. Cipollone, Counsel to the President, to Bill Burck, Counsel for John Eisenberg (Nov. 3, 2019); Letter from Pat A. Cipollone, Counsel to the President, to Charles J. Cooper, Counsel for Charles Kupperman (Oct. 25, 2019).

[294] *See generally* Memorandum for John D. Ehrlichman, Assistant to the President for Domestic Affairs, from William H. Rehnquist, Assistant Attorney General, Office of Legal Counsel, *Re: Power of Congressional Committee to Compel Appearance or Testimony of "White House Staff,"* at 8 (Feb. 5, 1971) (Rehnquist Memorandum) ("The President and his immediate advisers—that is, those who customarily meet with the President on a regular or frequent basis—should be deemed absolutely immune from testimonial compulsion by a congressional committee.").

[295] Letter from Steven A. Engel, Assistant Attorney General, to Pat A. Cipollone, Counsel to the President (Nov. 7, 2019) (regarding Acting White House Chief of Staff Mulvaney); Letter from Steven A. Engel, Assistant Attorney General, to Pat A. Cipollone, Counsel to the President (Nov. 3, 2019) (regarding Legal Advisor to the National Security Council Eisenberg); Letter from Steven A. Engel, Assistant Attorney General, to Pat A. Cipollone, Counsel to the President (October 25, 2019) (regarding Deputy National Security Advisor Kupperman). These letters are attached, *infra*, at Appendix D.

[296] *Testimonial Immunity Before Congress of the Former Counsel to the President*, 43 Op. O.L.C. __, *1 (May 20, 2019) (*2019 OLC Immunity Opinion*); *see also Immunity of the Assistant to the President and Director of the Office of Political Strategy and Outreach from Congressional Subpoena*, 38 Op. O.L.C. __ (July 15, 2014) (*2014 OLC Immunity Opinion*); *Immunity of the Former Counsel to the President from Compelled Congressional Testimony*, 31 Op. O.L.C. 191, 192 (2007); *Immunity of the Counsel to the President from Compelled Congressional Testimony*, 20 Op. O.L.C. 308, 308 (1996); Memorandum for Fred F. Fielding, Counsel to the President, from Theodore B. Olson, Assistant Attorney General, Office of Legal Counsel, *Re: Congressional Testimony by Presidential Assistants* at 1 (Apr. 14, 1981); Memorandum for All Heads of Offices, Divisions, Bureaus and Boards of the Department of Justice, from John M. Harmon, Acting Assistant Attorney General, Office of Legal Counsel, *Re: Executive Privilege*, at 5 (May 23, 1977); Rehnquist Memorandum, *supra* note 294.

[297] *See 2014 OLC Immunity Opinion*, 38 Op. O.L.C. at *3.

[298] *See Assertion of Executive Privilege with Respect to Clemency Decision*, 23 Op. O.L.C. 1, 5 (1999) (emphasis added).

problems, ***no matter what the assertion of congressional need***."[299]

This immunity exists because senior advisers "function as the President's alter ego."[300] Allowing Congress to summon the President's senior advisers would be tantamount to permitting Congress to subpoena the President, which would be intolerable under the Constitution: "Congress may no more summon the President to a congressional committee room than the President may command Members of Congress to appear at the White House."[301]

In addition, immunity is essential to protect the President's ability to secure candid and confidential advice and have frank discussions with his advisers. It thus serves, in part, to protect the same interests that underlie Executive Privilege.[302] As the Supreme Court has explained, the protections for confidentiality embodied in the doctrine of Executive Privilege are "fundamental to the operation of Government and inextricably rooted in the separation of powers under the Constitution."[303] The subpoenas issued to the President's senior advisers in this inquiry necessarily implicated three core areas of Executive Privilege—presidential communications, national security and foreign policy information, and deliberative process.

First, one of the House Democrats' obvious objectives was to find out about presidential communications. The document subpoena sent to Acting White House Chief of Staff Mulvaney, for instance, sought materials reflecting the President's discussions with advisers,[304] and Chairman Schiff's report specifically identified documents that House Democrats sought, including "briefing materials for President Trump," a "presidential decision memo," and presidential call records.[305]

Courts have long recognized constitutional limits on Congress's ability to obtain presidential communications. As the Supreme Court has explained, executive decisionmaking requires the candid exchange of ideas, and "[h]uman experience teaches that those who expect public dissemination of their remarks may well temper candor with a concern for appearances and for their own interests to the detriment of the decisionmaking process."[306] Protecting the confidentiality of communications ensures the President's ability to receive candid advice.[307]

---

[299] *Id.* at 5–6 (emphasis added); *see also Immunity of the Counsel to the President from Compelled Congressional Testimony*, 20 Op. O.L.C. at 308 ("It is the longstanding position of the executive branch that the President and his immediate advisors are absolutely immune from testimonial compulsion by a Congressional committee." (quotations and citations omitted)).

[300] *2014 OLC Immunity Opinion*, 38 Op. O.L.C. at *3 (quotations and citation omitted); *see also Assertion of Executive Privilege with Respect to Clemency Decision*, 23 Op. O.L.C. at 5 ("[A] senior advisor to the President functions as the President's alter ego . . . .").

[301] *2019 OLC Immunity Opinion*, 43 Op. O.L.C. at *5 (citations omitted).

[302] *Id.* at *4 ("Like executive privilege, the immunity protects confidentiality within the Executive Branch and the candid advice that the Supreme Court has acknowledged is essential to presidential decision-making." (citing *Nixon*, 418 U.S. at 705)).

[303] *Nixon*, 418 U.S. at 708.

[304] Subpoena from the House Committee on Oversight and Reform to John Michael Mulvaney, Acting White House Chief of Staff (Oct. 4, 2019) (requesting documents concerning a May 23 Oval Office meeting, among other presidential communications).

[305] H.R. Permanent Select Comm. on Intelligence, *The Trump-Ukraine Impeachment Inquiry Report*, H.R. Rep. No. 116-335, 116th Cong. 181–82 (2019) (HPSCI Report).

[306] *Nixon*, 418 U.S. at 705.

[307] *See, e.g.*, *2014 OLC Immunity Opinion*, 38 Op. O.L.C. at *6 ("[S]ubjecting an immediate presidential adviser to Congress's subpoena power would threaten the President's autonomy and his ability to receive sound and candid advice.").

Second, there can be no dispute that the matters at issue here implicate national security and foreign policy. As Deputy National Security Adviser Kupperman has explained, House Democrats were "seeking testimony relating to confidential national security communications concerning Ukraine."[308] But OLC has established that "immunity is particularly justified" where a senior official's "duties concern national security" or "relations with a foreign government"[309]— subject areas where the President's authority is at its zenith under the Constitution.[310] As the Supreme Court explained in *United States v. Nixon*, the "courts have traditionally shown the utmost deference to Presidential responsibilities" for foreign policy and national security, and claims of privilege in this area thus receive a higher degree of deference than invocations of "a President's generalized interest in confidentiality."[311]

The House's inquiry involved communications with a foreign leader and the development of foreign policy toward a foreign country. There are few areas where the President's powers under the Constitution are greater and his obligation to protect internal Executive Branch deliberations more profound.

Third, House Democrats were seeking deliberative process information. For instance, the committees requested White House documents reflecting internal deliberations about foreign aid, the delegation to President Zelenskyy's inauguration, and potential meetings with foreign leaders.[312] Courts have long recognized that the "deliberative process privilege" applies across the Executive Branch and protects "materials that would reveal advisory opinions, recommendations and deliberations comprising part of a process by which governmental decisions and policies are formulated."[313] The privilege prevents "injury to the quality of agency decisions by allowing government officials freedom to debate alternative approaches in private,"[314] and the privilege has been consistently recognized by administrations of both political parties.[315]

---

[308] *See* Compl. at 11, *Kupperman v. U.S. House of Representatives*, No. 19-cv-3224 (D.D.C. Oct. 25, 2019), ECF No. 1.

[309] Letter from Steven A. Engel, Assistant Attorney General, to Pat A. Cipollone, Counsel to the President, at 3 (Nov. 3, 2019) (regarding Legal Advisor to the National Security Council Eisenberg); Letter from Steven A. Engel, Assistant Attorney General, to Pat A. Cipollone, Counsel to the President, at 2 (Oct. 25, 2019) (regarding Deputy National Security Advisor Kupperman). These letters are attached, *infra*, at Appendix D.

[310] *See Chicago & S. Air Lines v. Waterman S.S. Corp.*, 333 U.S. 103, 109 (1948).

[311] 418 U.S. at 710–11; *see also Harlow v. Fitzgerald*, 457 U.S. 800, 812 (1982) ("For aides entrusted with discretionary authority in such sensitive areas as national security or foreign policy, absolute immunity might well be justified to protect the unhesitating performance of functions vital to the national interest."); *Committee on Judiciary v. Miers*, 558 F. Supp. 2d 53, 101 (D.D.C. 2008) (noting that "[s]ensitive matters of 'discretionary authority' such as 'national security or foreign policy' may warrant absolute immunity in certain circumstances.").

[312] Subpoena from the House Committee on Oversight and Reform to John Michael Mulvaney, Acting White House Chief of Staff (Oct. 4, 2019).

[313] *In re Sealed Case*, 121 F.3d 729, 737 (D.C. Cir. 1997) (internal quotation marks and citations omitted).

[314] *Id.*

[315] *See Assertion of Executive Privilege Over Documents Generated in Response to Congressional Investigation into Operation Fast and Furious*, 36 Op. O.L.C. __, at *3 (June 19, 2012) ("The threat of compelled disclosure of confidential Executive Branch deliberative material can discourage robust and candid deliberations."); *Assertion of Executive Privilege Over Communications Regarding EPA's Ozone Air Quality Standards and California's Greenhouse Gas Waiver Request*, 32 Op. O.L.C. __, *2 (June 19, 2008) ("Documents generated for the purpose of assisting the President in making a decision are protected" and these protections also "encompass[] Executive Branch deliberative communications that do not implicate presidential decisionmaking").

(c) **Administration Officials Properly Instructed Employees Not to Testify Before Committees that Improperly Excluded Agency Counsel.**

Subpoenas for testimony from other Executive Branch officials suffered from a distinct flaw. They impermissibly demanded that officials testify without agency counsel present.[316] OLC has determined that congressional committees "may not bar agency counsel from assisting an executive branch witness without contravening the legitimate prerogatives of the Executive Branch," and that attempting to enforce a subpoena while barring agency counsel "would be unconstitutional."[317] As OLC explained, that principle applies in the context of the House's purported impeachment inquiry just as it applies in more routine congressional oversight requests.[318]

The requirement for congressional committees to permit agency counsel to attend depositions of Executive Branch officials is firmly grounded in the President's constitutional authorities "to protect privileged information from disclosure" and to "control the activities of subordinate officials within the Executive Branch."[319] As OLC has explained, without the assistance of agency counsel, an Executive Branch employee might not be able to determine when a question invaded a privileged area.[320] It is the vital role of agency counsel to ensure that constitutionally based confidentiality interests are protected. Congressional rules do not override these constitutional principles, and there is no legitimate reason for House Democrats to seek to deprive these officials of the assistance of appropriate counsel.[321]

The important role of agency counsel in congressional inquiries has been recognized by administrations of both political parties. During the Obama Administration, for instance, OLC stated that exclusion of agency counsel "could potentially undermine the Executive Branch's ability to protect its confidentiality interests in the course of the constitutionally mandated accommodation process, as well as the President's constitutional authority to consider and assert executive privilege where appropriate."[322]

Requiring agency counsel to be present when Executive Branch employees testify does not

---

[316] *See, e.g.*, Letter from Eliot L. Engel, Chairman, H.R. Comm. on Foreign Relations, et al., to John Michael Mulvaney, Acting White House Chief of Staff, at 4 (Nov. 5, 2019) (explaining that House rules "do not permit agency counsel to participate in depositions").

[317] *Exclusion of Agency Counsel from Congressional Depositions in the Impeachment Context*, 43 Op. O.L.C. __, *4 (Nov. 1, 2019).

[318] *Id.* at *2; *see generally Attempted Exclusion of Agency Counsel from Congressional Depositions of Agency Employees*, 43 Op. O.L.C. __ (May 23, 2019) (same, in the oversight context).

[319] *Exclusion of Agency Counsel from Congressional Depositions in the Impeachment Context*, 43 Op. O.L.C. at *2.

[320] *Attempted Exclusion of Agency Counsel from Congressional Depositions of Agency Employees*, 43 Op. O.L.C. at *10 ("[I]n many cases, agency employees will have only limited experience with executive privilege and may not have the necessary legal expertise to determine whether a question implicates a protected privilege.").

[321] *See INS v. Chadha*, 462 U.S. 919, 955 n.21 (1983) (Congress's power to "determin[e] specified internal matters" is limited because the Constitution "only empowers Congress to bind itself"); *United States v. Ballin*, 144 U.S. 1, 5 (1892) (Congress "may not by its rules ignore constitutional restraints"); HJC Report at 198 (Dissenting Views) ("The Constitution's grant of the impeachment power to the House of Representatives does not temporarily suspend the rights and powers of the other branches established by the Constitution.").

[322] *Authority of the Department of Health and Human Services to Pay for Authority of the Department of Health and Human Services to Pay for Private Counsel to Represent an Employee Before Congressional Committees*, 41 Op. O.L.C. __, *5 n.6 (Jan. 18, 2017).

raise any insurmountable problems for congressional information gathering. To the contrary, as recently as April 2019, the House Committee on Oversight and Government Reform and the Trump Administration were able to work out an accommodation that satisfied both an information request and the need to have agency counsel present for an interview. In that case, after initially threatening contempt proceedings over a dispute, the late Chairman Elijah Cummings allowed White House attorneys to attend a transcribed interview of the former Director of the White House Personnel Security Office.[323] House Democrats could have eliminated a significant legal defect in their subpoenas simply by following Chairman Cummings' example. They did not take this step, so the Administration properly accepted the advice of OLC that House Democrats' actions were unconstitutional and directed witnesses not to appear without agency counsel present.

2. Asserting Legal Defenses and Immunities Grounded in the Constitution's Separation of Powers Is Not an Impeachable Offense.

House Democrats' theory that it is "obstruction" for the President to assert legal rights—especially rights and immunities grounded in the separation of powers—turns the law on its head and would do permanent damage to the structure of our government.

(a) Asserting Legal Defenses and Privileges Is Not "Obstruction."

Under fundamental principles of our legal system, asserting legal defenses cannot be labeled unlawful "obstruction." In a government of laws, asserting legal defenses is a fundamental right. As the Supreme Court has explained: "[F]or an agent of the State to pursue a course of action whose objective is to penalize a person's reliance on his legal rights is 'patently unconstitutional.'"[324] As Harvard Law Professor Laurence Tribe correctly explained in 1998, the same basic principles apply in impeachment:

> The allegations that invoking privileges and otherwise using the judicial system to shield information . . . is an abuse of power that should lead to impeachment and removal from office is not only frivolous, but also dangerous.[325]

Similarly, in 1998, now-Chairman Nadler of the House Judiciary Committee agreed that a president **cannot** be impeached for asserting a legal privilege. As he put it, "the use of a legal privilege is not illegal or impeachable by itself, a legal privilege, executive privilege."[326]

House Democrats, however, ran roughshod over these principles. They repeatedly threatened Executive Branch officials with obstruction charges if the officials dared to assert legal rights against defective subpoenas. They claimed that any "failure or refusal to comply with [a]

---

[323] Letter from Rep. Elijah E. Cummings, Chairman, H.R. Comm. on Oversight & Reform, to Carl Kline, at 2 (Apr. 27, 2019) ("Both your personal counsel and attorneys from the White House Counsel's office will be permitted to attend."); *see also* Kyle Cheney, *Cummings Drops Contempt Threat Against Former W.H. Security Chief*, Politico (Apr. 27, 2019), https://perma.cc/F273-EJZW.

[324] *Bordenkircher v. Hayes*, 434 U.S. 357, 363 (1978) (citations omitted); *see also, e.g., United States v. Goodwin*, 357 U.S. 368, 372 (1982) ("For while an individual certainly may be penalized for violating the law, he just as certainly may not be punished for exercising a protected statutory or constitutional right.").

[325] Harvey Berkman, *Top Profs: Not Enough to Impeach*, The National Law J. (Oct. 5, 1998) (quoting Professor Tribe), *reprinted in* 144 Cong. Rec. H10031 (1998).

[326] *Impeachment Inquiry: William Jefferson Clinton, President of the United States, Consideration of Articles of Impeachment*, 105th Cong. 398 (1998) (statement of Rep. Jerrold Nadler).

subpoena, including at the direction or behest of the President or others at the White House, shall constitute evidence of obstruction."[327] Even worse, Chairman Schiff made the remarkable claim that any action "that forces us to litigate or have *to consider* litigation, will be considered further evidence of obstruction of justice."[328] Those assertions turn core principles of the law inside out.

(b) House Democrats' Radical Theory of "Obstruction" Would Do Grave Damage to the Separation of Powers.

More important, in the context of House demands for information from the Executive Branch, House Democrats' radical theory that asserting legal privileges should be treated immediately as impeachable "obstruction" would do lasting damage to the separation of powers.

The Legislative and Executive Branches have frequently clashed on questions of constitutional interpretation, including on issues surrounding congressional demands for information, since the very first presidential administration.[329] Such interbranch conflicts are not evidence of an impeachable offense. To the contrary, they are part of the constitutional design. The Founders anticipated that the branches might have differing interpretations of the Constitution and might come into conflict. As Madison explained, "the Legislative, Executive, and Judicial departments . . . must, in the exercise of its functions, be guided by the text of the Constitution *according to its own interpretation of it*."[330] Friction between the branches on such points is part of the separation of powers at work.[331]

When the Legislative and Executive Branches disagree about their constitutional duties with respect to sharing information, the proper and historically accepted solution is not an article of impeachment. Instead, it is for the branches to engage in a constitutionally mandated accommodation process in an effort to resolve the disagreement.[332] As courts have explained, this "[n]egotiation between the two branches" is "a dynamic process affirmatively furthering the constitutional scheme."[333]

Where the accommodation process fails, Congress has other tools at its disposal to address

---

[327] *See, e.g.*, Letter from Rep. Elijah E. Cummings, Chairman, H.R. Comm. on Oversight & Reform, et al., to John Michael Mulvaney, Acting White House Chief of Staff, at 1 (Oct. 4, 2019).

[328] Transcript of Pelosi Weekly Press Conference, *supra* note 251 (statement of Rep. Adam Schiff) (emphasis added).

[329] *See History of Refusals by Executive Branch Officials to Provide Information Demanded by Congress, Part I—Presidential Invocations of Executive Privilege Vis-à-Vis Congress*, 6 Op. O.L.C. 751, 753 (1982) (explaining that in response to a request for documents relating to negotiation of the Jay Treaty with Great Britain, President Washington sent a letter to the House stating, "[t]o admit, then, a right in the House of Representatives to demand, and to have, as a matter of course, all the papers respecting a negotiation with a foreign Power, would be to establish a dangerous precedent" (citation omitted)); Jonathan L. Entin, *Separation of Powers, the Political Branches, and the Limits of Judicial Review*, 51 Ohio St. L.J. 175, 186–209 (1990).

[330] Letter from James Madison to Mr. —— (1834), *in* 4 Letters and other Writings of James Madison 349 (1884) (emphasis added).

[331] *Myers v. United States*, 272 U.S. 52, 85 (1926) ("The purpose was not to avoid friction, but, by means of the inevitable friction incident to the distribution of the governmental powers among three departments, to save the people from autocracy."); The Federalist No. 51, at 320–21 (James Madison) (Clinton Rossiter ed., 1961) (arguing that "liberty" requires that the government's "constituent parts . . . be the means of keeping each other in their proper places").

[332] *United States v. Am. Tel. & Tel. Co.*, 567 F.2d 121, 127 (D.C. Cir. 1977) (when Congress asks for information from the Executive Branch, that request triggers the "implicit constitutional mandate to seek optimal accommodation . . . of the needs of the conflicting branches.").

[333] *Id.* at 130.

a disagreement with the Executive. Historically, the House has held Executive Branch officials in contempt.[334] The process of holding a formal vote of the House on a contempt resolution ensures that the House itself examines the subpoena in question and weighs in on launching a full-blown confrontation with the Executive Branch.[335] In addition, in recent times, the House of Representatives has taken the view that it may sue in court to obtain a judicial determination of the validity of its subpoenas and an injunction to enforce them.[336]

In this case, if House Democrats had actually been interested in securing information (rather than merely adding a phony count to their impeachment charge sheet), the proper course would have been to engage with the Administration in one or more of these mechanisms for resolving the interbranch conflict.[337] House Democrats rejected any effort to pursue *any* of these avenues. Instead, they simply announced that constitutional accommodation, contempt, and litigation were all too inconvenient for their politically driven timetable and that they must impeach the President immediately.[338]

---

[334] *Congressional Requests for Confidential Executive Branch Information*, 13 Op. O.L.C. 153, 162 (1989) ("If after assertion of executive privilege the committee remains unsatisfied with the agency's response, it may vote to hold the agency head in contempt of Congress.").

[335] As the Minority Views on the House Judiciary Committee's Report in the Nixon proceedings pointed out, it is important to have a body other than the committee that issued a subpoena evaluate the subpoena before there is a move to contempt. "[I]f the Committee were to act as the final arbiter of the legality of its own demand, the result would seldom be in doubt. . . . It is for the reason just stated that, when a witness before a Congressional Committee refuses to give testimony or produce documents, the Committee cannot itself hold the witness in contempt. . . . Rather, the established procedure is for the witness to be given an opportunity to appear before the full House or Senate, as the case may be, and give reasons, if he can, why he should not be held in contempt." H.R. Rep. No. 93-1305, at 484 (1974) (Minority Views); *see also id.* at 516 (additional views of Rep. William Cohen).

[336] As examples of such lawsuits, *see* Compl., *Comm. on Oversight and Gov't Reform v. Holder*, No. 1:12-cv-1332 (D.D.C. August 13, 2012), ECF No. 1 (suing to enforce subpoenas in the Fast and Furious investigation during the Obama Administration); Compl., *Comm. on the Judiciary v. McGahn*, No. 19-cv-2379 (D.D.C. Aug. 7, 2019), ECF No. 1. Additionally, for Senate subpoenas, Congress has affirmatively passed legislation creating subject matter jurisdiction in federal court to hear such cases. *See* 28 U.S.C. § 1365 (2018). The Trump Administration, like the Obama Administration, has taken the position that a suit by a congressional committee attempting to enforce a subpoena against an Executive Branch official is not a justiciable controversy in an Article III court. *See Comm. on Oversight & Gov't Reform v. Holder*, 979 F. Supp. 2d 1, 9–10 (D.D.C. 2013) ("The defendant . . . maintains that Article III of the Constitution actually prohibits the Court from exercising jurisdiction over what he characterizes as 'an inherently political dispute.'"). The House of Representatives, however, has taken the opposite view. *See* Pl.'s Opp'n to Def.'s Mot. to Dismiss, *Comm. on Oversight & Gov't Reform v. Holder*, No. 12-cv-1332 (D.D.C. Nov. 21, 2012), ECF No. 17. Unless and until the justiciability question is resolved by the Supreme Court, the House cannot simultaneously (i) insist that the courts may decide whether any particular refusal to comply with a congressional committee's demand for information was legally proper *and* (ii) claim that the House can treat resistance to any demand for information from Congress as a "high crime and misdemeanor" justifying impeachment *without* securing any judicial determination that the Executive Branch's action was improper.

[337] *See Am. Tel. & Tel. Co.*, 567 F.2d at 127 ("[E]ach branch should take cognizance of an implicit constitutional mandate to seek optimal accommodation through a realistic evaluation of the needs of the conflicting branches in the particular fact situation.").

[338] *See Transcript: Nancy Pelosi's Public and Private Remarks on Trump Impeachment*, NBC News (Sept. 24, 2019), https://www.nbcnews.com/politics/trump-impeachment-inquiry/transcript-nancy-pelosi-s-speech-trump-impeachment-n1058351 ("[R]ight now, we have to strike while the iron is hot. . . . And, we want this to be done expeditiously. Expeditiously."); Ben Kamisar, *Schiff Says House Will Move Forward with Impeachment Inquiry After 'Overwhelming' Evidence from Hearings*, NBC News (Nov. 24, 2019), https://www.nbcnews.com/politics/meet-the-press/schiff-says-house-will-move-forward-impeachment-inquiry-after-overwhelming-n1090221 ("[T]here are still other witnesses, other documents that we'd like to obtain. But we are not willing to go the months and months and months of rope-a-dope in the courts, which the administration would love to do.").

Permitting that approach and treating the President's response to the subpoenas as an impeachable offense would do grave damage to the separation of powers. Suggesting that every congressional demand for information must automatically be obeyed on pain of impeachment would undermine the foundational premise that the Legislative and Executive Branches are co-equal branches of the government, neither of which is subservient to the other. As Madison explained, where the Executive and the Legislative Branches come into conflict "neither of them, it is evident, can pretend to an exclusive or superior right of settling the boundaries between their respective powers."[339] That is why the courts have insisted on an accommodations process by which the two branches work to reach a compromise in which the interest of each branch is addressed.[340] House Democrats, by contrast, have declared the House supreme not only over the Executive Branch, but also over the Judicial Branch, by baldly proclaiming that, whenever a committee chairman invokes the possibility of impeachment, the House itself is the sole judge of its own powers, because (in their view) "the Constitution gives the House the final word."[341]

House Democrats' theory is unprecedented and dangerous for our structure of government. There is no reason to believe that the House, acting as judge in its own case, will properly acknowledge limits on its own powers. That is evident from numerous cases in which courts have refused to enforce congressional subpoenas because they are invalid or overbroad.[342] More important, the House Democrats' theory means that the House could dangle the threat of impeachment over every congressional demand for information. Trivializing impeachment in this manner would functionally transform our government into precisely the type of parliamentary system the Framers rejected.

In his testimony before the House Judiciary Committee, Professor Turley rightly pointed out that, by "claiming Congress can demand any testimony or documents and then impeach any president who dares to go to the courts," House Democrats were advancing a position that was "entirely untenable and abusive [of] an impeachment."[343] Other scholars agree. In the Clinton impeachment, for example, Professor Susan Low Bloch testified that "impeaching a president for invoking lawful privileges is a dangerous and ominous precedent."[344]

In the past, the House itself has agreed and has recognized that a President cannot be

---

[339] The Federalist No. 49, at 314 (James Madison) (Clinton Rossiter ed., 1961).

[340] *Am. Tel. & Tel. Co.*, 567 F.2d at 127.

[341] HJC Report at 154.

[342] *See, e.g., Senate Select Comm. on Presidential Campaign Activities v. Nixon*, 498 F.2d 725, 733 (D.C. Cir. 1974) (holding that a congressional committee's need for subpoenaed material "is too attenuated and too tangential to its functions to permit a judicial judgment that the President is required to comply with the Committee's subpoena"); *Gojack v. United States*, 384 U.S. 702, 716 (1966) (reversing Petitioner's contempt of Congress conviction because "the subcommittee was without authority which can be vindicated by criminal sanctions"); *United States v. Rumely*, 345 U.S. 41, 47–48 (1953) (holding that a congressional committee subpoena sought materials outside the scope of the authorizing resolution); *United States v. McSurely*, 473 F.2d 1178, 1194 (D.C. Cir. 1972) (reversing a congressional contempt conviction and applying Fourth Amendment protections to a congressional investigation).

[343] Turley Written Statement, *supra* note 252, at 39.

[344] *Background and History of Impeachment: Hearing Before the Subcomm. on the Const. of the H.R. Comm. on Judiciary*, 105th Cong. 236 (1998) (*Clinton Judiciary Comm. Hearing on Background of Impeachment*) (written statement of Professor Susan Low Bloch, Georgetown University Law Center); *see also* Alan Dershowitz, *Supreme Court Ruling Pulls Rug out from under Article of Impeachment*, The Hill (Dec. 16, 2019), https://perma.cc/H5BA-TKVX (stating that "the House Judiciary Committee has arrogated to itself the power to decide the validity of subpoenas, and the power to determine whether claims of executive privilege must be recognized" and arguing that those authorities "properly belong with the judicial branch of our government, not the legislative branch").

impeached for asserting a privilege. For example, the House Judiciary Committee rejected as a ground for impeachment the allegation that President Clinton had "frivolously and corruptly asserted executive privilege" in connection with a criminal investigation.[345] Although the Committee believed that "the President ha[d] improperly exercised executive privilege,"[346] it nevertheless determined that this was not an "impeachable offense[]."[347] Similarly, over 175 years ago, the House rejected an attempt to impeach President Tyler "for abusing his powers based on his refusals to share with the House inside details on whom he was considering to nominate to various confirmable positions and his vetoing of a wide range of Whig-sponsored legislation."[348]

If House Democrats' unprecedented theory of "obstruction of Congress" were correct, virtually every President could have been impeached. Throughout our history, Presidents have refused to share information with Congress. For example, when Congress investigated Operation Fast and Furious during the last administration, President Obama invoked Executive Privilege with respect to documents responsive to a congressional subpoena.[349] Instead of a rash rush to impeachment, House Republicans secured a favorable court ruling on President Obama's assertion of privilege.[350] President Trump's actions are entirely consistent with such steps taken by his predecessors. As Professor Turley explained, "[i]f this Committee elects to seek impeachment on the failure to yield to congressional demands in an oversight or impeachment investigation, it will have to distinguish a long line of cases where prior presidents sought . . . [judicial] review while withholding witnesses and documents."[351]

House Democrats fare no better in claiming that President Trump announced a more "categorical" refusal to cooperate with House demands than any past president.[352] That claim misunderstands the law and misrepresents both the President's conduct and history. On the law, there is nothing impermissible about asserting rights consistently and "categorically." There is no requirement for a President to cede Executive Branch confidentiality interests some of the time lest he be too "categorical" in their defense. On the facts, the President did not issue a categorical refusal. As noted above, the Counsel to the President made clear to House Democrats that, if they sought to pursue regular oversight, the Administration would "stand ready to engage in that process as we have in the past, in a manner consistent with well-established bipartisan constitutional protections."[353] It was House Democrats who refused to engage in the accommodation process. And as for history, past Presidents—such as Presidents Truman, Coolidge, and Jackson—*did* announce categorical refusals to cooperate at all with congressional inquiries.[354] None was

---

[345] H.R. Rep. No. 105-830, at 85.

[346] *Id.* at 84 (quoting Rep. Bob Goodlatte).

[347] *Id.*

[348] *Clinton Judiciary Comm. Hearing on Background of Impeachment, supra* note 344, at 54 (written statement of Professor Michael J. Gerhardt, The College of William and Mary School of Law).

[349] *See Assertion of Executive Privilege Over Documents Generated in Response to Congressional Investigation into Operation Fast and Furious*, 36 Op. O.L.C. at *1, *8.

[350] *See, e.g.,* Harper Neidig, *Judge Rules Against Obama on 'Fast and Furious'*, The Hill (Jan. 19, 2016), https://perma.cc/FSA2-YQFT ("A federal judge on Tuesday ruled President Obama cannot use executive privilege to keep records on the 'Fast and Furious' gun-tracking program from Congress . . . House Republicans launched the suit after voting to hold then-Attorney General Eric Holder in contempt for refusing to turn over the records.").

[351] Turley Written Statement, *supra* note 252, at 42.

[352] *See* Trial Mem. of the U.S. House of Representatives at 33–34; HJC Report at 136–37.

[353] Oct. 8, 2019 Letter from Pat A. Cipollone, *supra* note 291, at 8.

[354] *History of Refusals*, 6 O.L.C. Op. at 771 ("President Truman issued a directive providing for the confidentiality of all loyalty files and requiring that all requests for such files from sources outside the Executive Branch be referred

impeached as a result.

Contrary to House Democrats' assertions, it also makes no difference that the subpoenas here were purportedly issued as part of an impeachment inquiry.[355] The defenses and immunities the President has asserted are grounded in the separation of powers and protect confidentiality interests that are vital for the functioning of the Executive Branch. Those defenses and immunities do not disappear the instant the House opens an impeachment inquiry. Just as with the judicial need for evidence in a criminal trial, the House's interest in investigating does not mean Executive Privilege goes away; instead, "it is necessary to resolve those competing interests in a manner that preserves the essential functions of each branch."[356] If anything, the interbranch conflict inherent in an impeachment inquiry *heightens* the need for scrupulous adherence to principles preserving each branch's mechanisms for protecting its own legitimate sphere of authority.

House Democrats' insistence that the Constitution assigns the House the "sole Power of Impeachment"[357] does nothing to advance their argument. That provision simply makes clear that the power of impeachment is assigned to the House and not anywhere else. It does not make the power of impeachment a paramount authority that sweeps away the constitutionally based privileges of other branches.[358] The fundamental Madisonian principle that each branch must place checks on the others—that "[a]mbition must be made to counteract ambition"—continues to apply even when the House invokes the power of impeachment.[359] The mere fact that impeachment provides an ultimate check on the Executive does not mean the Framers made it a

---

to the Office of the President, for such response as the President may determine . . . At a press conference held on April 22, 1948, President Truman indicated that he would not comply with the request to turn the papers over to the Committee." (citations omitted)); *id.* at 769 (noting President Coolidge refused to provide the Senate "a list of all companies in which the Secretary of the Treasury 'was interested'" and instead sent a letter "calling the Senate's investigation an 'unwarranted intrusion,' born of a desire other than to secure information for legitimate legislative purposes" (quoting 65 Cong. Rec. 6087 (1924))); *id.* at 757 (noting President Jackson refused to provide to the Senate a paper purportedly read by the President to his Cabinet and instead asserted "the Legislature had no constitutional authority to 'require of me an account of any communication, either verbally or in writing, made to the heads of Departments acting as a Cabinet council . . . [nor] might I be required to detail to the Senate the free and private conversations I have held with those officers on any subject relating to their duties and my own.'").

[355] As explained above, many of the subpoenas were *not* authorized as part of any impeachment inquiry because they were issued when the House had not voted to authorize any such inquiry. *See supra* Part I.B.1(a).

[356] *Nixon*, 418 U.S. at 707.

[357] *See, e.g.*, Trial Mem. of the U.S. House of Representatives at 33–34; HJC Report at 136–37.

[358] House Democrats' reliance on *Kilbourn v. Thompson* is misplaced. *Kilbourn* merely states that, when conducting an impeachment inquiry, the House or Senate may "compel the attendance of witnesses, and their answer to proper questions, in the same manner and by the use of the same means that courts of justice can in like cases.'" Trial Mem. of the U.S. House of Representatives at 32 (quoting *Kilbourn*, 103 U.S. 168, 190 (1880)). But constitutionally based privileges apply in "courts of justice," so *Kilbourn* does not foreclose the assertion of privileges and immunities in impeachment proceedings. Regardless, the statement quoted by House Democrats is dictum and, therefore, not binding. Additionally, House Democrats point to an 1846 statement by President Polk to support the proposition that "[p]revious Presidents have acknowledged their obligation to comply with an impeachment investigation." *Id.* at 32–33. OLC has clarified that, when read in context, President Polk's statement actually "acknowledg[es] the continued availability of executive privilege" because President Polk explained that "even in the impeachment context, 'the Executive branch would adopt all wise precautions to prevent the exposure of all such matters the publication of which might injuriously affect the public interest, except so far as this might be necessary to accomplish the great ends of public justice.'" *Impeachment Inquiry Authorization, infra* Appendix C, at 11 n.13 (quoting Memorandum for Elliot Richardson, Attorney General, from Robert G. Dixon, Jr., Assistant Attorney General, Office of Legal Counsel, *Re: Presidential Immunity from Coercive Congressional Demands for Information* at 22–23 (July 24, 1973)).

[359] The Federalist No. 51, *supra* note 331, at 322.

blank check for the House to expand its power without limit.

OLC has determined that Executive Privilege principles continue to apply in an impeachment inquiry.[360] And scholars agree that Presidents may assert privileges in response to demands for information in an impeachment inquiry, as Executive Privilege is "essential to the . . . dignified conduct of the presidency and to the free flow of candid advice to the President."[361]

None of the excuses House Democrats have offered justifies their unprecedented leap to impeachment while bypassing any effort either to seek constitutionally mandated accommodations or to go to court. Their claim that there was no *time* is no justification.[362] As Professor Turley has explained, "[t]he decision to adopt an abbreviated schedule for the investigation and not to seek to compel such testimony [in court] is a strategic choice of the House leadership. It is not the grounds for an impeachment."[363] Nor is their claim about urgency credible. The only constraint on timing here came from House Democrats' self-imposed deadline to ensure that this impeachment charade would not drag on into the Democratic primary season. They also showed no urgency when they waited four weeks to send the Articles of Impeachment to the Senate. If House Democrats had cared about constitutional precedent, they would have adhered to the ordinary timetable for something as momentous as a presidential impeachment and would have taken the time to work out disputes with the Executive Branch on subpoenas. House Democrats arbitrarily decided to skip that step.

Next, Democrats falsely claim that that "the House has *never* before relied on litigation to compel witness testimony or the production of documents in a Presidential impeachment proceeding."[364] But the House *has* filed such lawsuits, including just last year. In one case, the House made a court filing asserting that its impeachment inquiry entitled it to certain grand jury information on the same day the House Judiciary Committee issued its report.[365] And in another case purportedly based on an impeachment inquiry, House Democrats recently argued that, when at an impasse, disputes with the Executive Branch can "only be resolved by the courts."[366] These filings are flatly inconsistent with House Democrats' position here, where they claim that any

---

[360] *Exclusion of Agency Counsel from Congressional Depositions in the Impeachment Context*, 43 Op. OLC at *2 (discussing how the "same principles apply to a congressional committee's effort to compel the testimony of an executive branch official in an impeachment inquiry" as in other contexts).

[361] Black & Bobbitt, *supra* note 191, at 20; *see also* Turley Written Statement, *supra* note 252, at 40 ("Congress cannot substitute its judgment as to what a President can withhold.").

[362] HJC Report at 129–31.

[363] Turley Written Statement, *supra* note 252, at 41.

[364] HJC Report at 155 (emphasis in original).

[365] Appellee Br. at 13, *In re: Application of the Comm. on the Judiciary*, No. 19-5288 (D.C. Cir. Dec. 16, 2019) ("If the House approves Articles of Impeachment, relevant grand-jury material that the Committee obtains in this litigation could be used during the subsequent Senate proceedings. And the Committee continues its impeachment investigation into Presidential misconduct . . . . Material that the Committee obtains in this litigation could be used in that investigation as well.").

[366] Pl.'s Reply in Support of its Mot. for Expedited Partial Summary Judgment at 3, *Comm. on the Judiciary v. McGahn*, No. 19-cv-2379 (D.D.C. Oct. 16, 2019), ECF No. 38 ("The President has stated that the Executive Branch will not 'participate in' the House's ongoing impeachment inquiry, and has declared that McGahn is *absolutely* immune from Congressional process. The parties are currently at an impasse that can only be resolved by the courts." (emphasis in original)); *see also* Compl. ¶ 1, *Comm. on the Judiciary v. McGahn*, No. 19-cv-2379 (D.D.C. Aug. 7, 2019), ECF No. 1 (arguing that witness testimony is needed because "[t]he Judiciary Committee is now determining whether to recommend articles of impeachment against the President").

impasse should lead to impeachment.

Lastly, House Democrats also find no support for their theory of "obstruction" in the Clinton and Nixon impeachment proceedings.[367] To the contrary, the Clinton proceedings establish conclusively that there is no plausible basis for an article of impeachment based on the assertion of rights and privileges. In 1997 and 1998, there had been numerous court rulings rejecting various assertions of Executive Privilege by President Clinton.[368] The House Judiciary Committee concluded that Clinton's assertions of Executive Privilege were frivolous, especially because they related to "purely private" matters—not official actions.[369] Nevertheless, the Committee decided that the assertions of privilege did not constitute an "impeachable offense[]."[370]

Nothing from the Nixon impeachment proceedings supports House Democrats either. The record there included evidence that, as part of efforts to cover up the Watergate break-in, the President had (among other things): provided information from the Department of Justice to subjects of criminal investigations to help them evade justice; used the FBI, Secret Service, and Executive Branch personnel to conduct illegal electronic surveillance; and illegally attempted to secure access to tax return information in order to influence individuals.[371] Moreover, the Committee had transcripts of tapes on which the President discussed asserting privileges, not to protect governmental decision making, but solely to stymie the investigation into the break-in.[372] It was only in that context that the House Judiciary Committee narrowly recommended an article of impeachment asserting that President Nixon had "failed without lawful cause or excuse to produce papers and things" sought by Congress.[373] There is nothing remotely comparable in this case. Among other things, every step the Trump Administration has taken has been well-founded in law and supported by the opinion of the Department of Justice. Moreover, the subpoenas here attempted to probe into matters involving the conduct of foreign relations—matters squarely at the core of Executive Privilege where the President's powers and need to preserve confidentiality are at their apex.

(c) The President Cannot Be Removed from Office Based on a Difference in Legal Opinion.

House Democrats' reckless "obstruction" theory is further flawed because it asks the Senate to remove a duly elected President from office based on differences of legal opinion in which the President acted on the advice of OLC. As explained above, the Framers restricted

---

[367] *See* HJC Report at 146–48.

[368] *See, e.g.*, *Clinton v. Jones*, 520 U.S. 681, 692 (1997) (holding that a sitting president does not have immunity during his term from civil litigation about events occurring prior to entering office); *In re Grand Jury Proceedings*, 5 F. Supp. 2d 21 (D.D.C. 1998) (rejecting the privilege for information sought from a Deputy White House Counsel pertaining to potential presidential criminal misconduct), *aff'd in part, rev'd in part sub nom. In re Lindsey*, 158 F.3d 1263 (D.C. Cir. 1998).

[369] H.R. Rep. No. 105-830, at 92 ("[I]ndeed, the President repeatedly argued that he should not be impeached precisely because these matters are purely private in nature."); *id.* (quoting Rep. Bill McCollum) ("With regard to executive privilege, I don't think that there is any question that the President abused executive privilege here, because it can only be used to protect official functions.").

[370] *Id.* at 84 (quoting Rep. Bob Goodlatte).

[371] H.R. Rep. No. 93-1305, at 1–4.

[372] *Id.* at 203–04 (quoting President Nixon as saying "I want you all to stonewall it, let them plead the Fifth Amendment, cover-up or anything else, if it'll save it—save the plan. That's the whole point.").

[373] *Id.* at 188 (reflecting a vote of 21-17).

impeachment to remedy solely egregious conduct that endangers the constitutional structure of government. No matter how House Democrats try to dress up their claim, a difference of legal opinion over an assertion of grounds to resist subpoenas does not rise to that level. The Framers themselves recognized that differences of opinion could not justify impeachment. As Edmund Randolph explained in the Virginia ratifying convention, "[n]o man ever thought of impeaching a man for an opinion."[374]

Until now, that principle has prevailed, as the House has expressly rejected attempts to impeach presidents based on legal disputes over assertions of privilege. As noted above, in the Clinton impeachment, the House Judiciary Committee rejected a draft article alleging that President Clinton had "frivolously and corruptly asserted executive privilege."[375] Even though the Committee concluded that "the President ha[d] improperly exercised executive privilege,"[376] it decided that this was not an "impeachable offense[]."[377] The Committee concluded it did not have "the ability to second guess the rationale behind the President or what was in his mind in asserting that executive privilege" and it "ought to give . . . the benefit of the doubt [to the President] in the assertion of executive privilege."[378] As the Committee recognized, members of Congress need not agree that a President's assertion of a privilege or immunity is *correct* to recognize that making the assertion of legal privileges itself an impeachable offense is a dangerous and unwarranted step.

The House took a similar view in rejecting an attempt to impeach President Tyler in 1843 when he refused congressional demands for information. As Professor Gerhardt has explained:

> Tyler's attempts to protect and assert what he regarded as the prerogatives of his office *were a function of his constitutional and policy judgments*; they might have been wrong-headed or even poorly conceived (at least in the view of many Whigs in Congress), but they were not malicious efforts to abuse or expand his powers. . . .[379]

President Trump's resistance to congressional subpoenas here was similarly "a function of his constitutional and policy judgments." As the House recognized in the cases of President Tyler and President Clinton, divergent views on such matters cannot possibly be sufficient to remove a duly elected president from office. And that is especially the case here, where President Trump's actions were expressly based on advice from the Department of Justice.

II. The Articles Resulted from an Impeachment Inquiry that Violated All Precedent and Denied the President Constitutionally Required Due Process.

Three defects make the House's purported impeachment inquiry irredeemably flawed. *First*, as the Department of Justice advised at the time, the House's investigating committees compelled testimony and documents by issuing subpoenas that were invalid when issued and are

---

[374] 3 *The Debates in the Several State Conventions on the Adoption of the Federal Constitution*, at 401 (Jonathan Elliot 2nd ed. 1987).

[375] H.R. Rep. No. 105-830, at 85.

[376] *Id.* at 84 (quoting Rep. Bob Goodlatte).

[377] *Id.*

[378] *Id.* at 92 (quoting Rep. George Gekas).

[379] *Clinton Judiciary Comm. Hearing on Background of Impeachment*, *supra* note 344, at 54 (written statement of Professor Michael J. Gerhardt, The College of William & Mary School of Law) (emphasis added).

invalid today. *See* Parts I.B.1(a), II.A. ***Second***, the impeachment inquiry failed to provide due process to the President as required by the Constitution. *See* Part II.B. Contrary to 150 years of precedent, the House excluded the President from the process, denying him any right to participate or defend himself. House Democrats only pretended to provide the President any rights ***after*** the entire factual record had been compiled in *ex parte* hearings and ***after*** Speaker Pelosi had pre-determined the result by instructing the Judiciary Committee to draft articles of impeachment. ***Third***, the House's factual investigation was supervised by an interested fact witness, Chairman Schiff, who—after falsely denying it—admitted that his staff had been in contact with the whistleblower and had given him guidance. *See* Part II.C. These three fundamental errors infected the underpinnings of this trial, and the Senate cannot constitutionally rely upon House Democrats' tainted record to reach any verdict other than acquittal. *See* Part II.D. Nor is it the Senate's role to give House Democrats a "do-over" to develop the record anew in the Senate. These errors require rejecting the Articles and acquitting the President.

A. The Purported Impeachment Inquiry Was Unauthorized at the Outset and Compelled Testimony Based on Nearly Two Dozen Invalid Subpoenas.

It is emblematic of the rush to judgment throughout the House's slap-dash impeachment inquiry that Chairman Schiff's investigating committees began issuing subpoenas and compelling testimony when they plainly had no authority to do so. The House committees built their one-sided record by purporting to compel testimony and documents using nearly two dozen subpoenas "[p]ursuant to the House of Representatives' impeachment inquiry."[380] But their only authority was Speaker Pelosi's announcement at a press conference on September 24, 2019. As a result, the inquiry and the almost two dozen subpoenas issued before October 31, 2019 came ***before*** the House delegated any authority under its "sole Power of Impeachment" to any committee.[381] As OLC summarized:

> The Constitution vests the "sole Power of Impeachment" in the House of Representatives. U.S. Const. art. I, § 2, cl. 5. For precisely that reason, the House itself must authorize an impeachment inquiry, as it has done in virtually every prior impeachment investigation in our Nation's history, including every one involving a President. A congressional committee's "right to exact testimony and to call for the production of documents" is limited by the "controlling charter" the committee has received from the House. *United States v. Rumely*, 345 U.S. 41, 44 (1953). Yet the House, by its rules, has authorized its committees to issue subpoenas only for matters within

---

[380] *E.g.*, Oct. 4, 2019 Letter from Elijah E. Cummings, *supra* note 281; *see infra* Appendix B (listing subpoenas). The HPSCI Majority Report also relies on several "[d]ocument [p]roduction[s]" from AT&T and Verizon, reportedly in response to subpoenas issued by Chairman Schiff beginning in September before House Resolution 660 was passed. *See* Editorial Bd., *Schiff's Surveillance State*, Wall St. J. (Dec. 4, 2019), https://perma.cc/2ZQP-JW5V; HPSCI Report at 31 n.49, 80 n.529.

[381] U.S. Const. art. I, § 2, cl. 5.

their *legislative* jurisdiction. Accordingly, no committee may undertake the momentous move from legislative oversight to impeachment without a delegation by the full House of such authority.[382]

Thus, as explained above, all subpoenas issued before the adoption of House Resolution 660 on October 31, 2019, purportedly to advance an "impeachment inquiry," were unauthorized and invalid.

B. House Democrats' Impeachment Inquiry Deprived the President of the Fundamentally Fair Process Required by the Constitution.

The next glaring defect in House Democrats' impeachment proceedings was the wholly unfair procedures used to conduct the inquiry and compile the record. The Constitution requires that something as momentous as impeaching the President be done in a fundamentally fair way. Both the Due Process Clause and separation of powers principles require the House to provide the President with fair process and an opportunity to defend himself. Every modern presidential impeachment inquiry—and every impeachment investigation for the last 150 years—has expressly preserved the accused's rights to a fundamentally fair process and ensured a balanced development of the evidence. These included the rights to cross-examine witnesses, to call witnesses, to be represented by counsel at all hearings, to make objections relating to the examination of witnesses or the admissibility of evidence, and to respond to evidence and testimony received. There is no reason to think that the Framers designed a mechanism for the profoundly disruptive act of impeaching the President that could be accomplished through any unfair and arbitrary means that the House might invent.[383]

---

[382] Memorandum from Steven A. Engel, Assistant Attorney General, Office of Legal Counsel, to Pat A. Cipollone, Counsel to the President, *Re: House Committees' Authority to Investigate for Impeachment*, at 1 (Jan. 19, 2020) (emphasis in original) (*Impeachment Inquiry Authorization*), *infra* Appendix C.

[383] Impeachment is not just a political process unconstrained by law. "The subjects of [an impeachment trial] are those offenses which proceed from the misconduct of public men, or, in other words, from the abuse or violation of some public trust"—that is, "POLITICAL, as they relate chiefly to injuries done immediately to the society itself." The Federalist No. 65, at 396 (Alexander Hamilton) (Clinton Rossiter ed., 1961). But "Hamilton didn't say the *process* of impeachment is entirely political. He said the *offense* has to be political." Alan M. Dershowitz, *Hamilton Wouldn't Impeach Trump*, Wall St. J. (Oct. 9, 2019), https://perma.cc/97PH-QPGT (emphasis in original). "Hamilton's description in Federalist 65 should not be taken to mean that impeachments have a conventional political nature, unmoored from traditional criminal process." J. Richard Broughton, *Conviction, Nullification, and the Limits of Impeachment As Politics*, 68 Case W. Res. L. Rev. 275, 288 (2017). Federalist No. 65 goes to "pains to show that the Senate can act in 'their judicial character as a court for the trial of impeachments,'" and "[t]he entire essay is an attempt to show that the Senate can *overcome* its political nature as an elected body . . . and act as a proper 'court for the trial of impeachments.'" Charles L. Black, Jr. & Philip Bobbitt, *Impeachment: A Handbook* 102 (2018) (emphasis in original). Hamilton emphasized that impeachment and removal of "the accused" must be based on partially legal considerations involving "real demonstrations of innocence or guilt" rather than purely political factors like "the comparative strength of parties." *Id.* at 102–03 (quoting The Federalist No. 65). Thus, "one should not diminish the significance of impeachment's legal aspects, particularly as they relate to the formalities of the criminal justice process. It is a hybrid of the political and the legal, a political process moderated by legal formalities . . . ." Broughton, *supra* note 383, at 289.

1. **The Text and Structure of the Constitution Demand that the House Ensure Fundamentally Fair Procedures in an Impeachment Inquiry.**

   (a) **The Due Process Clause Requires Fair Process.**

The federal Due Process Clause broadly states that "[n]o person shall . . . be deprived of life, liberty, or property, without due process of law"[384] and applies to every part of the federal government. In any proceeding that may lead to deprivation of a protected interest, it requires fair procedures commensurate with the interests at stake.[385] There is no exemption from the clause for Congress. Thus, for example, the Supreme Court has held that due process protections apply to congressional investigations and provide witnesses in such investigations certain rights.[386] Congress's "power to investigate, broad as it may be, is also subject to recognized limitations"— including those "found in the specific individual guarantees of the Bill of Rights."[387] It would be anomalous if the Due Process Clause applied to investigations conducted under Congress's legislative power—which aim merely to gather information for legislation—but somehow did not apply to impeachment investigations aimed at stripping individuals of their government positions. An impeachment investigation against the President potentially seeks to charge the President with "Treason, Bribery, or other high Crimes and Misdemeanors,"[388] and to strip the President of both (1) his constitutionally granted right to "hold his Office during the Term of Four years,"[389] and (2) his eligibility to "hold and enjoy any Office of honor, Trust or Profit under the United States,"[390] including to be re-elected as President.[391]

Those actions plainly involve deprivations of property and liberty interests protected by the Due Process Clause.[392] As a threshold matter, it is settled law that even the lowest level "public employees who can be discharged only for cause have a constitutionally protected property interest in their tenure and cannot be fired without due process."[393] Nothing in the Constitution suggests that the impeachment process for addressing charges crossing the extraordinarily high threshold of "Treason, Bribery, or other high Crimes and Misdemeanors"[394] should involve *less* fair process than what the Constitution requires for every lower-level federal employee. The Constitution also explicitly gives the President (and every individual) a protected liberty interest in eligibility for election to the Office of President—so long as the individual meets the qualifications established

---

[384] U.S. Const. amend. V.

[385] *See, e.g., Walters v. Nat'l Ass'n of Radiation Survivors*, 473 U.S. 305, 320 (1985) ("[T]he processes required by the Clause with respect to the termination of a protected interest will vary depending upon the importance attached to the interest and the particular circumstances under which the deprivation may occur."); *Mathews v. Eldridge*, 424 U.S. 319, 334 (1976) ("Due process is flexible and calls for such procedural protections as the particular situation demands.") (quoting *Morrissey v. Brewer*, 408 U.S. 471, 481 (1972)).

[386] *See, e.g., Watkins v. United States*, 354 U.S. 178, 188 (1957); *Quinn v. United States*, 349 U.S. 155, 161 (1955).

[387] *Quinn*, 349 U.S. at 161.

[388] U.S. Const. art. II, § 4.

[389] U.S. Const. art. II, § 1, cl. 1.

[390] U.S. Const. art. I, § 3, cl. 7.

[391] *See* U.S. Const. art. II, § 1, cl. 5.

[392] *See generally Board of Regents of State Colleges v. Roth*, 408 U.S. 564, 571–72 (1972) ("The Court has also made clear that the property interests protected by procedural due process extend well beyond actual ownership of real estate, chattels, or money."); *Bolling v. Sharpe*, 347 U.S. 497, 499 (1954) ("Although the Court has not assumed to define 'liberty' with any great precision, that term is not confined to mere freedom from bodily restraint.").

[393] *Gilbert v. Homar*, 520 U.S. 924, 928–29 (1997).

[394] U.S. Const. art. II, § 4.

by the Constitution.[395] Finally, every federal officer has a protected liberty interest in his reputation that would be directly impaired by impeachment charges.[396] Impeachment by the House alone has an impact warranting the protections of due process.[397] The House's efforts to deprive the President of these constitutionally protected property and liberty interests necessarily implicate the Due Process Clause. The fact that impeachment is a constitutionally prescribed mechanism for removing federal officials from office does not make it any the less a mechanism affecting rights within the ordinary ambit of the clause.

The gravity of the deprivation at stake in an impeachment—especially a presidential impeachment—buttresses the conclusion that some due process limitations must apply. It would be incompatible with the Framers' understanding of the "delicacy and magnitude of a trust which so deeply concerns the political reputation and existence of every man engaged in the administration of public affairs"[398] to think that they envisioned a system in which the House was free to devise any arbitrary or unfair mechanism it wished for impeaching individuals. The Supreme Court has described due process as "the protection of the individual against arbitrary action."[399] There is no reason to think that protection was not intended to extend to impeachments.

Similarly, the momentous impact of a presidential impeachment on the operation of the government suggests that the drafters of the Constitution expected the process to be governed by procedures that would ensure a fair assessment of evidence. The Bill of Rights guarantees due process, not out of an abstract, academic interest in process as an end in itself, but rather due to a belief, deeply rooted in the Anglo-American system of law, that procedural protections reduce the chances of erroneous decision-making.[400] The Framers surely did not intend to approve a process for determining impeachments that would be wholly cut loose from all traditional mechanisms deemed essential in our legal heritage for discovering the truth.

The sole judicial opinion to reach the question held that the Due Process Clause applies to impeachment proceedings.[401] In *Hastings v United States*, the district court held that the Due Process Clause imposes an independent constitutional constraint on how the Senate exercises its "sole Power to try all Impeachments."[402] In 1974, the Department of Justice suggested the same view, opining that "[w]hether or not capable of judicial enforcement, due process standards would seem to be relevant to the manner of conducting an impeachment proceeding" in the House— including "the ability of the President to be represented at the inquiry of the House Committee, to cross-examine witnesses, and to offer witnesses and evidence," completely separate from the trial

---

[395] *Cf. U.S. Term Limits, Inc. v. Thornton*, 514 U.S. 779, 789 (1995).

[396] *See, e.g., Roth*, 408 U.S. at 573; *see also, e.g., Doe v. Dep't of Justice*, 753 F.2d 1092, 1106–07 (D.C. Cir. 1985); *McGinnis v. D.C.*, 65 F. Supp. 3d 203, 213 (D.D.C. 2014).

[397] *See, e.g.,* Message of Protest from Andrew Jackson, President, to the U.S. Senate (Apr. 15, 1834) (noting that the Framers were "undoubtedly aware" that impeachment, "whatever might be its result, would in most cases be accompanied by so much of dishonor and reproach, solicitude and suffering, as to make the power of preferring it one of the highest solemnity and importance."); 2 Joseph Story, *Commentaries on the Constitution* § 686 (1833) (observing the "notoriety of the [impeachment] proceedings" and "the deep extent to which they affect the reputations of the accused," even apart from the "ignominy of a conviction").

[398] The Federalist No. 65, *supra* note 383, at 397 (Alexander Hamilton).

[399] *Ohio Bell Tel. Co. v. Pub. Serv. Comm'n*, 301 U.S. 292, 302 (1937).

[400] *See Marshall v. Jerrico, Inc.*, 446 U.S. 238, 242 (1980) (one of the "central concerns of procedural due process" is "the prevention of unjustified or mistaken deprivations"); *Carey v. Piphus*, 435 U.S. 247, 259–60 (1978) (similar).

[401] *See Hastings v. United States*, 802 F. Supp. 490, 504 (D.D.C. 1992), *vacated and remanded on other grounds by Hastings v. United States*, 988 F.2d 1280 (D.C. Cir. 1993) (per curiam).

[402] *Id.*; U.S. Const. art. I, § 3, cl. 6.

in the Senate.[403]

(b) The Separation of Powers Requires Fair Process.

A proper respect for the head of a co-equal branch of the government also requires that the House use procedures that are not arbitrary and that are designed to permit the fair development of evidence. The Framers intended the impeachment power to be limited to "guard[] against the danger of persecution, from the prevalency of a factious spirit."[404] The Constitution places the power of impeachment in the entire House precisely to ensure that a majority of the elected representatives of the people decide to move an impeachment forward. That design would be undermined if a House vote were shaped by an investigatory process so lopsided that it effectively empowered only one faction to develop evidence and foreclosed the ability of others—including the accused—to develop the facts. Rather than promoting deliberation by a majority of the people's representatives, that approach would foster precisely the factionalism that the Framers foresaw as one of the greatest dangers in impeachments. "By forcing the House and Senate to act as tribunals rather than merely as legislative bodies, the Framers infused the process with notions of due process to prevent impeachment from becoming a common tool of party politics."[405]

The need for fair process as a reflection of respect for the separation of powers is further buttressed by the unique role of the President in the constitutional structure. As explained above,[406] "presidential impeachments are qualitatively different from all others" because they overturn a national election and risk grave disruption of the government.[407] It is unthinkable that a process carrying such grave risks for the Nation should not be regulated by any constitutional limits. And the need for fair process is even more critical where, as here, impeachment turns on how the President has exercised authorities within his exclusive constitutional sphere. The President is "the constitutional representative of the United States in its dealings with foreign nations."[408] Preserving the President's ability to carry out this constitutional function requires that he be provided fair process and an opportunity to defend himself in any investigation into how he has exercised his authority to conduct foreign affairs. Otherwise, a partisan faction could smear the President with one-sided allegations with no opportunity for the President to respond. That would threaten to "undermine the President's capacity" for "effective diplomacy" and "compromise the very capacity of the President to speak for the Nation with one voice in dealing with other governments."[409]

---

[403] Dep't of Justice, Office of Legal Counsel, *Legal Aspects of Impeachment: An Overview*, at 45 (1974), https://perma.cc/X4HU-WVWS.

[404] The Federalist No. 66, at 402 (Alexander Hamilton) (Clinton Rossiter ed., 1961).

[405] John O. McGinnis, *Impeachment: The Structural Understanding*, 67 Geo. Wash. L. Rev. 650, 663 (1999).

[406] *See supra* Standards Part B.2.

[407] Akhil Reed Amar, *On Impeaching Presidents*, 28 Hofstra L. Rev. 291, 304 (1999).

[408] *United States v. Louisiana*, 363 U.S. 1, 35 (1960); *see also United States v. Curtiss-Wright Corp.*, 299 U.S. 304, 319 (1936) ("The President is the sole organ of the nation in its external relations, and its sole representative with foreign nations.") (quoting 10 Annals of Cong. 613 (1800) (statement of Rep. John Marshall)); *Ex parte Hennen*, 38 U.S. (13 Pet.) 225, 235 (1839).

[409] *Crosby v. Nat'l Foreign Trade Council*, 530 U.S. 363, 381 (2000).

(c) The House's Sole Power of Impeachment and Power to Determine Rules of Its Own Proceedings Do Not Eliminate the Constitutional Requirement of Due Process.

Nothing in the House's "sole Power of Impeachment"[410] and power to "determine the Rules of its Proceedings"[411] undermines the House's obligation to use fundamentally fair procedures in impeachment. Those provisions simply mean that the House, and no other entity, has these powers. The Supreme Court has made clear that independent constitutional constraints limit otherwise plenary powers committed to one of the political branches.[412] For example, even though "[t]he [C]onstitution empowers each house to determine its rules of proceedings," each House "may not by its rules ignore constitutional restraints or violate fundamental rights."[413] Similarly, the doctrine of Executive Privilege, which is rooted in the separation of powers, constrains Congress's exercise of its constitutionally assigned powers. A congressional committee cannot simply demand access to information protected by Executive Privilege. Instead, if it can get access to such information at all, it must show that the information "is demonstrably critical to the responsible fulfillment of the Committee's functions."[414] The House could not evade that constraint by invoking its plenary authority to "determine the Rules of its Proceedings"[415] and adopting a rule allowing its committees to override Executive Privilege.[416] Executive Privilege, which is itself grounded in the Constitution, similarly constrains the House's ability to demand information pursuant to its "sole Power of Impeachment."[417]

Nixon v. United States, in any case, does not suggest otherwise.[418] *Nixon* addressed whether the use of a committee to take evidence in a Senate impeachment trial violated the direction in the Constitution that the Senate shall have "sole Power to try all Impeachments."[419] The Court held that the challenge presented a non-justiciable political question[420]—specifically, that "*[i]n the case before us*, there is no separate provision of the Constitution that could be defeated by allowing the Senate final authority to determine the meaning of the word 'try' in the Impeachment Trial Clause."[421] But *Nixon* did not hold that ***all*** questions related to impeachment are non-justiciable[422] or that there are no constitutional constraints on impeachment. To the contrary, the Court "agree[d] with Nixon that courts possess power to review either legislative or

---

[410] U.S. Const. art. I, § 2, cl. 5.

[411] U.S. Const. art. I, § 5, cl. 2.

[412] *See, e.g., INS v. Chadha*, 462 U.S. 919, 940–41 (1983); *Buckley v. Valeo*, 424 U.S. 1, 132 (1976), *superseded on other grounds by statute as stated in McConnell v. FEC*, 540 U.S. 93 (2003).

[413] *United States v. Ballin*, 144 U.S. 1, 5 (1892); *see also Barry v. United States ex rel. Cunningham*, 279 U.S. 597, 614 (1929); *Morgan v. United States*, 801 F.2d 445, 451 (D.C. Cir. 1986) (Scalia, J.).

[414] *Senate Select Comm. on Presidential Campaign Activities v. Nixon*, 498 F.2d 725, 731 (D.C. Cir. 1974).

[415] U.S. Const. art I, § 5, cl. 2.

[416] *See Attempted Exclusion of Agency Counsel from Congressional Depositions of Agency Employees*, 43 Op. O.L.C. ___, *2 (2019).

[417] *See supra* Part I.B.2(b).

[418] 506 U.S. 224 (1993).

[419] U.S. Const. art. I, § 3, cl. 6; *see Nixon*, 506 U.S. at 226.

[420] *Nixon*, 506 U.S. at 228–29.

[421] *Id.* at 237 (emphasis added).

[422] In concurrence, Justice Souter explained that some approaches by the Senate might be so extreme that they would merit judicial review under the Impeachment Trial Clause. As he explained: "If the Senate were to act in a manner seriously threatening the integrity of its results, convicting, say, upon a coin toss, or upon a summary determination that an officer of the United States was simply 'a bad guy,' . . . judicial interference might well be appropriate." *Id.* at 253–54 (Souter, J., concurring in judgment) (quoting *Nixon*, 506 U.S. at 239 (White, J., concurring in judgment)).

executive action that transgresses identifiable textual limits," but merely concluded "that the word 'try' in the Impeachment Trial Clause does not provide an identifiable textual limit on the authority which is committed to the Senate."[423] More importantly, the justiciability of such questions is irrelevant. Constitutional obligations need not be enforceable by the judiciary to exist and constrain the political branches. As Madison explained, "as the Legislative, Executive, and Judicial departments of the United States are co-ordinate, and each equally bound to support the Constitution, it follows that each must in the exercise of its functions, be guided by the text of the Constitution according to its own interpretation of it."[424] Particularly in the impeachment context, "we have to divest ourselves of the common misconception that constitutionality is discussable or determinable only in the courts, and that anything is constitutional which a court cannot or will not overturn. . . . Congress's responsibility to preserve the forms and the precepts of the Constitution is greater, rather than less, when the judicial forum is unavailable, as it sometimes must be."[425] A holding that a particular question is a non-justiciable political question leaves that question to the political branches to use "nonjudicial methods of working out their differences"[426] and does not relieve the House of its constitutional obligation.

2. The House's Consistent Practice of Providing Due Process in Impeachment Investigations for the Last 150 Years Confirms that the Constitution Requires Due Process.

Historical practice provides a gloss on the requirements of the Constitution and strongly confirms that House impeachment investigations must adhere to basic forms of due process. "In separation-of-powers cases, th[e] [Supreme] Court has often put significant weight upon historical practice."[427] As James Madison explained, it "was foreseen at the birth of the Constitution, that difficulties and differences of opinion might occasionally arise in expounding terms [and] phrases necessarily used in such a charter . . . and that it might require a regular course of practice to liquidate [and] settle the meaning of some of them."[428] The Constitution "contemplates that practice will integrate the dispersed powers [of the federal government] into a workable government."[429] The Supreme Court has thus explained that historical practice reflects "an admissible view of the Constitution,"[430] and "consistent congressional practice requires our respect."[431] Although constitutional requirements governing House impeachment proceedings may have been unsettled when the Constitution was adopted, by the 1870s consistent practice in the House (unbroken since then) gave meaning to the Constitution and settled the minimum procedures that must be afforded for a fair impeachment inquiry.

---

[423] *Id.* at 237–38. *Nixon* did not address whether the Due Process Clause constrained the conduct of an impeachment trial in the Senate because no due process claim was raised by the parties.

[424] Letter from James Madison to Mr. —— (1834), *in* 4 Letters and Other Writings of James Madison 349, 349 (Philadelphia, J.B. Lippincott & Co. 1865); *see also* William Baude, *Constitutional Liquidation*, 71 Stan. L. Rev. 1, 21, 35 (2019).

[425] Charles L. Black & Philip Bobbitt, *Impeachment: A Handbook, New Edition* 22–23 (2018).

[426] *Zivotofsky ex rel. Zivotofsky v. Clinton*, 566 U.S. 189, 219 (2012) (*Zivotofsky I*) (Breyer, J., dissenting); *see also Coleman v. Miller*, 307 U.S. 433, 454 (1939).

[427] *Zivotofsky ex rel. Zivotofsky v. Kerry*, 135 S. Ct. 2076, 2091 (2015) (*Zivotofsky II*) (internal quotation marks omitted); *see also McCulloch v. Maryland*, 17 U.S. 316, 401 (1819).

[428] *Noel Canning*, 573 U.S. at 525 (quoting Letter to Spencer Roane (Sept. 2, 1819), *in* 8 Writings of James Madison 450 (G. Hunt ed. 1908)).

[429] *Youngstown Sheet & Tube Co. v. Sawyer*, 343 U.S. 579, 635 (1952) (Jackson, J., concurring).

[430] *Curtiss-Wright Export Corp.*, 299 U.S. at 329.

[431] *Bahlul v. United States*, 840 F.3d 757, 765 (D.C. Cir. 2016) (Kavanaugh, J., concurring).

The Framers, who debated impeachment with reference to the contemporaneous English impeachment of Warren Hastings,[432] knew that "the House of Commons did hear the accused, and did permit him to produce testimony, before they voted an impeachment against him."[433] And practice in the United States rapidly established that the accused in an impeachment must be allowed fair process. Although a few early impeachment investigations were *ex parte*,[434] the House provided the accused with notice and an opportunity to be heard in the majority of cases starting as early as 1818.[435]

By Judge Peck's impeachment in 1830, House Members, explicitly acknowledging that "it was obvious that it had not yet been settled by precedent," had an extensive debate to "settle[]" "[t]he practice in cases of impeachments, so far as regards the proceedings in this House."[436] Judge Peck had asked for the House to give him the ability to submit a "written exposition of the whole case, embracing both the facts and the law, and give him, also, process to call his witnesses from Missouri in support of his statements."[437] The Judiciary Committee Chairman, James Buchanan, pointed out that "in the case of Warren Hastings" in England, "the House of Commons did hear the accused, and did permit him to produce testimony, before they voted an impeachment against him."[438] Mr. Ingersoll explained that, in a prior impeachment inquiry against Vice President Calhoun, "a friend of the Vice President had been permitted to appear, and represent him throughout the whole investigation," that "[w]itnesses, also, had been examined on the part of the accused," and that "witnesses in favor of the Vice President had been examined, as well as against him, and that his representative had been allowed to present before the committee through every stage of the examination."[439] He noted that "[t]he committee at that time took some pains to ascertain what was the proper mode of proceeding, and they became satisfied that the party accused had, in these preliminary proceedings, a *right* to be thus heard."[440] Mr. Pettis similarly concluded that "[t]he request of the Judge is supported by the whole train of English decisions in cases of a like kind" and that he should be given those rights here as well.[441] The debate was thus settled in favor of due process rights for Judge Peck.[442]

By at least the 1870s, despite some unsettled practice in the interim, the House Judiciary Committee concluded that an opportunity for the "accused by himself and his counsel [to] be heard" had "become the ***established practice*** of the [Judiciary Committee] in cases of

---

[432] 2 *Records of the Federal Convention of 1787*, at 550 (M. Farrand ed. 1966); *see, e.g.*, Richard M. Pious, *Impeaching the President: The Intersection of Constitutional and Popular Law*, 43 St. Louis L.J. 859, 872 (1999); *see also, e.g.*, *Proceedings of the Senate Sitting for the Trial of William W. Belknap, Late Secretary of War, on the Articles of Impeachment Exhibited by the House of Representatives*, 44th Cong. 98 (1876) (statement of Sen. Timothy Howe); Scott S. Barker, *An Overview of Presidential Impeachment*, 47 Colo. Lawyer 30, 32 (Sept. 2018).

[433] 6 Reg. Deb. 737 (1830) (statement of Rep. James Buchanan).

[434] *See* III Hinds' Precedents § 2319, at 681 (Judge Pickering); *id.* § 2343, at 716 (Justice Chase).

[435] *See* 32 Annals of Cong. 1715, 1715–16 (1818); *see, e.g.*, III Hinds' Precedents § 2491, at 988 (Judge Thurston, 1825); *id.* § 1736, at 97–98 (Vice President Calhoun, 1826); *id.* §§ 2365–2366 (Judge Peck, 1830–1831); *id.* § 2491, at 989 (Judge Thurston, 1837); *id.* § 2495, at 994 & n.4 (Judge Watrous, 1852); Cong. Globe, 35th Cong., 1st Sess. 2167 (1858) (statement of Rep. Horace Clark) (Judge Watrous, 1858); III Hinds' Precedents § 2496, at 999 (Judge Watrous, 1858); *id.* § 2504, at 1008 (Judge Delahay, 1873).

[436] 6 Reg. Deb. 738 (1830) (statement of Rep. Spencer Pettis).

[437] III Hinds' Precedents § 2366, at 776.

[438] 6 Reg. Deb. 737 (1830) (statement of Rep. James Buchanan).

[439] *Id.* at 737–38 (statement of Rep. Charles Ingersoll).

[440] *Id.* at 738 (emphasis added).

[441] *Id.* (statement of Rep. Spencer Pettis).

[442] *See* III Hinds' Precedents § 2365, at 774.

impeachment" and thus "deemed it **due to the accused** that he should have" due process.[443] That "established practice" has been followed in every House impeachment investigation for the past 150 years[444] and has provided a fixed meaning for the constitutional requirements governing House impeachment proceedings.[445] The fact that the House has not followed a perfectly consistent practice dating all the way back to 1789, or that there were early outliers, is irrelevant.[446]

The House's Parliamentarian acknowledges that while "the committee sometimes made its

---

[443] Cong. Globe, 42d Cong., 3d Sess. 2122 (1873) (emphasis added); III Hinds' Precedents § 2506, at 1011 (noting, in Judge Durrell's impeachment in 1873, that "[i]t has been the practice of the Committee on the Judiciary to hear the accused in matters of impeachment whenever thereto requested, by witnesses or by counsel, or by both").

[444] *E.g.*, H.R. Rep. No. 111-427, 111th Cong. 11–12 (2010) (Judge Porteous); 155 Cong. Rec. H7055, H7056 (2009) (Judge Kent) (statement of Rep. Adam Schiff); H.R. Rep. No. 101-36, 101st Cong. 15 (1989) (Judge Nixon); *Impeachment Inquiry: Hearings Before the Subcomm. on Criminal Justice of H.R. Comm. on the Jud.*, 100th Cong. 10–12; H.R. Rep. No. 100-810, 100th Cong. 11–12 (1988) (Judge Hastings); *Conduct of Harry E. Claiborne, U.S. Dist. Judge, D. Nev.: Hearing Before the Subcomm. on Courts, Civil Liberties, & Admin. of Justice of H.R. Comm. on the Jud.*, 99th Cong. 2–3, 6–7, 48–78; H.R. Rep. No. 99-688, 99th Cong. 4-5 (1986) (Judge Claiborne); *Justice William O. Douglas: First Report by the Special Subcomm. on H.R. Res. 920 of H.R. Comm. on the Judiciary*, 91st Cong. 12 (Comm. Print 1970); *Conduct of Albert W. Johnson & Albert L. Watson, U.S. Dist. Judges, M.D. Pa.: Hearing Before the Subcomm. of H.R. Comm. on the Judiciary*, 79th Cong. 3 (1946); *Conduct of Halsted L. Ritter, U.S. Dist. Judge, S.D. Fla.: Hearing Before the Subcomm. of H.R. Comm. on the Judiciary*, 73d Cong. 2–3, 12, 39, 86, 102, 148, 233 (1933); *Hearing Before the H.R. Special Comm. Appointed to Inquire into the Official Conduct of Judge Harold Louderback*, 72d Cong. 10–11, 33–34, 92, 109, 131–33, 329–30 (1932); *Conduct of Hon. Wright Patman Against the Sec'y of the Treasury: Hearings on H.R. Res. 92 Before the H.R. Comm. on the Judiciary*, 72d Cong. 6, 13–14, 53, 62–69, 152–177, 197 (1932) (Sec'y of Treasury Andrew W. Mellon); *Conduct of Grover M. Moscowitz: Hearing Before H.R. Special Comm.*, 70th Cong. 1–2, 4, 15, 18 (1929); *Conduct of Harry B. Anderson: Hearing Before H.R. Comm. on Judiciary*, 71st Cong. 2, 5–7, 48–49 (1931); *Charges Against Hon. Frank Cooper: Hearing on H.R. Res. 398 & 415 Before H.R. Comm. on the Judiciary*, 69th Cong. 1, 12 (1927); *Charges of Impeachment Against Frederick A. Fenning: Hearing on H.R. Res. 228 Before H.R. Comm. on the Judiciary*, 69th Cong. 10, 153, 366, 520–21, 523, 566–70, 1092–93 (1926); *Conduct of George W. English: Hearing Before the H. Special Comm.*, 69th Cong. 5–7, 48–53, 81–84, 95–96, 106–08, 126–27, 149–55, 212–216, 239–40, 243–45 (1925); *Hearing Before H.R. Comm. on the Judiciary*, 68th Cong. 1, 9–10, 26, 36–37 (1925) (Judge Baker); VI Cannon's Precedents § 537, at 771 (Att'y Gen. Daugherty); *Conduct of Judge Kenesaw Mountain Landis: Hearing Before H.R. Comm. on Judiciary*, 66th Cong. 7 (1921); H.R. Rep. No. 66-544, 64th Cong. (1916), *in* 53 Cong. Rec. 6137 (1916) (U.S. Dist. Att'y Marshall); *Judge Alston G. Dayton: Hearings Before H.R. Comm. on Judiciary & Special Subcomm. Thereof*, 63d Cong. 210 (1915); *Daniel Thew Wright: Hearings Before Subcomm. of H.R. Comm. on the Judiciary*, 63d Cong. 8–9 (1914); *Conduct of Emory Speer: Hearings Before Subcomm. of H.R. Comm. on the Judiciary*, 63d Cong. 23 (1914); 48 Cong. Rec. 8907 (1912) (Judge Archbald); VI Cannon's Precedents § 526, at 745 (Judge Hanford); *Hearings Before Subcomm. of H.R. Comm. on the Judiciary upon the Articles of Impeachment of Lebbeus R. Wilfley, Judge of U.S. Ct. for China*, 60th Cong. 3–4 (1908); *Impeachment of Judge Charles Swayne: Evidence Before the Subcomm. of H.R. Comm. on the Judiciary*, 58th Cong. III (1904); III Hinds' Precedents § 2520, at 1034 (Judge Ricks); *id.* § 2518, at 1031 (Judge Boarman); *id.* § 2516, at 1027 (Judge Blodgett); *id.* § 2445, at 904 (Sec'y of War Belknap); *id.* § 2514, at 1024 (Consul-Gen. Seward); H.R. Rep. No. 43-626, 43d Cong. V (1874) (Judge W. Story, J.); III Hinds' Precedents § 2507, at 1011 (Judge Durell); *id.* § 2512, at 1021 (Judge Busteed); Cong. Globe, 42d Cong., 3d Sess. 2124 (1873) (Judge Sherman); III Hinds Precedents § 2504, at 1008 (Judge Delahay).

[445] *See, e.g.*, William Baude, *Rethinking the Federal Eminent Domain Power*, 122 Yale L.J. 1738, 1811 (2013) (explaining that the Founders envisioned that "post-ratification practice can serve to give concrete meaning to a constitutional provision even if it was vague as an original matter" and that "this is consistent with an originalist theory of constitutional construction"); Caleb Nelson, *Originalism and Interpretive Conventions*, 70 U. Chi. L. Rev. 519, 521 (2003); *see generally* Baude, *Constitutional Liquidation, supra* note 424.

[446] *See NLRB v. Noel Canning*, 573 U.S. 513, 525 (2014) ("These precedents show that this Court has treated practice as an important interpretive factor even when the nature or longevity of that practice is subject to dispute, and even when that practice began after the founding era."); *Free Enter. Fund v. Public Co. Accounting Oversight Bd.*, 561 U.S. 477, 505 (2010) (a "handful of isolated" examples cannot overcome the otherwise settled "past practice of Congress"); *see also, e.g., Dames & Moore v. Regan*, 453 U.S. 654, 684 (1981).

inquiry *ex parte*" in "earlier practice" before the 1870s, the practice dating to the 1870s "is to permit the accused to testify, present witnesses, cross-examine witnesses, and be represented by counsel."[447] Current House Democrats are already on record agreeing that due process protections apply in the House's impeachment inquiries. Chairman Nadler has admitted that "[t]he power of impeachment is a solemn responsibility, assigned to the House by the Constitution," and "[t]hat responsibility demands a rigorous level of due process."[448] He has rightly acknowledged, expressly in the context of impeachment, that "[t]he Constitution guarantees the right of anyone who is accused of any wrongdoing, and fundamental fairness guarantees the right of anyone, to have the right to confront the witness against him."[449] Rep. Hank Johnson—a current Judiciary Committee member—has similarly recognized that "[t]here is a reason for a careful process when it comes to the most drastic action of impeachment; it is called due process."[450]

The two modern presidential impeachment inquiries also abundantly confirm the due process protections that apply to the accused in an impeachment inquiry. In fact, every President who has asked to participate in an impeachment investigation has been afforded extensive rights to do so.[451] The House Judiciary Committee adopted explicit procedures to provide Presidents Clinton and Nixon with robust opportunities to defend themselves, including the rights "to attend all hearings, including any held in executive session"; "respond to evidence received and testimony adduced by the Committee"; "submit written requests" for "the Committee to receive additional testimony or other evidence";[452] "question any witness called before the Committee"; and raise "[o]bjections relating to the examination of witnesses, or to the admissibility of testimony and evidence."[453] President Clinton was given access to the grand-jury evidence that underpinned the Starr report.[454] The Committee also ensured that the minority could fully participate in the investigation and hearings, including by submitting evidence, objecting to witness examination

---

[447] Charles W. Johnson et al., *House Practice: A Guide to the Rules, Precedents, and Procedures of the House*, 115th Cong., 1st Sess., ch. 27, § 7, at 616 (2017), https://perma.cc/RB2S-Q965 (*House Practice*) (citing, as support for this "modern practice," the 1876 impeachment investigation of William Belknap in III Hinds' Precedents § 2445, at 904).

[448] *Impeachment Articles Referred on John Koskinen (Part II): Hearing Before the H.R. Comm. on the Judiciary*, 114th Cong. 3 (2016) (statement of Rep. Jerrold Nadler).

[449] *Hearing Pursuant to H.R. Res. 581 Before the H.R. Comm. on the Judiciary: Appearance of Independent Counsel*, 105th Cong. 6 (Nov. 19, 1998) (*Clinton Independent Counsel Hearing*) (statement of Rep. Jerrold Nadler).

[450] *Impeachment Articles Referred on John Koskinen (Part III): Hearing Before the H.R. Comm. on the Judiciary*, 114th Cong. 30 (2016) (statement of Rep. Hank Johnson).

[451] President Johnson was apparently "notified of what was going on, but never asked to appear"—a fact that Judiciary Committee members later found significant in discounting President Johnson's impeachment as a precedent. Cong. Globe, 42d Cong., 3d Sess., 2122–23 (1873) (statement of Mr. Butler during impeachment investigation of Judge Sherman).

[452] *Authorization of an Inquiry into Whether Grounds Exist for the Impeachment of William Jefferson Clinton, President of the United States: Meeting of the H.R. Comm. on the Judiciary; Presentation by Inquiry Staff Consideration of Inquiry Resolution; Adoption of Inquiry Procedures*, 105th Cong. 220 (Comm. Print 1998) (*Clinton Impeachment Inquiry Procedures*); *see also* H.R. Rep. No. 105-795, at 25–26; 3 Deschler's Precedents ch. 14, § 6.5, at 2046 (same); H.R. Comm. on the Judiciary, *Impeachment of Richard M. Nixon, President of the United States*, H.R. Rep. No. 93-1305, 93d Cong. 8–9 (1974) (same, Nixon impeachment).

[453] *Clinton Impeachment Inquiry Procedures*, *supra* note 452, at 220; 3 Deschler's Precedents ch. 14, § 6.5, at 2045–47 (Nixon Impeachment Inquiry Procedures); *see also* H.R. Rep. No. 93-1305, at 8–9 (affording the President Nixon's counsel the "opportunity to . . . ask such questions of the witnesses as the Committee deemed appropriate").

[454] *See Impeachment Inquiry Pursuant to H.R. Res. 581: Presentations by Investigative Counsel*, 105th Cong. 93 (Dec. 10, 1998); *Hearing Before the H.R. Comm. on the Judiciary: Impeachment Inquiry Pursuant to H.R. Res. 581: Presentation on Behalf of the President*, 105th Cong. 69 (Dec. 8–9, 1998) (*Clinton Presentation on Behalf of the President*).

and evidence, and exercising co-equal subpoena authority to issue a subpoena subject to overruling by the full Committee.[455] Both Presidents were thus able to present robust defenses before the Committee.[456] Indeed, President Clinton's counsel gave an opening statement, the President called 14 expert witnesses over two days, and the President's counsel also gave a closing statement[457] and cross-examined the witnesses, including "question[ing] Judge Starr for an hour."[458] In this impeachment inquiry, the House Intelligence Committee fulfilled the investigatory role that the House Judiciary Committee filled in prior impeachments, and thus, these rights should have been available in the proceedings before the Intelligence Committee.

3.   **The President's Counsel Must Be Allowed to Be Present at Hearings, See and Present Evidence, and Cross-Examine All Witnesses.**

The exact contours of the procedural protections required during an impeachment investigation must, of course, be adapted to the nature of that proceeding. The hallmarks of a full blown trial are not required, but procedures must reflect, at a minimum, basic protections that are essential for ensuring a fair process that is designed to get at the truth.

The Supreme Court's "precedents establish the general rule that individuals must receive notice and an opportunity to be heard *before* the Government deprives them" of a constitutionally protected interest.[459] That means, at a minimum, that the evidence must be disclosed to the accused, and the accused must be permitted an opportunity to test and respond to the evidence—particularly through "[t]he rights to confront and cross-examine witnesses," which "have long been recognized as essential to due process."[460] For 250 years, "the policy of the Anglo-American system of evidence has been to regard the necessity of testing by cross-examination as a vital feature of the law."[461] Cross-examination is "the greatest legal engine ever invented for the discovery of truth,"[462] "shed[ding] light on the witness' perception, memory and narration"[463] and

---

[455]   H.R. Res. 581 § 2(b); 3 Deschler's Precedents ch. 14, § 6.5, at 2046; H.R. Res. 803 § 2(b).

[456]   President Clinton's counsel gave opening and closing statements, called 14 expert witnesses, and cross-examined the witnesses. *See generally Clinton Presentation on Behalf of the President, supra* note 454; *Submission by Counsel for President Clinton to the H.R. Comm. on the Judiciary*, H.R. Comm. on the Judiciary, Comm. Print, Ser. No. 16, 105th Cong., 2nd Sess. (1998) (*Submission by Counsel for President Clinton*); H.R. Comm. on the Judiciary, *Impeachment of William Jefferson Clinton, President of the United States*, H.R. Rep. No. 105-830, 105th Cong. 127 (1998); *Clinton Judiciary Comm. Hearing Appearance of Independent Counsel, supra* note 449. President Nixon's counsel attended all Committee hearings to hear the initial presentation of evidence, submitted an 800-plus page response, gave a two-day oral argument, questioned witnesses, objected to testimony, submitted a 151-page closing brief, and was given all "the time that you want" to argue. *See Statement of Information Submitted on Behalf of President Nixon: Hearings Pursuant to H.R. Res. 803 Before the H.R. Comm. on the Judiciary*, 93d Cong. (1974) (Books I–IV); *Hearings Pursuant to H.R. Res. 803 Before the H.R. Comm. on the Judiciary*, 93d Cong. 1719–1866 (June 27–28, 1974); *Testimony of Witnesses: Hearings Pursuant to H.R. Res. 803 Before the H.R. Comm. on the Judiciary*, 93d Cong. (1974); *id.*, Book I at 70–90, 135–42, 232–41; *id.*, Book II at 29–55, 160–65, 196–98, 216–17, 257–88; *id.*, Book III at 107–23, 134, 179–81, 399–45, 517–18, 669–92, 1888; 10 Weekly Comp. Pres. Docs. 840 (1974).

[457]   *See Clinton Presentation on Behalf of the President, supra* note 454; *Submission by Counsel for President Clinton, supra* note 456.

[458]   H.R. Rep. No. 105-830, at 127; *see generally Clinton Independent Counsel Hearing, supra* note 449.

[459]   *United States v. James Daniel Good Real Prop.*, 510 U.S. 43, 48 (1993) (emphasis added).

[460]   *Chambers v. Miss.*, 410 U.S. 284, 294 (1973); *see also, e.g., Greene v. McElroy*, 360 U.S. 474, 496 (1959).

[461]   *Perry v. Leeke*, 488 U.S. 272, 283 n.7 (1989) (quoting 5 Wigmore, *Evidence* § 1367 (Chadbourn rev. 1974)).

[462]   *Id.*

[463]   *Id.* (quoting 4 J. Weinstein, *Evidence* ¶ 800[01] (1988)).

"expos[ing] inconsistencies, incompleteness, and inaccuracies in his testimony."[464] Thus, "[i]n almost every setting where important decisions turn on questions of fact, due process requires an opportunity to confront and cross-examine adverse witnesses."[465] It is unthinkable that the Framers, steeped in the history of Anglo-American jurisprudence, would create a system that would allow the Chief Executive and Commander-in-Chief of the armed forces to be impeached based on a process that developed evidence without providing any of the elementary procedures that the common law developed over centuries for ensuring the proper testing of evidence in an adversarial process.

The most persuasive source indicating what the Constitution requires in an impeachment investigation is the record of the House's own past practice, as explained above.[466] The due process rights consistently afforded by the House to the accused for the past 150 years have generally included the right to appear and to be represented by counsel at all hearings, to have access to and respond to the evidence, to submit evidence and testimony, to question witnesses and object to evidence, and to make opening statements and closing arguments.[467] Chairman Nadler, Chairman Schiff, other House Democrats, and then-Representative Schumer have repeatedly confirmed these procedural requirements.[468]

4.   The House Impeachment Inquiry Failed to Provide the Due Process Demanded by the Constitution and Generated a Fundamentally Skewed Record that Cannot Be Relied Upon in the Senate.

Despite clear precedent mandating due process for the accused in any impeachment inquiry—and especially in a presidential impeachment inquiry—House Democrats concocted a wholly unprecedented three-stage process in this case that denied the President fair process at every step of the way. Indeed, because the process started without any actual authorization from the House, committees initially made up the process as they went along. In the end, all three phases of the House's inquiry failed to afford the President even the most rudimentary procedures demanded by the Constitution, fundamental fairness, and over 150 years of precedent.

(a)   Phase I: Secret Hearings in the Basement Bunker

The first phase involved secret proceedings in a basement bunker where the President was not given any rights at all. This phase consisted of depositions taken by joint hearings of the House Permanent Select Committee on Intelligence (HPSCI), the House Committee on Foreign Affairs, and the House Committee on Oversight and Reform. To ensure there would be no transparency for the President or the American people, depositions were conducted in a facility designed for securing highly classified information—even though **all** of the depositions were "conducted entirely at the unclassified level."[469] The President was denied any opportunity to participate. He

---

464   *Id.*

465   *Goldberg v. Kelly*, 397 U.S. 254, 269 (1970).

466   *See supra* Part II.B.2.

467   *See generally supra* notes 443–454 and accompanying text.

468   *See, e.g., Background and History of Impeachment: Hearing Before the Subcomm. on the Constitution of the H.R. Comm. on the Judiciary*, 105th Cong. 17 (1998) (statement of Rep. Jerrold Nadler) (in the context of a House impeachment investigation, "due process mean[s] . . . the right to be informed of the law, of the charges against you, the right to confront the witnesses against you, to call your own witnesses, and to have the assistance of counsel"); H.R. Rep. No. 111-427, 111th Cong. 11–12 (2010); H.R. Rep. No. 111-159, 111th Cong. 14 (2009); H.R. Rep. No. 105-830, at 265–66 ("[I]mpeachment not only mandates due process, but [] 'due process quadrupled.'").

469   *See, e.g.,* T. Morrison Dep. Tr. at 8:14-15 (Oct. 31, 2019).

was denied the right to have counsel present. He was denied the right to cross-examine witnesses, call witnesses, and present evidence. He was even denied the right to have Executive Branch counsel present during depositions of Executive Branch officials, thereby undermining any ability for the President to protect longstanding constitutional privileges over Executive Branch information.[470] Members in the Republican minority on the investigating committees could not provide a counterweight to remedy the lack of process for the President. They were denied subpoena authority to call witnesses, and they were blocked even from asking questions that would ensure a balanced development of the facts. For example, Chairman Schiff repeatedly shut down any line of questioning that would have exposed personal self-interest, prejudice, or bias of the whistleblower.[471]

Finally, House Democrats made clear that the proceedings' secrecy was just a partisan stratagem. Daily leaks describing purported testimony of witnesses were calculated to present the public with a distorted view of what was taking place behind closed doors and further the narrative that the President had done something wrong.[472]

House Democrats' assertions that the basement Star Chamber hearings were justified because the House "serves in a role analogous to a grand jury and prosecutor"[473] are baseless. The House's unbroken practice of providing due process over the last 150 years confirms that the House is not merely a grand jury.[474] Chairman Nadler, other House Democrats, and then-Representative Schumer rejected such analogies as a "cramped view of the appropriate role of the House [that] finds no support in the Constitution and is completely contrary to the great weight of historical precedent."[475] The Judiciary Committee's own impeachment consultant and staff have rejected "[g]rand jury analogies" as "badly misplaced when it comes to impeachment."[476]

More importantly, the narrow rationales that justify limiting procedural protections in grand juries simply do not apply here.[477] For example, it is primarily grand jury secrecy—not the preliminary nature of grand jury proceedings in developing the basis for a charge—that "justif[ies] the limited procedural safeguards available to . . . persons under investigation."[478] That secrecy, in turn, promotes two primary objectives. It allows an investigation to proceed without notice to those under suspicion and thus may further the investigation.[479] In addition, a "cornerstone" of

---

[470] 116th Congress Regulations for Use of Deposition Authority ¶ 3, *in* 165 Cong. Rec. H1216 (2019).

[471] *See, e.g.*, A. Vindman Dep. Tr. at 77–80, 82, 274–75 (Oct. 29, 2019); Morrison Dep. Tr. at 69:23–70:5.

[472] *See* David M. Drucker, *Impeachment Spin Win: Democrats Killing GOP in Testimony Leak Game*, Wash. Examiner (Nov. 1, 2019), https://perma.cc/FC7T-FZ49 ("House Democrats are crushing Republicans with the use of testimony to frame the impeachment of President Trump for American voters, weaponizing selective leaks from closed-door depositions to portray a commander in chief that abused his power."); *see also, e.g.*, The Editorial Bd., *Schiff's Secret Bombshells*, Wall St. J. (Oct. 23, 2019), https://perma.cc/T964-8DMS; Russell Berman & Elaine Godfrey, *The Closed-Door Impeachment*, The Atlantic (Oct. 19, 2019), https://perma.cc/JPT8-W7KB.

[473] HJC Report at 37.

[474] *See supra* Part II.B.2; *see supra* note 443–454 and accompanying text.

[475] H.R. Rep. No. 105-830, at 210–11 (Minority Views).

[476] Laurence Tribe & Joshua Matz, *To End a Presidency: The Power of Impeachment* 78 (2018).

[477] "[T]he invocation of grand jury interests is not 'some talisman that dissolves all constitutional protections.'" *Butterworth v. Smith*, 494 U.S. 624, 630 (1990) (quoting *United States v. Dionisio*, 410 U.S. 1, 11 (1973)). Grand juries do not "enjoy blanket exemption from the commands of due process." *United States v. Briggs*, 514 F.2d 794, 804 (5th Cir. 1975); Sara Sun Beale et al., *Grand Jury Law and Practice* § 2:4 n.1 (2d ed. 2019); *see, e.g., United States v. Calandra*, 414 U.S. 338, 346 (1974); *Peters v. Kiff*, 407 U.S. 493, 504 (1972) (plurality opinion of Marshall, J.); *United States v. Hodge*, 496 F.2d 87, 88 (5th Cir. 1974).

[478] *Illinois v. Abbott & Assocs., Inc.*, 460 U.S. 557, 566 n.11 (1983).

[479] *See, e.g., United States v. Procter & Gamble Co.*, 356 U.S. 677, 681 n.6 (1958).

grand jury secrecy is the policy of protecting the public reputations of those who may be investigated but never charged.[480]

Neither rationale applied to Chairman Schiff's proceedings for a straightforward reason: in relevant respects, the proceedings were entirely public. Chairman Schiff made no secret that the target of his investigation was President Trump. He and his colleagues held news conferences to announce that fact, and they leaked information intended to damage the President from their otherwise secret hearings.[481] In addition, the exact witness list with the dates, times, and places of witness testimony were announced to the world long in advance of each hearing. And witnesses' opening statements, as well as slanted summaries of their testimony, were selectively leaked to the press in real time. The entire direction of the investigation, as well as specific testimony, was thus telegraphed to the world. These acts would have violated federal criminal law if grand jury rules had applied.[482]

It is also well settled that the one-sided procedures employed by Chairman Schiff were not designed to be the best mechanism for getting at the truth. Grand jury procedures have never been justified on the theory that they are well adapted for uncovering ultimate facts. To the contrary, as explained above, the Anglo-American legal system has long recognized that "adversarial testing," particularly cross-examination, "will ultimately advance the public interest in truth and fairness."[483] Those essential procedural rights are no less necessary in impeachment proceedings unless one adopts the counterintuitive assumption that the Framers did not intend an impeachment inquiry to use any of the familiar mechanisms developed over centuries in the common law to get at the truth.

(b) Phase II: The Public, *Ex Parte* Show Trial Before HPSCI

After four weeks of secret—and wholly unauthorized—hearings, House Democrats finally introduced a resolution to have the House authorize an impeachment inquiry and to set procedures for it. House Resolution 660, however, merely compounded the fundamentally unfair procedures from the secret cellar hearings by subjecting the President to a *second* round of *ex parte* hearings before Chairman Schiff's committee. The only difference was that this second round took place in public.[484] Thus, after screening witnesses' testimony behind closed doors, Chairman Schiff moved on to a true show trial—a stage-managed inquisition in front of the cameras, choreographed with pre-screened testimony to build a narrative aiming at a pre-determined result. The President was *still* denied any opportunity to participate, to cross-examine witnesses, to present witnesses or evidence, or to protect constitutionally privileged Executive Branch information by having agency counsel present. All of this was directly contrary to the rules that had governed the Nixon and Clinton impeachment inquiries. There, the President had been allowed to cross-examine *any* fact witnesses called by the committee.[485] In addition, the President had been permitted to call witnesses, and the ranking member on the investigating committee had been permitted co-equal

---

[480] *In re Am. Historical Ass'n*, 62 F. Supp. 2d 1100, 1103 (S.D.N.Y. 1999); *see also, e.g., Procter & Gamble Co.*, 356 U.S. at 681 n.6; *Douglas Oil Co. of Cal. v. Petrol Stops Nw.*, 441 U.S. 211, 219 (1979).

[481] *See supra* note 472 and accompanying text.

[482] *See* Fed. R. Crim. P. 6(e); 18 U.S.C. §§ 401(3), 641, 1503 (2018); *see, e.g., United States v. Jeter*, 775 F.2d 670, 675–82 (6th Cir. 1985); *Martin v. Consultants & Adm'rs, Inc.*, 966 F.2d 1078, 1097 (7th Cir. 1992); *In re Sealed Case No. 99–3091*, 192 F.3d 995, 1001 (D.C. Cir. 1999) (per curiam); Beale et al., *supra* note 477, § 5:6, at 5–28.

[483] *Polk Cty. v. Dodson*, 454 U.S. 312, 318 (1981); *see supra* notes 459–465 and accompanying text.

[484] H.R. Res. 660 § 2(1).

[485] H.R. Rep. No. 105-830, at 126–127; 3 Deschler's Precedents ch. 14, § 6.5, at 2046–47.

subpoena authority.[486]

(c) Phase III: The Ignominious Rubber Stamp from the Judiciary Committee

The House Committee on the Judiciary simply rubber-stamped the *ex parte* record compiled by Chairman Schiff and, per the Speaker's direction, relied on it to draft articles of impeachment. Under House Resolution 660, it was only during this third phase that the President was even nominally allowed a chance to participate and some rudimentary elements of process.[487] With fact-finding already over, there was no meaningful way to allow the President to use those rights for a balanced factual inquiry. Instead, the Judiciary Committee doubled down on using the skewed, one-sided record developed by Chairman Schiff. Thus, the only procedural protections that House Resolution 660 provided the President were inadequate from the outset because they came far too late in the proceedings to be effective. Procedural protections such as cross-examination are essential *as the factual record is being developed*. Providing process only *after* the record has been compiled and *after* charges are being drafted can do little to remedy the distortions built into the record. Here, most witnesses testified *twice* under oath on the same topics—once in a secret rehearsal to preview their testimony, and again in public—without any cross-examination by the President's counsel. Locking witnesses into their stories by having them testify twice vastly reduces the benefit of cross-examination. Any deviation from prior testimony potentially exposes a witness to a double perjury charge, and, worse, the prior *ex parte* testimony becomes fixed in each witness's mind in place of actual memory.

While it would have been next to impossible for a proceeding before the Judiciary Committee to remedy the defects in the prior two rounds of hearings, Chairman Nadler had no interest in even attempting to do that. His only interest was following marching orders to report articles of impeachment to the House so they could be voted on before Christmas. Thus, he repeatedly provided vague and inadequate notice about what proceedings were planned until he ultimately informed the President that he had no plans for any evidentiary hearings at all.

For example, on November 26, 2019—two days before Thanksgiving—Chairman Nadler informed the President and the Ranking Member that the Judiciary Committee would hold a hearing on December 4 vaguely limited to "the historical and constitutional basis of impeachment."[488] The Chairman provided no further information about the hearing, including the identities of the witnesses, but nonetheless required the President to indicate whether he wished to participate by Sunday, December 1. Every aspect of the planning for this hearing departed from the Clinton and Nixon precedents. The Committee afforded the President no scheduling input, no meaningful information about the hearing, and so little time to prepare that it effectively denied the Administration a fair opportunity to participate. The Committee ultimately announced the identities of the witnesses less than two days before the hearing.[489] For a similar hearing with scholars in the Clinton impeachment, the Committee provided two-and-a-half weeks' notice to

---

[486] *See supra* notes 452–458 and accompanying text.

[487] *See* 165 Cong. Rec. E1357 (2019) (Impeachment Inquiry Procedures in the Committee on the Judiciary Pursuant to H.R. Res. 660).

[488] Letter from Jerrold Nadler, Chairman, H.R. Comm. on Judiciary, to President Donald J. Trump, at 1 (Nov. 26, 2019).

[489] *See* Press Release, House Judiciary Committee, Wednesday: House Judiciary to Hold Hearing on Constitutional Grounds for Presidential Impeachment (Dec. 2, 2019), https://perma.cc/5PFE-LCS5.

prepare and scheduled the hearing on a date suggested by the President's attorneys.[490] President Trump understandably declined to participate in that biased constitutional law seminar because he could not "fairly be expected to participate in a hearing while the witnesses are yet to be named and while it remains unclear whether the Judiciary Committee will afford the President a fair process through additional hearings."[491]

Meanwhile, in a separate letter on November 29, 2019, Chairman Nadler asked the President to specify, by December 6, how he would participate in future undefined "proceedings" and which "privileges" in the Judiciary Committee's Impeachment Procedures the President's counsel would seek to exercise.[492] At the same time, he gave no indication as to what these "proceedings" would involve, what subjects they would address, whether witnesses would be heard (or who they would be), or when any hearings would be held.[493] To inform the President's decision, the President's counsel asked Chairman Nadler for information about the "scope and nature of the proceedings" he planned, including topics of hearings, whether he intended "to allow for fact witnesses to be called," and whether he would allow "the President's counsel the right to cross examine fact witnesses."[494] The President's counsel even offered to meet with Chairman Nadler to discuss a plan for upcoming hearings.[495] All to no avail—Chairman Nadler did not even bother to respond.

And the Judiciary Committee continued to hide the ball. Throughout the week of December 2, the President's counsel were in contact with Committee counsel trying to get answers concerning what hearings were planned, so that the President could determine whether and how to participate. But all that Committee staff were authorized to convey was: (i) a hearing on an unknown topic had been publicly announced for December 9; (ii) before that hearing, the Committee might be issuing two additional reports (one based on the December 4 constitutional law seminar and one dredging up unspecified aspects of Special Counsel Mueller's report); and (iii) they would not have an answer to any other questions about the subjects of the December 9 hearing or whether any other hearings would be scheduled until after the close of business on Thursday, December 5.

On the morning of December 5, Speaker Pelosi instructed the Judiciary Committee to begin drafting articles of impeachment **before** the Committee had received any presentation on the HPSCI report, heard any fact witness, or heard a single word from the President in his defense.[496] Later that day, Committee counsel informed the President's counsel that—other than a report addressing the meaning of "high Crimes and Misdemeanors" based on the December 4 constitutional law seminar and other than a hearing on December 9 involving a presentation of the HPSCI majority and minority reports solely by staff—there were no immediate plans to issue any

---

[490] Letter from Charles F.C. Ruff, Counsel to the President, et al., to Henry J. Hyde, Chairman, H.R. Comm. on Judiciary, et al. (Oct. 21, 1998); Guy Gugliotta, *House Hearing Set on Impeachment History*, Wash. Post (Oct. 24, 1998), https://perma.cc/2LDX-XDL2.

[491] Letter from Pat A. Cipollone, Counsel to the President, to Jerrold Nadler, Chairman, H.R. Comm. on Judiciary, at 4 (Dec. 1, 2019).

[492] Letter from Jerrold Nadler, Chairman, H.R. Comm. on Judiciary, to President Donald J. Trump (Nov. 29, 2019).

[493] *See id.*

[494] Dec. 1, 2019 Letter from Pat A. Cipollone, *supra* note 491, at 4.

[495] *Id.* ("We stand ready to meet with you to discuss a plan for these proceedings at your convenience.").

[496] Nicholas Fandos, *Pelosi Says House Will Draft Impeachment Charges Against Trump*, N.Y. Times (Dec. 5, 2019), https://perma.cc/L8PG-23DL (Speaker Pelosi: "Today, I am asking our Chairman to proceed with articles of impeachment.").

other reports or have any other hearings.

Meanwhile, Chairman Nadler was also playing hide-the-ball with the minority members of his own Committee. The Committee's Ranking Member, Doug Collins, sent at least seven letters to Chairman Nadler trying to find out about the process the Committee would follow and requesting specific rights to ensure a balanced presentation of the law and facts, including requesting witnesses.[497] Chairman Nadler simply ignored them. He offered only an after-the-fact response[498] that denied his request for witnesses in part on the misleading claim that "the President is not requesting any witnesses," when it was Chairman Nadler who had refused to commit to allowing the President to call witnesses in the first place.[499]

As a backdrop to all of this, Chairman Nadler had threatened to invoke the unprecedented provision of the Committee's Impeachment Inquiry Procedures Pursuant to House Resolution 660 that allowed him to deny the President any due process rights if the President continued to assert longstanding privileges and immunities to protect Executive Branch information and to challenge the validity of the investigating committees' subpoenas.[500] This approach also departed from all precedent in the Clinton and Nixon proceedings.[501] Even though both Presidents had asserted numerous privileges, the Judiciary Committee never contemplated that offering the opportunity to present a defense and to have a fair hearing should be conditioned on forcing the President to abandon the longstanding constitutional rights and privileges of the Executive Branch. The Supreme Court has already addressed such Catch-22 choices and has made clear that it is "intolerable that one constitutional right should have to be surrendered in order to assert another."[502] Conditioning access to basic procedural rights on an agreement to waive other fundamental rights is the same as denying procedural rights altogether.

As a result, by the December 6 deadline, the President had been left with no meaningful choice at all. The Committee was already under instructions to draft articles of impeachment before hearing any evidence; Chairman Nadler had kept the President in the dark until the last minute about how and when the Committee would proceed; and Committee counsel had finally confirmed that the Committee's plan was to hear solely a staff presentation of the HPSCI report and not to hold any other hearings. It was abundantly clear that, if the President asked to present

---

[497]   Letter from Doug Collins, Ranking Member, H.R. Comm. on Judiciary, et al., to Jerrold Nadler, Chairman, H.R. Comm. on Judiciary, at 2 (Nov. 12, 2019); Letter from Doug Collins, Ranking Member, H.R. Comm. on Judiciary, to Jerrold Nadler, Chairman, H.R. Comm. on Judiciary, at 1–2 (Nov. 14, 2019); Letter from Doug Collins, Ranking Member, H.R. Comm. on Judiciary, to Jerrold Nadler, Chairman, H.R. Comm. on Judiciary, at 6 (Nov. 18, 2019); Letter from Doug Collins, Ranking Member, H.R. Comm. on Judiciary, to Jerrold Nadler, Chairman, H.R. Comm. on Judiciary (Dec. 2, 2019); Letter from Doug Collins, Ranking Member, H.R. Comm. on Judiciary, to Jerrold Nadler, Chairman, H.R. Comm. on Judiciary (Dec. 4, 2019); Letter from Doug Collins, Ranking Member, H.R. Comm. on Judiciary, to Jerrold Nadler, Chairman, H.R. Comm. on Judiciary (Dec. 5, 2019); Letter from Doug Collins, Ranking Member, H.R. Comm. on Judiciary, to Jerrold Nadler, Chairman, H.R. Comm. on Judiciary (Dec. 6, 2019).
[498]   Letter from Jerrold Nadler, Chairman, H.R. Comm. on Judiciary, to Doug Collins, Ranking Member, H.R. Comm. on Judiciary (Dec. 8, 2019).
[499]   *See supra* notes 491–495, 497–498 and accompanying text.
[500]   Nov. 26, 2019 Letter from Jerrold Nadler, *supra* note 488.
[501]   *See* 165 Cong. Rec. E1357 (2019) (Impeachment Inquiry Procedures in the Committee on the Judiciary Pursuant to H.R. Res. 660 ¶ F) ("Should the President unlawfully refuse to make witnesses available for testimony to, or to produce documents requested by, the investigative committees . . . , the chair shall have the discretion to impose appropriate remedies, including by denying specific requests by the President or his counsel under these procedures to call or question witnesses."), *and* H.R. Rep. No. 116-266, 116th Cong. 9–10 (2019).
[502]   *Simmons v. United States*, 390 U.S. 377, 394 (1968); *see also Bourgeois v. Peters*, 387 F.3d 1303, 1324 (11th Cir. 2004).

or cross examine any witnesses, any future hearings would merely be window-dressing designed to place a veneer of fair process on a stage-managed show trial already hurtling toward a pre-ordained result. The President would not be given any meaningful opportunity to question fact witnesses or otherwise respond to the one-sided factual record transmitted by HPSCI. The Judiciary Committee's assertion that the President "could have had his counsel make a presentation of evidence or request that other witnesses be called"[503] is thus entirely disingenuous. Under those circumstances, the President determined that he would not condone House Democrats' violations of due process—and that he would not lend legitimacy to their unprecedented procedures—by participating in their show trial.

Chairman Nadler ultimately refused to allow the Committee to hear from a single fact witness or hear any evidence first-hand. He also blatantly violated House Rules by refusing to allow the minority to have a minority hearing day.[504] Instead, the Judiciary Committee simply relied on the *ex parte* evidence gathered by Chairman Schiff's show trial with no procedural protections at all. And there could be no clearer admission that the evidence simply did not matter than Speaker Pelosi's instruction to begin drafting articles of impeachment *before* the Committee had even heard any evidence whatsoever.[505]

All of this conduct highlights rank hypocrisy by Chairman Nadler, who, during the Clinton impeachment, decried the fact that there had been "no witness called in front of this committee against the President" and declared it "a failure of the Chairman of this committee that we are going to consider voting impeachment, having heard no witnesses whatsoever against the President."[506] Then, Chairman Nadler argued that the Judiciary Committee cannot simply receive a report compiled by another entity (there, the Independent Counsel) and proceed to judgment. That, in his words, "would be to say that the role of this committee of the House is a mere transmission belt or rubber stamp,"[507] and would "conclude the inquiry expeditiously, but not fairly, and not without trashing the Constitution and every principle of due process and fundamental fairness that we have held sacred since the Magna Carta."[508] House Democrats on the Judiciary Committee made the same point just a few years ago in 2016: "[i]n all modern cases, the Committee has conducted an independent, formal investigation into the charges underlying a resolution of impeachment—again, *even when* other authorities and other congressional committees have already investigated the underlying issue."[509]

The House's constitutionally deficient proceedings have so distorted the factual record compiled in the House that it cannot constitutionally be relied upon for the Senate to reach any

---

[503] HJC Report at 23–24.

[504] *See* Rules of the House of Representatives, Rule XI, cl. 2(j)(1) ("[M]inority members of the committee *shall be entitled*, upon request to the chair by a majority of them before the completion of the hearing, to call witnesses selected by the minority to testify with respect to that measure or matter during at least one day of hearing thereon." (emphasis added)).

[505] *E.g.*, *Pelosi Says House Will Draft Impeachment Charges Against Trump*, *supra* note 496.

[506] *Impeachment Inquiry Pursuant to H.R. Res. 581: Consequences of Perjury and Related Crimes: Hearing Before the H.R. Comm. on the Judiciary*, 105th Cong. 18–19 (1998) (*Clinton Judiciary Comm. Hearing on Perjury*) (statement of Rep. Jerrold Nadler).

[507] *Id.* at 19.

[508] *Clinton Judiciary Comm. Hearing on Background of Impeachment*, *supra* note 468, at 17 (statement of Rep. Jerrold Nadler).

[509] Press Release, Committee on the Judiciary, U.S. House of Representatives, Fact Sheet: GOP Attacks on IRS Commissioner are Not Impeachment Proceedings (Sept. 21, 2016) (emphasis added), https://perma.cc/6VYE-9JQV.

verdict other than acquittal.

C.   **The House's Inquiry Was Irredeemably Defective Because It Was Presided Over by an Interested Fact Witness Who Lied About Contact with the Whistleblower Before the Complaint Was Filed.**

The House's entire factual investigation was carefully orchestrated—and restricted—by an interested fact witness: Chairman Schiff. His repeated falsehoods about the President leave him with no credibility whatsoever. In March 2017, Chairman Schiff lied, announcing that he already had evidence that the Trump campaign colluded with Russia.[510] That was proved false when the Mueller Report was released and the entire Russian hoax Chairman Schiff had been peddling was disproved.

In this proceeding, Chairman Schiff violated basic fairness by overseeing and prosecuting the proceedings while secretly being a witness in the case. Before public release of the whistleblower complaint, when asked whether he had "heard from the whistleblower," Chairman Schiff falsely denied having "heard from the whistleblower," saying: "We have not spoken directly with the whistleblower. We would like to . . . . But yes, we would love to talk directly with the whistleblower."[511] As multiple media outlets concluded, that statement was "flat-out false"[512]—a "[w]hopper" of a lie that earned "four Pinnochios" from *The Washington Post*[513]—because it "wrongly implied the committee had not been contacted" by the whistleblower before the complaint was filed.[514] Subsequent reporting showed that Chairman Schiff's staff had not only had contact with the whistleblower, but apparently played some still-unverified role in advising the whistleblower before the complaint was filed.[515] And Chairman Schiff began the hearings in this matter by lying once again and reading a fabricated version of the President's telephone conversation with President Zelenskyy to the American people.[516]

Given the role that Chairman Schiff and his staff apparently played in advising the whistleblower, Chairman Schiff made himself a fact witness in these proceedings. The American people understand that Chairman Schiff cannot covertly assist with the submission of a complaint, mislead the public about his involvement, and then pretend to be a neutral "investigator." No wonder Chairman Schiff repeatedly denied requests to subpoena the whistleblower and shut down any questions that he feared might identify the whistleblower. Questioning the whistleblower

---

510   Madeline Conway, *Schiff: There Is Now 'More Than Circumstantial Evidence' of Trump-Russia Collusion*, Politico (Mar. 22, 2017), https://perma.cc/P5SL-BNM6.

511   *Rep. Schiff on MSNBC Morning Joe: Trump Must Come to Congress for Any Strike Against Iran*, YouTube (Sept. 17, 2019), https://perma.cc/J7X4-F6N2 (at 0:36–1:07).

512   *Schiff's False Claim His Committee Had Not Spoken to the Whistleblower*, Wash. Post (Oct. 4, 2019), https://www.washingtonpost.com/politics/2019/10/04/schiffs-false-claim-his-committee-had-not-spoken-whistleblower/.

513   Glenn Kessler, *About The Fact Checker* (Jan. 21, 2017), https://perma.cc/VCD4-N3NB.

514   Lori Robertson, *Schiff Wrong on Whistleblower Contact*, FactCheck.org (Oct. 6, 2019), https://perma.cc/BZ8F-SWJW.

515   *See, e.g.*, Julie E. Barnes et al., *Schiff Got Early Account of Accusations as Whistle-Blower's Concerns Grew*, N.Y. Times (Oct. 2, 2019), https://perma.cc/7ZZ4-BLRC; Ellen Nakashima, *Whistleblower Sought Informal Guidance from Schiff's Committee Before Filing Complaint Against Trump*, Wash. Post (Oct. 2, 2019), https://perma.cc/SM2B-6BJN.

516   *"Whistleblower Disclosure": Hearing of the H.R. Permanent Select Comm. on Intelligence*, 116th Cong. (Sept. 26, 2019) (statement of Rep. Adam Schiff); *see also, e.g.*, Daniel Dale, *Fact Check: Breaking Down Adam Schiff's Account of Trump's Ukraine Call*, CNN (Sept. 27, 2019), https://perma.cc/SM2B-6BJN.

would have exposed before the American people the role Chairman Schiff and his staff had in concocting the very complaint they purported to be investigating.

D. The Senate May Not Rely on a Factual Record Derived from a Procedurally Deficient House Impeachment Inquiry.

The Senate may not rely on a corrupted factual record derived from constitutionally deficient proceedings to support a conviction of the President of the United States. Nor is it the Senate's role to attempt to remedy the House's errors by providing a "do-over" to develop the record anew in the Senate. In the courts, comparable fundamental errors underpinning the foundations of a case would require throwing the case out. The denial of "basic protections" of due process "necessarily render[s]" a proceeding "fundamentally unfair," precluding it from "reliably serv[ing] its function as a vehicle for determination of guilt or innocence."[517] A "proceeding infected with fundamental procedural error, like a void judicial judgment, is a legal nullity."[518] That is why, for example, criminal indictments may not proceed to trial when they result from "fundamental" errors that cause "the structural protections of the grand jury [to] have been so compromised as to render the proceedings fundamentally unfair."[519] The same principles should apply in the impeachment trial context. The Senate cannot rely on a record developed in a hopelessly defective House proceeding to convict the President.

E. House Democrats Used an Unprecedented and Unfair Process Because Their Goal to Impeach at Any Cost Had Nothing To Do with Finding the Truth.

House Democrats' impeachment inquiry was never a quest for the truth. Instead it was an inquisition in pursuit of an offense to justify a pre-ordained outcome—impeaching President Trump by any means necessary. The procedural protections that the House has afforded to the accused in every impeachment for the last 150 years were incompatible with that agenda. Ensuring a fair process that uses time-tested methods for getting at the truth—like adversarial cross examination of witnesses by counsel for the accused—takes time and it also risks undermining the accusers' preferred version of the facts. But House Democrats had no time. By September 2019, when the President released the transcript of his telephone call with President Zelenskyy, the 2020 campaign for the presidency was already well underway, and they needed a fast and tightly controlled process that would yield their political goal: impeachment by Christmas.

In fact, House Democrats have been on a crusade to impeach the President since *the moment he took office three years ago*. As Speaker Pelosi recently confirmed, her party's quest for impeachment had "been going on for 22 months . . . [t]wo and a half years, actually."[520] The moment that the President was sworn in, two liberal advocacy groups launched a campaign to impeach him.[521] The current proceedings began with a complaint prepared with the assistance of

---

[517] *Rose v. Clark*, 478 U.S. 570, 577–78 (1986); *see also, e.g., United States v. Cronic*, 466 U.S. 648, 659 (1984) (holding that denial of representation by counsel "makes the adversary process itself presumptively unreasonable").

[518] *Winterberger v. Gen. Teamsters Auto Truck Drivers & Helpers Local Union 162*, 558 F.2d 923, 925 (9th Cir. 1977) (administrative law).

[519] *Bank of Nova Scotia v. United States*, 487 U.S. 250, 256 (1988); *see also, e.g., Beck v. Washington*, 369 U.S. 541, 546 (1962); *United States v. Estepa*, 471 F.2d 1132, 1137 (2d Cir. 1972) (Friendly, J.) (reversing judgment of conviction because the government's argument before the grand jury relied upon hearsay).

[520] Zack Stanton, *Pelosi: Unless We Impeach Trump, 'Say Hello to a President-King'*, Politico (Dec. 18, 2019), https://perma.cc/3R3M-D356.

[521] Matea Gold, *The Campaign to Impeach President Trump Has Begun*, Wash. Post (Jan. 20, 2017), https://perma.cc/HW4U-LBX6.

a lawyer who declared in 2017 that he was already planning to use "impeachment" to effect a "coup."[522] The first resolution proposing articles of impeachment against President Trump was filed before he had been in office for six months.[523] As soon as Democrats gained control of the House in the 2018 midterm elections, they made clear that they would stop at nothing to impeach the President. Rep. Rashida Tlaib, for example, announced in January 2019: "[W]e're going to go in there and we're gonna impeach the motherf****r."[524]

Over the past three years, House Democrats have filed at least eight resolutions to impeach the President, alleging a vast range of preposterous purported offenses. They have repeatedly charged the President with obstruction of justice in connection with the Mueller investigation[525]— an allegation that the Department of Justice resoundingly rejected.[526] One resolution sought to impeach the President for protecting national security by restricting U.S. entry by nationals of eight countries[527]—an action upheld by the Supreme Court.[528] Another tried to impeach the President for publishing disparaging tweets about Democrat House members in response to their own attacks on the President.[529] Still another gathered a hodge-podge of absurd charges, including failing to nominate persons to fill vacancies and insulting the press.[530]

In this case, House Democrats ran the fastest presidential impeachment fact-finding on record. They raced through their entire process in less than three months from the beginning of their fact-finding investigation on September 24, 2019 to the adoption of articles on December 18—meeting their deadline of impeachment by Christmas. That rushed three-month process stands apart from *every* prior presidential impeachment—the fastest of which took place after a fact-finding period *nearly four* times as long. Independent Counsel Ken Starr received authorization to investigate the charges that led to President Clinton's impeachment in January 1998,[531] almost a full year before the House impeached President Clinton in December 1998.[532] Congress began investigating President Nixon's conduct in February 1973,[533] more than one year before July 1974, when the House Judiciary Committee voted to recommend articles of

[522] Mark S. Zaid (@MarkSZaidEsq), Twitter (Jan. 30, 2017, 6:54 PM), https://perma.cc/TUF2-NLP3.

[523] H.R. Res. 438, 115th Cong. (2017).

[524] Caitlin Oprysko, *Freshman Rep. Tlaib: Dem Majority Will 'Impeach the Motherf---er'*, Politico (Jan. 4, 2019), https://perma.cc/MAW7-WLQY.

[525] H.R. Res. 438, 115th Cong. (2017).

[526] Press Release, Dep't of Justice, Attorney General William P. Barr Delivers Remarks on the Release of the Report on the Investigation into Russian Interference in the 2016 Presidential Election (Apr. 18, 2019), https://perma.cc/K5ZJ-2KA2 ("[T]he evidence developed by the Special Counsel is not sufficient to establish that the President committed an obstruction-of-justice offense.").

[527] H.R. Res. 705, 115th Cong. (2018).

[528] *See Trump v. Hawaii*, 138 S. Ct. 2392 (2018).

[529] H.R. Res. 498, 116th Cong. (2019).

[530] H.R. Res. 396, 116th Cong. (2019).

[531] *In re Madison Guar. Sav. & Loan Ass'n*, No. 94-1, 1998 WL 472444, at *1 (D.C. Cir. Special Div. Jan. 16, 1998); *see also* H.R. Doc. No. 105-310, *Communication from Kenneth W. Starr, Independent Counsel, Transmitting A Referral*, 105th Cong., at 3 (1998). The House authorized the House Judiciary Committee's review of the Independent Counsel's referral two days after receiving it. H.R. Res. 525, 105th Cong. (1998).

[532] H.R. Res. 611, 105th Cong. (1998).

[533] The Senate Select Committee on Presidential Campaign Activities was established by the U.S. Senate on February 7, 1973 to investigate 1972 presidential campaign fundraising practices, the Watergate break-in, and the concealment of evidence relating to the break-in. H.R. Rep. No. 93-1305, at 116. Prior to the conclusion of that Committee's investigation, the House authorized the House Judiciary Committee's impeachment inquiry in February 1974. *Id.* at 6.

impeachment.[534] The investigation into President Johnson also exceeded 12 months. Except for a two-month break between a vote rejecting articles of impeachment in 1867 and the authorization of a second impeachment inquiry,[535] President Johnson's impeachment was investigated over 14 months from January 1867[536] to the adoption of articles of impeachment in March 1868.[537] The two inquiries were closely related,[538] and one article of impeachment was carried over from the first impeachment inquiry.[539] The Democrats' need for speed only underscores that, unlike prior impeachments, these proceedings were never about conducting a serious inquiry into the truth.

Although they tried everything, Democrats pinned their impeachment dreams primarily on the Mueller investigation and their dogmatic faith in the myth that President Trump—or at least his campaign—was somehow in league with Russia. After $32 million, 2,800 subpoenas, nearly 500 search warrants, 230 orders for communications records, and 500 witness interviews, that inquisition disproved the myth of collusion between the President or his campaign and Russia. As the Mueller Report informed the public, Special Counsel Mueller and his team of investigators and FBI agents could not find any evidence of collusion between the Trump Campaign and the Russian government.[540] While the Mueller investigation was pending, though, Chairman Schiff flatly lied to the American people, telling them that he was privy to "'more than circumstantial evidence' that the President's associates colluded with Russia."[541] He played up the Mueller investigation, promising that it would show wrongdoing "of a size and scope probably beyond Watergate."[542]

The damage caused by Democrats' Russian collusion delusion stretches far beyond anything directly attributable to the Mueller investigation. The Mueller investigation itself was triggered by an FBI investigation, known as Crossfire Hurricane, that involved gross abuses of FBI investigative tools—including FISA orders and undercover agents. The FBI abused its extraordinary authorities to spy on American citizens and a major-party presidential campaign.[543] According to a report from the Inspector General of the Department of Justice, these abuses included "multiple instances" of factual assertions to the FISA court that were knowingly

---

[534] *Id.* at 10–11.

[535] The House voted against President Johnson's impeachment in December 1867. III Hinds' Precedents § 2407, at 843. In February 1868, the House transferred the record from the first impeachment inquiry to the Committee on Reconstruction as part of President Johnson's second impeachment inquiry. *Id.* § 2408, at 845.

[536] *Id.* § 2400, at 823.

[537] *Id.* § 2416, at 855–56.

[538] *Impeachment Inquiry into President Donald J. Trump: Constitutional Grounds for Presidential Impeachment: Hearing Before the H.R. Comm. on the Judiciary*, 116th Cong. (Dec. 4, 2019) (written statement of Professor Jonathan Turley, George Washington Univ. Law School, at 4 n.7, https://perma.cc/QU4H-FZC4); III Hinds' Precedents § 2408, at 845 (referring evidence from the first impeachment inquiry to committee conducting second impeachment inquiry); *cf.* HJC Report at 47–48.

[539] Raoul Berger, *Impeachment: The Constitutional Problems* 271–72 (1973).

[540] Special Counsel Robert S. Mueller, III, *Report on the Investigation into Russian Interference in the 2016 Presidential Election*, vol. I at 2 (Mar. 2019), https://perma.cc/EGB4-WA76.

[541] Kailani Koenig, *Schiff: 'More Than Circumstantial Evidence' Trump Associates Colluded With Russia*, NBC News (Mar. 22, 2017), https://perma.cc/P5KE-6BE4.

[542] Tim Hains, *Adam Schiff: Republicans in Congress (Ryan, Gowdy, Nunes, Meadows, Jordan) Are Complicit in Trump's Lies*, RealClearPolitics (May 27, 2018), https://perma.cc/H5JM-RZHK.

[543] *See* U.S. Dep't of Justice Office of the Inspector General, Review of Four FISA Applications and Other Aspects of the FBI's Crossfire Hurricane Investigation (Dec. 2019) (OIG FISA Report); *id.* at vii–viii, 95–96, 172, 256 n.400; Order, *In re Accuracy Concerns Regarding FBI Matters Submitted to the FISC*, No. Misc. 19-02 (FISA Ct. Dec. 17, 2019).

"inaccurate, incomplete, or unsupported by appropriate documentation"[544]—in other words, *lies* to the FISA court. One FBI official, who openly advocated for "resistance" against the President, even fabricated evidence to persuade the FISA court to maintain surveillance on an American citizen connected with the Trump Campaign.[545] Tellingly, the Inspector General could not rule out the possibility that Crossfire Hurricane was corrupted by political bias, because the FBI could not provide "satisfactory explanations" for the extraordinary litany of errors and abuses that plagued the investigation from its inception—all of which indicated bias against the President.[546]

Despite all of this, House Democrats have refused to accept the conclusions of the Mueller Report. They held hearings and issued subpoenas hoping to uncover collusion where Mueller had found none. Failing that, they tried to keep the impeachment flame alive by manufacturing an obstruction charge—even though the Department of Justice had already rejected such a claim.[547] They embarked on new fishing expeditions, such as demanding the President's tax returns, investigating the routine Executive Branch practice of granting case-by-case exceptions to the President's voluntarily undertaken ethics guidelines, and the costs of the July 4 "Salute to America" event—all in the hope that rummaging through those records might give them some new basis for attacking the President.

Democrats have been fixated on impeachment and Russia for the past three years for two reasons. First, they have never accepted the results of the 2016 election and have been consumed by an insatiable need to justify their continued belief that President Trump could not "really" have won. Long before votes had been cast, Democrats had taken it as an article of faith that Hillary Clinton would be the next President. House Democrats' impeachment and Russia obsessions thus stem from a pair of false beliefs held as dogma: that Donald Trump should not be President and that he is President only by virtue of foreign interference.

The second reason for Democrats' fixations is that they desperately need an illegitimate boost for their candidate in the 2020 election, whoever that may be. Put simply, Democrats have no response to the President's record of achievement in restoring growth and prosperity to the American economy, rebuilding America's military, and confronting America's adversaries abroad. They have no policies and no ideas to compete against that. Instead, they are held hostage by a radical left wing that has foisted on the party a radical agenda of socialism at home and appeasement abroad that Democrat leaders know the American people will never accept. For Democrats, President Trump's record of success made impeachment an electoral imperative. As Congressman Al Green explained it: "if we don't impeach the [P]resident, he will get re-

---

544 OIG FISA Report, *supra* note 543, at viii.

545 *Id.* at 160, 256 n.400; *see also* Jerry Dunleavy, *FBI Lawyer Under Criminal Investigation Altered Document to Say Carter Page 'Was Not a Source' for Another Agency*, Wash. Exam. (Dec. 9, 2019), https://perma.cc/3J4Z-WZCJ.

546 OIG FISA Report, *supra* note 543, at xiii; *Inspector General Report on Origins of FBI's Russia Inquiry: Hearing Before S. Comm. on the Judiciary*, C-SPAN at 1:19:22, 3:49:34 (Dec. 11, 2019), https://www.c-span.org/video/?466593-1/justice-department-ig-horowitz-defends-report-highlights-fisa-problems; *id.* at 4:59:16 (Inspector General Horowitz: "There is such a range of conduct here that is inexplicable. And the answers we got were not satisfactory that we're left trying to understand how could all these errors have occurred over a nine-month period or so, among three teams, hand-picked, one of the highest profile, if not the highest profile, case in the FBI, going to the very top of the organization, involving a presidential campaign.").

547 Press Release, Dep't of Justice, Attorney General William P. Barr Delivers Remarks on the Release of the Report on the Investigation into Russian Interference in the 2016 Presidential Election (Apr. 18, 2019), https://perma.cc/K5ZJ-2KA2.

elected."[548]

The result of House Democrats' relentless pursuit of their obsessions—and their willingness to sacrifice every precedent, every principle, and every procedural right standing in their way—is exactly what the Framers warned against: a wholly partisan impeachment. The Articles of Impeachment now before the Senate were adopted without a single Republican vote. Indeed, the only bipartisan aspect of these articles was congressional opposition to their adoption.[549]

Democrats used to recognize that the momentous act of overturning a national election by impeaching a President should never take place on a partisan basis, and that impeachment should not be used as a partisan tool in electoral politics. As Chairman Nadler explained in 1998:

> The effect of impeachment is to overturn the popular will of the voters. We must not overturn an election and remove a President from office except to defend our system of government or our constitutional liberties against a dire threat, and we must not do so without an overwhelming consensus of the American people. There must never be a narrowly voted impeachment or an impeachment supported by one of our major political parties and opposed by another. Such an impeachment will produce divisiveness and bitterness in our politics for years to come, and will call into question the very legitimacy of our political institutions.[550]

Senator Leahy agreed: "A partisan impeachment cannot command the respect of the American people. *It is no more valid than a stolen election*."[551] Chairman Schiff likewise recognized that a partisan impeachment would be "doomed for failure," adding that there was "little to be gained by putting the country through that kind of wrenching experience."[552] Earlier last year even Speaker Pelosi acknowledged that, "before I think we should go down any impeachment path," it "would have to be so clearly bipartisan in terms of acceptance of it."[553]

Now, however, House Democrats have completely abandoned those principles and placed before the Senate Articles of Impeachment that are partisan to their core. In their rush to impeach the President before Christmas, Democrats allowed speed and political expediency to conquer fairness and truth. As Professor Turley explained, this impeachment "stand[s] out among modern impeachments as the shortest proceeding, with the thinnest evidentiary record, and the narrowest grounds ever used to impeach a president."[554] And as the vote closed, House Democrats could not

---

[548] Rebecca Shabad & Alex Moe, *Impeachment Inquiry Ramps Up as Judiciary Panel Adopts Procedural Guidelines*, NBC News (Sept. 12, 2019), https://perma.cc/6694-SWXX.

[549] Clerk, H.R., Final Vote Results for Roll Call 695 on Agreeing to Article I of the Resolution (Dec. 18, 2019), http://clerk house.gov/evs/2019/roll695.xml; Clerk, H.R., Final Vote Results for Roll Call 696 on Agreeing to Article II of the Resolution (Dec. 18, 2019), http://clerk.house.gov/evs/2019/roll696.xml.

[550] 144 Cong. Rec. H11786 (1998) (statement of Rep. Jerrold Nadler).

[551] 145 Cong. Rec. S1582 (1999) (statement of Sen. Patrick Leahy) (emphasis added).

[552] Brooke Singman & Guerin Hays, *Dem. Rep. Brushes Off Pelosi Pushback, Says He'll Pursue Trump Impeachment*, Fox News (Mar. 12, 2019), https://perma.cc/2LK6-W4TR (brackets in original).

[553] Nicole Gaudiano & Eliza Collins, *Exclusive: Nancy Pelosi Vows 'Different World' for Trump, No More 'Rubber Stamp' in New Congress*, USA Today (Jan. 3, 2019), https://perma.cc/LF66-R7NU; *see also, e.g.*, Brian Fung, *Pelosi Tamps Down Talk of Impeachment*, Wash. Post (Jan. 6, 2019), https://perma.cc/8VQ3-RYZ5 (Pelosi: "If and when the time comes for impeachment, it will have to be something that has such a crescendo in a bipartisan way.").

[554] *Impeachment Inquiry into President Donald J. Trump: Constitutional Grounds for Presidential Impeachment*

contain their glee. Several Democrats clapped; others cheered; and still others raised exclamations of joy on the floor of the House of Representatives—until the Speaker shamed them into silence.[555]

The Framers foresaw clearly the possibility of such an improper, partisan use of impeachment. As Hamilton recognized, impeachment could be a powerful tool in the hands of determined "pre-existing factions."[556] The Framers fully recognized that "the persecution of an intemperate or designing majority in the House of Representatives" was a real danger.[557] That is why they chose the Senate as the tribunal for trying impeachments. Further removed from the politics of the day than the House, they believed the Senate could mitigate the "danger that the decision" to remove a President would be based on the "comparative strength of parties" rather "than by the real demonstrations of innocence or guilt."[558] The Senate would thus "guard[] against the danger of persecution, from the prevalency of a factious spirit" in the House.[559] It now falls to the Senate to fulfill the role of guardian that the Framers envisioned and to reject these wholly insubstantial Articles of Impeachment that have been propelled forward by nothing other than partisan enmity toward the President.

III. Article I Fails Because the Evidence Disproves House Democrats' Claims.

Despite House Democrats' unprecedented, rigged process, the record they compiled clearly establishes that the President did nothing wrong.

This entire impeachment charade centers on a telephone call that President Trump had with President Zelenskyy of Ukraine on July 25, 2019. There is no mystery about what happened on that call, because the President has been completely transparent: he released a transcript of the call months ago. And that transcript shows conclusively that the call was perfectly appropriate. Indeed, the person on the other end of the call, President Zelenskyy, has confirmed in multiple public statements that the call was perfectly normal. Before they had even seen the transcript, though, House Democrats concocted all their charges based on distortions peddled by a so-called whistleblower *who had no first-hand knowledge of the call*. And contrary to their claims, the transcript proves that the President did not seek to use either security assistance or a presidential meeting as leverage to pressure Ukrainians to announce investigations on two subjects: (i) possible Ukrainian interference in the 2016 election; or (ii) an incident in which then-Vice President Biden had forced the dismissal of a Ukrainian anti-corruption prosecutor who reportedly had been investigating a company (Burisma) that paid Biden's son, Hunter, to sit on its board.[560] The President did not even *mention* the security assistance on the call, and he invited President Zelenskyy to the White House without any condition whatsoever. When the President released the transcript of the call on September 25, 2019, it cut the legs out from under all of House Democrats' phony claims about a quid pro quo. That should have ended this entire matter.

Nevertheless, House Democrats forged ahead, determined to gin up some other evidence

---

Before the H.R. Comm. on the Judiciary, 116th Cong. (Dec. 4, 2019) (written statement of Professor Jonathan Turley, Geo. Wash. Univ. Law Sch., at 4, https://perma.cc/QU4H-FZC4).

[555] Justine Coleman, *Pelosi Reaction to Democrats Clapping After Impeachment Vote Goes Viral*, The Hill (Dec. 19, 2019), https://perma.cc/LJ5U-E8VA.

[556] The Federalist No. 65, at 396 (Alexander Hamilton) (Clinton Rossiter ed., 1961).

[557] *Id.* at 400.

[558] *Id.* at 396–97.

[559] The Federalist No. 66, at 402 (Alexander Hamilton) (Clinton Rossiter ed., 1961).

[560] H.R. Res. 755, 116th Cong. art. I (2019).

to prop up their false narrative. But even their rigged process failed to yield the evidence they wanted. Instead, the record affirmatively refutes House Democrats' claims. In addition to the transcript, the central fact in this case is this: there are only two people who have made statements on the record who say they spoke directly to the President about the heart of this matter—Ambassador Gordon Sondland and Senator Ron Johnson. And they both confirmed that the President stated unequivocally that he sought nothing and no quid pro quo of any kind from Ukraine. House Democrats' claims are built entirely on speculation from witnesses who had no direct knowledge about anything and who never even spoke to the President about this matter.

House Democrats' charges also rest on the fundamentally mistaken premise that it would have been illegitimate for the President to ask President Zelenskyy about either: (i) Ukrainian interference in the 2016 election or (ii) the Biden-Burisma affair. That is obviously wrong. Asking another country to examine potential interference in a past U.S. election is always permissible. Similarly, it would not have been improper for the President to ask the Ukrainians about an incident in which Vice President Biden had threatened withholding U.S. loan guarantees to secure the dismissal of a prosecutor when Biden had been operating under, at the very least, the appearance of a serious conflict of interest.

A. The Evidence Refutes Any Claim That the President Conditioned the Release of Security Assistance on an Announcement of Investigations by Ukraine.

The evidence squarely refutes the made-up claim that the President leveraged security assistance in exchange for Ukraine announcing an investigation into either interference in the 2016 election or the Biden-Burisma affair.

1. The July 25 Call Transcript Shows the President Did Nothing Wrong.

The most important piece of evidence demonstrating the President's innocence is the transcript of the President's July 25 telephone call with President Zelenskyy. In an unprecedented act of transparency, the President made that transcript public months ago.[561] President Trump did not even mention the security assistance on the call, and he certainly did not make any connection between the assistance and any investigation. Instead, the record shows that he raised two issues that are entirely consistent with both his authority to conduct foreign relations and his longstanding concerns about how the United States spends taxpayers' money on foreign aid: burden-sharing and corruption.

Burden-sharing has been a consistent theme of the President's foreign policy,[562] and he raised burden-sharing directly with President Zelenskyy, noting that "Germany does almost nothing for you" and "[a] lot of the European countries are the same way."[563] President Zelenskyy acknowledged that European countries should be Ukraine's biggest partner, but they surprisingly were not.[564]

---

[561] July 25 Call Mem., *infra* Appendix A.
[562] *See infra* Part III.B.2.
[563] July 25 Call Mem., *infra* Appendix A, at 2; *see also Impeachment Inquiry: Amb. Kurt Volker and Mr. Timothy Morrison Before the H.R. Permanent Select Comm. on Intelligence*, 116th Cong. 64 (Nov. 19, 2019) (Volker-Morrison Public Hearing) ("The President was concerned that the United States seemed to—to bear the exclusive brunt of security assistance to Ukraine. He wanted to see the Europeans step up and contribute more security assistance.").
[564] July 25 Call Mem., *infra* Appendix A, at 2.

President Trump also raised concerns about corruption. He first raised these concerns in connection with reports of Ukrainian actions in the 2016 presidential election. Numerous media outlets have reported that Ukrainian officials took steps to influence and interfere in the 2016 election to undermine then-candidate Trump, and three Senate committee chairmen are currently investigating this interference.[565] President Trump raised "this whole situation" and noted particularly that President Zelenskyy was "surrounding [him]self with some of the same people."[566] President Zelenskyy responded by noting that he had recalled the Ukrainian Ambassador to the United States—an individual who had sought to influence the U.S. election by authoring an anti-Trump op-ed.[567] As Democrats' witness Dr. Hill testified, many officials in the State Department and NSC were similarly concerned about individuals surrounding Zelenskyy.[568]

The President also mentioned an incident involving then-Vice President Joe Biden and a corruption investigation involving Burisma.[569] In that incident, a corruption investigation involving Burisma had reportedly been stopped after Vice President Biden threated to withhold one billion dollars in U.S. loan guarantees unless the Ukrainian government fired a prosecutor.[570] At the time, Vice President Biden's son, Hunter, was sitting on the Burisma's board of directors.[571] The fired prosecutor reportedly had been investigating Burisma at the time.[572] In fact, on July 22, 2019—just days before the July 25 call—*The Washington Post* reported that the prosecutor "said he believes his ouster was because of his interest in [Burisma]" and "[h]ad he remained in his post . . . he would have questioned Hunter Biden."[573] The incident raised important issues for anti-

---

[565] *See, e.g.*, Sharyl Attkisson, *Timeline of Alleged Ukrainian-Democrat Meddling in 2016 Presidential Election*, Epoch Times (Nov. 27, 2019), https://perma.cc/9EYP-9RUE; Andrew E. Kramer, *Ukraine Court Rules Manafort Disclosure Caused 'Meddling' in U.S. Election*, N.Y. Times (Dec. 12, 2018), https://perma.cc/87B2-XYAN; Kenneth P. Vogel & David Stern, *Ukrainian Efforts to Sabotage Trump Backfire*, Politico (Jan. 11, 2017), https://perma.cc/5K56-46YG; Roman Olearchyk, *Ukraine's Leaders Campaign Against 'Pro-Putin' Trump*, Financial Times (Aug. 28, 2016), https://www.ft.com/content/c98078d0-6ae7-11e6-a0b1-d87a9fea034f; Press Release, *Senators Seek Interviews on Reported Coordination Between Ukrainian Officials, DNC Consultant to Aid Clinton in 2016 Elections* (Dec. 6, 2019), https://perma.cc/PAE6-RV78?type=image.

[566] July 25 Call Mem., *infra* Appendix A, at 3.

[567] *See infra* note 737 and accompanying text; July 25 Call Mem., *infra* Appendix A at 3.

[568] F. Hill Dep. Tr. at 76:20–77:11 (Oct. 14, 2019); *see also* C. Croft Dep. Tr. at 125:12–126:15 (Oct. 30, 2019). Senator Johnson recalled similar concerns over "rumors that [President] Zelensky was going to appoint Andriy Bohdan, the lawyer for oligarch Igor Kolomoisky, as his chief of staff." Letter from Sen. Ron Johnson to Rep. Jim Jordan, Ranking Member, H.R. Comm. on Oversight & Reform, and Rep. Devin Nunes, Ranking Member, H.R. Permanent Select Comm. on Intelligence, at 3 (Nov. 18, 2019). And Ambassadors Taylor and Volker even discussed these concerns directly with President Zelenskyy. *See* W. Taylor Dep. Tr. at 86:13-22 (Oct. 22, 2019); K. Volker Interview Tr. at 137:15-25 (Oct. 3, 2019).

[569] *See* July 25 Call Mem., *infra* Appendix A, at 4 (President Zelenskyy understood President Trump's comments to be referring "specifically to the company").

[570] *See* Tim Hains, *FLASHBACK, 2018: Joe Biden Brags at CFR Meeting About Withholding Aid to Ukraine to Force Firing of Prosecutor*, RealClearPolitics (Sept. 27, 2019), https://www.realclearpolitics.com/video/2019/09/27/flashback_2018_joe_biden_brags_at_cfr_meeting_about_withh olding_aid_to_ukraine_to_force_firing_of_prosecutor.html.

[571] *See* Adam Taylor, *Hunter Biden's New Job at a Ukrainian Gas Company Is a Problem for U.S. Soft Power*, Wash. Post (May 14, 2014), https://perma.cc/Q4QS-4H3B.

[572] *See, e.g.*, Kenneth P. Vogel & Iuliia Mendel, *Biden Faces Conflict of Interest Questions That Are Being Promoted by Trump and Allies*, N.Y. Times (May 1, 2019), https://perma.cc/6A4G-2CRE ("Among those who had a stake in the outcome was Hunter Biden, Mr. Biden's younger son, who at the time was on the board of an energy company owned by a Ukrainian oligarch who had been in the sights of the fired prosecutor general.").

[573] Michael Kranish & David L. Stern, *As Vice President, Biden Said Ukraine Should Increase Gas Production. Then His Son Got a Job with a Ukrainian Gas Company*, Wash. Post (July 22, 2019), https://perma.cc/L24P-367Z

corruption efforts in Ukraine, as it raised at least the possibility that a U.S. official may have been involved in derailing a legitimate investigation of a foreign sovereign.

As these examples show, President Trump raised corruption issues with President Zelenskyy. House Democrats' claim that he did not address corruption because the incidents he raised were "not part of any official briefing materials or talking points" is nonsense.[574] President Trump spoke extemporaneously and used specific examples rather than following boilerplate talking points proposed by the NSC.[575] That is the President's prerogative. He is not bound to raise his concerns with a foreign leader in the terms a staffer placed on a briefing card.

More important, President Zelenskyy has publicly confirmed that he understood President Trump to be talking precisely about corruption. On the call, President Zelenskyy acknowledged that the incidents President Trump had raised highlighted "the issue of making sure to restore the honesty."[576] As President Zelenskyy later explained, he understood President Trump to be saying "we are tired of any corruption things."[577] President Zelenskyy explained that his response was essentially, "[w]e are not corrupt."[578]

In contrast to the explicit discussions about burden-sharing and corruption, there was *no* discussion of the paused security assistance on the July 25 call. To fill that gap, House Democrats seize on President Zelenskyy's statement that Ukraine was "almost ready to buy more Javelins," and President Trump's subsequent turn of the conversation as he said, "I would like you to do us a favor though because our country has been through a lot and Ukraine knows a lot about it."[579] According to House Democrats, that sequence alone somehow linked the security assistance to a "favor" for President Trump relating to "his reelection efforts."[580] That is nonsense.

First, President Trump asked President Zelenskyy to "do *us* a favor," and he made clear that "us" referred to "*our country*"—as he put it, "because *our country* has been through a lot."[581] *Second*, nothing in the flow of the conversation suggests that the President was drawing a connection between the Javelin sales and the next topics he turned to.[582] The President was clearly transitioning to a new subject. *Third*, as Democrats' own witnesses conceded, Javelins are *not* part of the security assistance that had been temporarily paused.[583] Accordingly, House

---

("In an email interview with The Post, Shokin [the fired prosecutor] said he believes his ouster was because of his interest in [Burisma]. . . . Had he remained in his post, Shokin said, he would have questioned Hunter Biden.").

[574] HJC Report at 121; *id.* at 101 ("He was given extensive talking points about corruption for his April 21 and July 25 calls, yet ignored them both times and did not mention corruption on either call.").

[575] *See* A. Vindman Dep. Tr. at 109, 241 (Oct. 29, 2019) (explaining that the NSC talking points discussed "deliver[ing] on the anticorruption agenda" and "reinforc[ing] efforts to root out corruption").

[576] July 25 Call Mem., *infra* Appendix A, at 4.

[577] Kyiv Post, *Zelensky Talks Trump, U.S. Elections, Giuliani at All-Day Press Marathon*, YouTube, at 0:17 (Oct. 10, 2019), https://youtu.be/iG5kVNm_R5Y?t=17.

[578] *Id.* at 0:33, https://youtu.be/iG5kVNm_R5Y?t=33.

[579] July 25 Call Mem., *infra* Appendix A, at 2–3.

[580] HPSCI Report at XI.

[581] July 25 Call Mem., *infra* Appendix A, at 3 (emphases added).

[582] *Id.* at 2–3.

[583] M. Yovanovitch Dep. Tr. at 314:15-18 (Oct. 11, 2019) ("[Q.] The foreign aid that was—has been reported as being held up, it doesn't relate to Javelins, does it? [A.] No. At least I'm not aware that it does."); *id.* at 315:4-7 ("[Q.] But it was actually aid that had been appropriated and it had nothing to do with Javelins. Would you agree

Democrats' assertion that "President Trump froze" Javelin sales "without explanation" is demonstrably false.[584] ***Fourth***, the President frequently uses variations of the phrase "do us a favor" in the context of international diplomacy, and the "favors" have nothing to do with the President's personal interests.[585] The President cannot be removed from office because House Democrats deliberately misconstrue one of his commonly used phrases.

Notably, multiple government officials were on the July 25 call, and only one of them—NSC Director for European Affairs Alexander Vindman—raised any concerns at the time about the substance of it.[586] His concerns were based primarily on policy disagreements and a misplaced belief that the President of the United States should have deferred to him on matters of foreign relations. Lt. Col. Vindman testified that he had "deep policy concerns"[587] about Ukraine retaining bipartisan support,[588] but he ultimately conceded that the President—not a staffer like him—sets policy.[589]

Mr. Morrison, Lt. Col. Vindman's supervisor, affirmed that "there was nothing improper that occurred during the call."[590] Similarly, National Security Advisor to the Vice President Keith Kellogg said that he "heard nothing wrong or improper on the call."[591]

> 2. **President Zelenskyy and Other Senior Ukrainian Officials Confirmed There Was No Quid Pro Quo and No Pressure on Them Concerning Investigations.**

The ***Ukrainian government*** also made clear that President Trump did not connect security assistance and investigations on the call. The Ukrainians' official statement did not reflect any such link,[592] and President Zelenskyy has been crystal clear about this in his public statements. He

---

with that? [A.] That's my understanding."); T. Morrison Dep. Tr. at 79:25–80:2 (Oct. 31, 2019) ("[Q.] Okay. In your mind, are the Javelins separate from the security assistance funds? [A.] Yes.").

[584] *See* HPSCI Report at XI.

[585] *See, e.g.*, Remarks By President Trump And Prime Minister Abe of Japan Before Bilateral Meeting, New York, NY (Sept. 25, 2019), https://perma.cc/6E4V-AYC4 ("So we did [China] a favor. But they're doing us a favor. But they're buying a lot of agricultural product and, in particular, where you are."); Remarks by President Trump at the 2019 White House Business Session With Our Nation's Governors (Feb. 25, 2019), https://perma.cc/WK7Z-L82N ("And I said to President Xi — I said, 'President, you have to do me a favor. As part of our trade deal…'"); Remarks by President Trump at Workforce Development Roundtable (July 26, 2018), https://perma.cc/AT2V-U4PQ ("I said to the Europeans, I said, 'Do me a favor. Would you go out to the farms in Iowa and all the different places in the Midwest? Would you buy a lot of soybeans, right now?'"); Geoff Brumfiel, *Trump Says North Korea Will Destroy Missile Site. But Which One?*, NPR (June 12, 2018), https://perma.cc/LKV5-7YAG ("I said, 'Do me a favor. You've got this missile engine testing site. . . .' I said, 'Can you close it up?'"); Transcript: Donald Trump's New York Press Conference (Sept. 26, 2018), https://perma.cc/G6Y9-XHST ("Japan just gave us some numbers that are incredible . . . . I said, 'You have to do me a favor. We don't want these big deficits. You're going to have to buy more.'").

[586] NSC Senior Director Morrison raised concerns "about a potential leak of the [transcript]," but he had no concern about the substance of the call. Morrison Dep. Tr. at 16:4-10.

[587] Vindman Dep. Tr. at 155.

[588] *Id.* at 18–19.

[589] *Impeachment Inquiry: Ms. Jennifer Williams & Lt. Col. Alexander Vindman Before the H.R. Permanent Select Comm. on Intelligence*, 116th Cong. 130–31 (Nov. 19, 2019) (Williams-Vindman Public Hearing); Vindman Dep. Tr. at 155.

[590] Morrison Dep. Tr. at 60.

[591] Press Release, The White House, Statement from Lt. Gen. Keith Kellogg, National Security Advisor to Vice President Mike Pence (Nov. 19, 2019), https://perma.cc/7FT8-U3QY.

[592] Press Release, President of Ukraine, Volodymyr Zelenskyy Had a Phone Conversation with President of the

has explained that he "never talked to the President from the position of a quid pro quo"[593] and stated that they did not discuss the security assistance on the call at all.[594] Indeed, President Zelenskyy has confirmed several separate times that his communications with President Trump were "good" and "normal," and "no one pushed me."[595] The day after the call, President Zelenskyy met with Ambassador Volker, Ambassador Sondland, and Ambassador Taylor in Kyiv. Ambassador Volker reported that the Ukrainians "thought [the call] went well."[596] Likewise, Ambassador Taylor reported that President Zelenskyy stated that he was "happy with the call."[597] And Ms. Croft, who met with President Zelenskyy's chief of staff Andriy Bohdan the day after the call, heard from Bohdan that the call "was a very good call, very positive, they had good chemistry."[598]

Other high ranking Ukrainian officials confirmed that they never perceived a connection between security assistance and investigations. Ukrainian Foreign Minister Vadym Prystaiko stated his belief that "there was no pressure,"[599] he has "never seen a direct link between investigations and security assistance," and "there was no clear connection between these events."[600] Similarly, when President Zelenskyy's adviser, Andriy Yermak, was asked if "he had ever felt there was a connection between the U.S. military aid and the requests for investigations," he was "adamant" that "[w]e never had that feeling" and "[w]e did not have the feeling that this aid was connected to any one specific issue."[601]

3. President Zelenskyy and Other Senior Ukrainian Officials Did Not Even *Know* that the Security Assistance Had Been Paused.

House Democrats' theory is further disproved because the evidence shows that President Zelenskyy and other senior Ukrainian officials did not even ***know*** that the aid had been paused until more than a month after the July 25, 2019 call, when the pause was reported in *Politico* at the

---

United States (July 25, 2019), https://perma.cc/DKP3-VKCH.

[593] Simon Shuster, *'I Don't Trust Anyone at All.' Ukrainian President Volodymyr Zelensky Speaks Out on Trump, Putin, and a Divided Europe*, Time (Dec. 2, 2019), https://perma.cc/Z65U-FKAR.

[594] *Ukraine President Downplays Trump Pressures in All-Day Media Marathon*, Politico (Oct. 10, 2019), https://perma.cc/QVM3-HFNK ("Responding to questions from The Associated Press, Zelenskiy said he only learned after their July 25 phone call that the U.S. had blocked hundreds of millions of dollars in military aid to Ukraine. 'We didn't speak about this' during the July call, Zelenskiy said. 'There was no blackmail.'").

[595] *See President Trump Meeting with Ukrainian President*, C-SPAN, at 08:10 (Sept. 25, 2019), https://www.c-span.org/video/?464711-1/president-trump-meets-ukrainian-leader-memo-release ("[W]e had, I think, [a] good phone call. It was normal. We spoke about many things. And I—so I think, and you read it, that nobody pushed—pushed me."); Meg Wagner et al., *Ukraine President Insists "No One Can Put Pressure on Me" to Investigate Bidens*, CNN (Oct. 1, 2019), https://perma.cc/AAV7-74G4 ("I don't feel pressure. . . . I have lots of people who'd like to put pressure on me here and abroad. I'm the president of an independent Ukraine — no one can put pressure on me.").

[596] Volker Interview Tr. at 313:2-9.

[597] Taylor Dep. Tr. at 31:6-8.

[598] Croft Dep. Tr. at 117:7-12.

[599] Matthias Williams, *Ukraine Minister Denies Trump Put Pressure on Zelenskiy During Call: Report*, Reuters (Sept. 21, 2019), https://perma.cc/J8TF-8SQ3.

[600] Mairead McArdle, *Ukrainian Foreign Minister Denies Sondland Linked Military Aid Delay to Biden Investigation*, National Rev. (Nov. 14, 2019), https://perma.cc/DPF6-GB5V (citing Interfax-Ukraine); *see also* Matthias Williams, *U.S. Envoy Sondland Did Not Link Biden Probe to Aid: Ukraine Minister*, Reuters (Nov. 14, 2019), https://perma.cc/2URG-9H5Y ("'I have never seen a direct relationship between investigations and security assistance,' [Ukraine Foreign Minister Vadym] Prystaiko was quoted as saying by Interfax.").

[601] Simon Shuster, *Exclusive: Top Ukraine Official Andriy Yermak Casts Doubt on Key Impeachment Testimony*, Time (Dec. 10, 2019), https://perma.cc/A93U-KVKF.

end of August.[602] The Ukrainians could not have been pressured by a pause on the aid they did not even know about.

The uniform and uncontradicted testimony from American officials who actually interacted with President Zelenskyy and other senior Ukrainian officials was that they had no reason to think that Ukraine knew of the pause until more than a month after the July 25 call. Ambassador Volker testified that he "believe[s] the Ukrainians became aware of the delay on August 29 and not before."[603] Ambassador Taylor agreed that, to the best of his knowledge, "nobody in the Ukrainian Government became aware of a hold on military aid until . . . August 29th."[604] Mr. Morrison concurred, testifying that he had "no reason to believe the Ukrainians had any knowledge of the review until August 28, 2019."[605] Deputy Assistant Secretary Kent and Ambassador Sondland agreed.[606]

Public statements from high-level Ukrainian officials have confirmed the same point. For example, adviser to President Zelenskyy Andriy Yermak told *Bloomberg* that President Zelenskyy and his key advisers learned of the pause only from the *Politico* article.[607] And then-Foreign Minister Pavlo Klimkin learned of the pause in the aid "by reading a news article," and Deputy Minister of Defense Oleh Shevchuk learned "through media reports."[608]

Further confirmation that the Ukrainians did not know about the pause comes from the fact that the Ukrainians did not raise the security assistance in any of the numerous high-level meetings held over the summer—something Yermak told *Bloomberg* they would have done had they known.[609] President Zelenskyy did not raise the issue in meetings with Ambassador Taylor on either July 26 or August 27.[610] And Volker—who was in touch with the highest levels of the Ukrainian government—explained that Ukrainian officials "would confide things" in him and

---

[602] *See* Caitlin Emma & Connor O'Brien, *Trump Holds up Ukraine Military Aid Meant to Confront Russia*, Politico (Aug. 28, 2019), https://perma.cc/9FFS-B9WT.

[603] Volker-Morrison Public Hearing, *supra* note 563, at 22; *see also id.* at 143; Volker Interview Tr. at 125:14-17 ("To my knowledge, the news about a hold on security assistance did not get into Ukrainian Government circles, as indicated to me by the current foreign minister, then diplomatic adviser, until the end of August.").

[604] Taylor Dep. Tr. at 119:21-24; *Impeachment Inquiry: Amb. William Taylor & Mr. George Kent Before the H.R. Permanent Select Comm. on Intelligence*, 116th Cong. 154:10-13 (Nov. 13, 2019) (Taylor-Kent Public Hearing) ("[Q.] Ambassador Taylor, earlier you were testifying that Ukrainian officials did not become aware of potential U.S. assistance being withheld until August 29th. Is that accurate? [A.] That's my understanding, Mr. Hurd.").

[605] Morrison Dep. Tr. at 17:11-12 ("I have no reason to believe the Ukrainians had any knowledge of the review until August 28, 2019."); *see also* Volker-Morrison Public Hearing, *supra* note 563, at 68 ("[Q.] You mentioned the August 28th Politico article. Was that the first time that you believe the Ukrainians may have had a real sense that the aid was on hold? [A.] Yes.").

[606] Taylor-Kent Public Hearing, *supra* note 604, at 154:19-23 ("[Q.] Mr. Kent, . . . when was the first time a Ukrainian official contacted you, concerned about potential withholding of USAID [sic]? [A.] It was after the article in Politico came out, in that first intense week of September."); G. Sondland Interview Tr. at 177:11-17 (Oct. 17, 2019) (testifying that "I don't recall exactly when I learned that the Ukrainians learned" but agreeing that "by the time there was a Politico report . . . everyone would have known.").

[607] Stephanie Baker & Daryna Krasnolutska, *Ukraine's Fraught Summer Included a Rogue Embassy in Washington*, Bloomberg (Nov. 22, 2019), https://perma.cc/YUB5-E92S.

[608] Andrew E. Kramer, *Trump's Hold on Military Aid Blindsided Top Ukrainian Officials*, N.Y. Times (Sept. 22, 2019), https://perma.cc/7PR9-DAAS.

[609] *Ukraine's Fraught Summer Included a Rogue Embassy in Washington*, *supra* note 607 ("Had the top people in Kyiv known about the holdup earlier, they said, the matter would have been raised with National Security Advisor John Bolton during his visit on Aug. 27.").

[610] Taylor-Kent Public Hearing, *supra* note 604, at 108:4-19.

"would have asked" if they had any questions about the aid.[611] Things changed, however, within hours of the publication of the *Politico* article, when Yermak, a top adviser to President Zelenskyy, texted Ambassador Volker to ask about the report.[612]

The House Democrats' entire theory falls apart because President Zelenskyy and other officials at the highest levels of the Ukrainian government did not even know about the temporary pause until shortly before the President released the security assistance. As Ambassador Volker said: "I don't believe . . . they were aware at the time, *so there was no leverage implied*."[613] These facts alone vindicate the President.

4. House Democrats Rely Solely on Speculation Built on Hearsay.

House Democrats' charge is further disproved by the straightforward fact that not a single witness with actual knowledge ever testified that the President suggested any connection between announcing investigations and security assistance. Assumptions, presumptions, and speculation based on hearsay are all that House Democrats can rely on to spin their tale of a quid pro quo.

House Democrats' claims are refuted first and foremost by the fact that there are only two people with statements on record who spoke directly with the President about the matter—and both have confirmed that the President expressly told them there was no connection whatsoever between the security assistance and investigations. Ambassador Sondland testified that he asked President Trump directly about these issues, and the President explicitly told him that he did not want anything from Ukraine:

> I want nothing. I want nothing. I want no quid pro quo. Tell
> Zelensky to do the right thing . . . .[614]

Similarly, Senator Ron Johnson has said that he asked the President "whether there was some kind of arrangement where Ukraine would take some action and the hold would be lifted," and the answer was clear and "[w]ithout hesitation": "(Expletive deleted)—No way. I would never do that."[615]

Although he did not speak to the President directly, Ambassador Volker also explained that President Trump never linked security assistance to investigations, and the Ukrainians never indicated that they thought there was any connection:

> [Q.] Did the President of the United States ever say to you that he
> was not going to allow aid from the United States to go to []
> Ukraine unless there were investigations into Burisma, the

---

[611] Volker Interview Tr. at 168:10–169:23.

[612] Volker-Morrison Public Hearing, *supra* note 563, at 68 ("I received a text message from one of my Ukrainian counterparts on August 29th forwarding that article, and that's the first they raised it with me."); Text Message from Andriy Yermak, Adviser to President Zelenskyy, to Kurt Volker, U.S. Special Rep. for Ukraine Negotiations, at KV00000020 (Aug. 29, 2019, 3:06:14 AM), https://perma.cc/PV4B-T6HM.

[613] Volker Interview Tr. at 124:11–125:1 (emphasis added).

[614] *Impeachment Inquiry: Amb. Gordon Sondland Before the H.R. Permanent Select Comm. on Intelligence*, 116th Cong. 40 (Nov. 20, 2019) (Sondland Public Hearing).

[615] Letter from Sen. Ron Johnson, *supra* note 568, at 6.

Bidens, or the 2016 elections?

[A.] No, he did not.

[Q.] Did the Ukrainians ever tell you that they understood that they would not get a meeting with the President of the United States, a phone call with the President of the United States, military aid or foreign aid from the United States unless they undertook investigations of Burisma, the Bidens, or the 2016 elections?

[A.] No, they did not.[616]

Against all of that unequivocal testimony, House Democrats base their case entirely on witnesses who offer nothing but speculation. Worse, it is speculation that traces back to one source: Sondland. Other witnesses repeatedly invoked things that Ambassador Sondland had said in a chain of hearsay that would never be admitted in any court. For example, Chairman Schiff's leading witness, Ambassador Taylor, acknowledged that, to the extent he thought there was a connection between the security assistance and investigations, his information came entirely from things that Sondland said—or (worse) second-hand accounts of what Morrison told Taylor that Sondland had said.[617] Similarly, Morrison testified that he "had no reason to believe that the release of the security-sector assistance might be conditioned on a public statement reopening the Burisma investigation until [his] September 1, 2019, conversation with Ambassador Sondland."[618]

Sondland, however, testified unequivocally that "the President did not tie aid to investigations." Instead, he acknowledged that any link that he had suggested was based entirely on his own *speculation*, unconnected to any conversation with the President:

[Q.] What about the aid? [Ambassador Volker] says that they weren't tied, that the aid was not tied --

[A.] And I didn't say they were conclusively tied either. *I said I was presuming it.*

[Q.] Okay. And so the President never told you they were tied.

[A.] That is correct.

[Q.] So your testimony and [Ambassador Volker's] testimony is consistent, and the President did not tie aid to investigations.

[A.] That is correct.[619]

Indeed, Sondland testified that he did "not recall any discussions with the White House on withholding U.S. security assistance from Ukraine in return for assistance with the President's

616 Volker-Morrison Public Hearing, *supra* note 563, at 106–07.
617 Taylor-Kent Public Hearing, *supra* note 604, at 109:18-20 (testifying that his "clear understanding" "came from Ambassador Sondland"); *id.* at 110:6-8 ("[Q.] You said you got this from Ambassador Sondland. [A.] That is correct."); Taylor Dep. Tr. at 297:21–298:1 ("[Q.] But if I understand this correctly, you're telling us that Tim Morrison told you that Ambassador Sondland told him that the President told Ambassador Sondland that Zelensky would have to open an investigation into Biden?" [A.] That's correct."); *see also, e.g., id.* at 35:20-25, 38:13-16.
618 Morrison Dep. Tr. at 17:13-16.
619 Sondland Public Hearing, *supra* note 614, at 148–49 (emphasis added).

2020 reelection campaign."[620] And he explained that he "did not know (and still do[es] not know) when, why, or by whom the aid was suspended," so he just "***presumed*** that the aid suspension had become linked to the proposed anti-corruption statement."[621] In his public testimony alone, Sondland used variations of "presume," "assume," "guess," or "speculate" over ***thirty*** times. When asked if he had any "testimony [] that ties President Trump to a scheme to withhold aid from Ukraine in exchange for these investigations," he stated that he has nothing "[o]ther than [his] own presumption," and he conceded that "[n]o one on this planet told [him] that Donald Trump was tying aid to investigations."[622] House Democrats' assertion that "President Trump made it clear to Ambassador Sondland—who conveyed this message to Ambassador Taylor—that everything was dependent on such an announcement [of investigations]," simply misrepresents the testimony.[623]

5. The Security Assistance Flowed Without Any Statement or Investigation by Ukraine.

The made-up narrative that the security assistance was conditioned on Ukraine taking some action on investigations is further disproved by the straightforward fact that the aid was released on September 11, 2019, without the Ukrainians taking any action on investigations. President Zelenskyy never made a statement about investigations, nor did anyone else in the Ukrainian government. Instead, the evidence confirms that the decision to release the aid was based on entirely unrelated factors. *See infra* Part III.B. The paused aid, moreover, was entirely distinct from U.S. sales of Javelin missiles and thus had no effect on the supply of those arms to Ukraine.[624]

6. President Trump's Record of Support for Ukraine Is Beyond Reproach.

Part of House Democrats' baseless charge is that the temporary pause on security assistance somehow "compromised the national security of the United States" by leaving Ukraine vulnerable to Russian aggression.[625] The record affirmatively disproves that claim. In fact, Chairman Schiff's hearings established beyond a doubt that the Trump Administration has been a stronger, more reliable friend to Ukraine than the prior administration. Ambassador Yovanovitch testified that "our policy actually got stronger" under President Trump, largely because, unlike the Obama administration, "this administration made the decision to provide lethal weapons to Ukraine" to help Ukraine fend off Russian aggression.[626] Yovanovitch explained that "we all felt [that] was very significant."[627] Ambassador Taylor similarly explained that the aid package provided by the Trump Administration was a "substantial improvement" over the policy of the prior

---

[620] Sondland Interview Tr. at 35:8-11.

[621] Declaration of Ambassador Gordon D. Sondland ¶ 4 (Nov. 4, 2019) (emphasis added).

[622] Sondland Public Hearing, *supra* note 614, at 150–51.

[623] HJC Report at 97 (quotations omitted).

[624] M. Yovanovitch Dep. Tr. at 314:15-18 (Oct. 11, 2019) ("[Q.] . . . The foreign aid that was—has been reported as being held up, it doesn't relate to Javelins, does it? [A.] No. At least I'm not aware that it does."); *id.* at 315:4-7 ("[Q.] But it was actually aid that had been appropriated and it had nothing to do with Javelins. Would you agree with that? [A.] That's my understanding."); Morrison Dep. Tr. at 79:25–80:2 (Oct. 31, 2019) ("Q. Okay. In your mind, are the Javelins separate from the security assistance funds? A. Yes.").

[625] H.R. Res. 755, 116th Cong. art. I (2019); *see also* HPSCI Report at 24; HJC Report at 76.

[626] Yovanovitch Dep. Tr. at 140:24–141:3 ("And I actually felt that in the 3 years that I was there, partly because of my efforts, but also the interagency team, and President Trump's decision to provide lethal weapons to Ukraine, that our policy actually got stronger over the last 3 years.").

[627] Yovanovitch Dep. Tr. at 144:14-16.

administration, because "this administration provided Javelin antitank weapons," which "are serious weapons" that "will kill Russian tanks."[628] Deputy Assistant Secretary Kent agreed that Javelins "are incredibly effective weapons at stopping armored advance, and the Russians are scared of them,"[629] and Ambassador Volker explained that "President Trump approved each of the decisions made along the way," and as a result, "America's policy towards Ukraine strengthened."[630] As Senator Johnson has noted, President Trump capitalized on a longstanding congressional authorization that President Obama did not: "In 2015, Congress overwhelmingly authorized $300 million of security assistance to Ukraine, of which $50 million was to be available only for lethal defensive weaponry. The Obama administration never supplied the authorized lethal defensive weaponry, but President Trump did."[631]

Thus, any claim that President Trump put the security of Ukraine at risk is flatly incorrect. The pause on security assistance (which was entirely distinct from the Javelin sales) was lifted by the end of the fiscal year, and the aid flowed to Ukraine without any preconditions. Ambassador Volker testified that the brief pause on releasing the aid was "not significant."[632] And Under Secretary of State for Political Affairs David Hale explained that "this [was] future assistance. . . . not to keep the army going now," disproving the false claim made by House Democrats that the pause caused any harm to Ukraine over the summer.[633] In fact, according to Oleh Shevchuk, the Ukrainian Deputy Minister of Defense who oversaw U.S. aid shipments, "the hold came and went so quickly" that he did not notice any change.[634]

B.   The Administration Paused Security Assistance Based on Policy Concerns and Released It After the Concerns Were Satisfied.

What the evidence actually shows is that President Trump had legitimate policy concerns about foreign aid. As Under Secretary Hale explained, foreign aid to all countries was undergoing a systematic review in 2019. As he put it, "the administration did not want to take a, sort of, business-as-usual approach to foreign assistance, a feeling that once a country has received a certain assistance package . . . it's something that continues forever."[635] Dr. Hill confirmed this review and explained that "there had been a directive for whole-scale review of our foreign policy, foreign policy assistance, and the ties between our foreign policy objectives and the assistance. This had been going on actually for many months."[636]

With regard to Ukraine, witnesses testified that President Trump was concerned about corruption and whether other countries were contributing their share.

---

[628] Taylor Dep. Tr. at 155:14-23.
[629] G. Kent Interview Tr. at 294:10-17 (Oct. 15, 2019).
[630] Volker-Morrison Public Hearing, *supra* note 563, at 58; *see also id.* at 58–59 ("[Q.] And for many years, there had been an initiative in the interagency to advocate for lethal defensive weaponry for Ukraine. Is that correct? [A.] That is correct. [Q.] And it wasn't until President Trump and his administration came in that that went through? [A.] That is correct.").
[631] Nov. 18, 2019 Letter from Sen. Ron Johnson, *supra* note 568, at 2.
[632] Volker Interview Tr. at 80:6-7.
[633] D. Hale Dep. Tr. at 85:2-3 (Nov. 6, 2019).
[634] *Trump's Hold on Military Aid Blindsided Top Ukrainian Officials*, *supra* note 608.
[635] Hale Dep. Tr. at 82:2-6.
[636] *Impeachment Inquiry: Dr. Fiona Hill and Mr. David Holmes Before the H.R. Permanent Select Comm. on Intelligence*, 116th Cong. 75:17-19 (Nov. 21, 2019) (Hill-Holmes Public Hearing).

1. **Witnesses Testified That President Trump Had Concerns About Corruption in Ukraine.**

Contrary to the bald assertion in the House Democrats' trial brief that "[b]efore news of former Vice President Biden's candidacy broke, President Trump showed no interest in corruption in Ukraine,"[637] multiple witnesses testified that the President has long had concerns about this issue. Dr. Hill, for instance, testified that she "think[s] the President has actually quite publicly said that he was very skeptical about corruption in Ukraine. And, in fact, he's not alone, because everyone has expressed great concerns about corruption in Ukraine."[638] Similarly, Ambassador Yovanovitch testified that "we all" had concerns about corruption in Ukraine and noted that President Trump delivered an anti-corruption message to former Ukraine President Petro Poroshenko in their first meeting in the White House on June 20, 2017.[639] NSC Senior Director Morrison confirmed that he "was aware that the President thought Ukraine had a corruption problem, as did many others familiar with Ukraine."[640] And Ms. Croft also heard the President raise the issue of corruption directly with then-President Poroshenko of Ukraine during a bilateral meeting at the United Nations General Assembly in September 2017.[641] She also understood the President's concern "[t]hat Ukraine is corrupt" because she had been "tasked[] and retasked" by then-National Security Advisor General McMaster "to write [a] paper to help [McMaster] make the case to the President" in connection with prior security assistance.[642]

Concerns about corruption in Ukraine were also entirely justified. As Dr. Hill affirmed, "eliminating corruption in Ukraine was one of, if [not] the central, goals of U.S. foreign policy" in Ukraine.[643] Virtually every witness agreed that confronting corruption should be at the forefront of U.S. policy with respect to Ukraine.[644]

2. **The President Had Legitimate Concerns About Foreign Aid Burden-Sharing, Including With Regard to Ukraine.**

President Trump also has well-documented concerns regarding American taxpayers being forced to cover the cost of foreign aid while other countries refuse to pitch in. In fact, "another factor in the foreign affairs review" discussed by Under Secretary Hale was "appropriate burden sharing."[645] The President's 2018 Budget discussed this precise issue:

> The Budget proposes to reduce or end direct funding for
> international programs and organizations whose missions do not

---

[637] Trial Mem. of the U.S. House of Representatives at 26.

[638] Hill Dep. Tr. at 118:19-22.

[639] Yovanovitch Dep. Tr. at 142:10-16 ("Q. Were you aware of the President's deep-rooted skepticism about Ukraine's business environment? A. Yes. Q. And what did you know about that? A. That he—I mean, he shared that concern directly with President Poroshenko in their first meeting in the Oval Office."); 143:8-10 (Q. The administration had concerns about corruption in Ukraine, correct? A. We all did.").

[640] Morrison Dep. Tr. at 16:16-17.

[641] Croft Dep. Tr. at 21:20–22:5; *see also* The White House, President Trump Meets with President Poroshenko of Ukraine (Sept. 22, 2017), https://perma.cc/A5AC-PNS2 ("The President recommended that President Poroshenko continue working to eliminate corruption and improve Ukraine's business climate.").

[642] Croft Dep. Tr. at 32:16-25.

[643] Hill Dep. Tr. at 34:7-13.

[644] *See, e.g.*, Yovanovitch Dep. Tr. at 17:9-12; Taylor Dep. Tr. at 87:20-25; Kent Interview Tr. at 105:15-18, 151:21-22.

[645] Hale Dep. Tr. at 82:18-22.

substantially advance U.S. foreign policy interests. The Budget also renews attention on the appropriate U.S. share of international spending at the United Nations, at the World Bank, and for many other global issues where the United States currently pays more than its fair share.[646]

Burden-sharing was reemphasized in the President's 2020 budget when it advocated for reforms that would "prioritize the efficient use of taxpayer dollars and increased burden-sharing to rebalance U.S. contributions to international organizations."[647]

House Democrats wrongly claim that "[i]t was not until September . . . that the hold, for the first time, was attributed to the President's concern about other countries not contributing more to Ukraine"[648] and that President Trump "never ordered a review of burden-sharing."[649] These assertions are demonstrably false.

Mr. Morrison testified that he was well aware of the President's "skeptical view"[650] on foreign aid generally and Ukrainian aid specifically. He affirmed that the President was "trying to scrutinize [aid] to make sure the U.S. taxpayers were getting their money's worth" and explained that the President "was concerned that the United States seemed to—to bear the exclusive brunt of security assistance to Ukraine. He wanted to see the Europeans step up and contribute more security assistance."[651]

There is other evidence as well. In a June 24 email with the subject line "POTUS follow up," a Department of Defense official relayed several questions from a meeting with the President, including "What do other NATO members spend to support Ukraine?"[652] Moreover, as discussed above, President Trump personally raised the issue of burden-sharing with President Zelenskyy on July 25.[653] Senator Johnson similarly related that the President had shared concerns about burden-sharing with him. He recounted an August 31 conversation in which President Trump described discussions he would have with Angela Merkel, Chancellor of Germany. According to Senator Johnson, President Trump explained: "Ron, I talk to Angela and ask her, 'Why don't you fund these things,' and she tells me, 'Because we know you will.' We're schmucks, Ron. We're schmucks."[654] And Ambassador Taylor testified that, when the Vice President met with President Zelenskyy on September 1, the Vice President reiterated that "President Trump wanted the

---

[646] Office of Mgmt. & Budget, *Budget of the U.S. Government Fiscal Year 2018*, at 13 (May 23, 2017), https://perma.cc/GE2U-MPMU.

[647] Office of Mgmt. & Budget, *Budget of the U.S. Government Fiscal Year 2020*, at 71 (Mar. 11, 2019), https://perma.cc/5ER6-7A3Q.

[648] Trial Mem. of the U.S. House of Representatives at 28.

[649] *Id.*

[650] Volker-Morrison Public Hearing, *supra* note 563, at 63.

[651] *Id.* at 64.

[652] Email from Eric Chewning, Chief of Staff, Office of the Secretary of Defense, to John Rood, Under Secretary of Defense for Policy, and Elaine McCusker, Under Secretary of Defense (Comptroller) (June 24, 2019), *available at* https://publicintegrity.org/national-security/trump-administration-officials-worried-ukraine-aid-halt-violated-spending-law (page 11); L. Cooper Dep. Tr. at 33 (Oct. 23, 2019) (summarizing follow-up questions from "a meeting with the President").

[653] *See supra* Part III.A.1.

[654] Nov. 18, 2019 Letter from Sen. Johnson, *supra* note 568, at 5.

Europeans to do more to support Ukraine."[655]

President Trump's burden-sharing concerns were entirely legitimate. The evidence shows that the United States pays more than its fair share for Ukrainian assistance. As Deputy Assistant Secretary Cooper testified, "U.S. contributions [to Ukraine] are far more significant than any individual country" and "EU funds tend to be on the economic side," rather than for "defense and security."[656] Even President Zelenskyy noted in the July 25 call that the Europeans were not helping Ukraine as much as they should and certainly not as much as the United States.[657]

3. Pauses on Foreign Aid Are Often Necessary and Appropriate.

Placing a temporary pause on aid is not unusual. Indeed, the President has often paused, re-evaluated, and even canceled foreign aid programs. For example:

- In September 2019, the Administration announced that it was withholding over $100 million in aid to Afghanistan over concerns about government corruption.[658]

- In August 2019, President Trump announced that the Administration and Seoul were in talks to "substantially" increase South Korea's share of the expense of U.S. military support for South Korea.[659]

- In June, President Trump cut or paused over $550 million in foreign aid to El Salvador, Honduras, and Guatemala because those countries were not fairly sharing the burdens of preventing mass migration to the United States.[660]

- In or around June, the Administration temporarily paused $105 million in military aid to Lebanon. The Administration lifted the hold in December, with one official explaining that the Administration "continually reviews and thoroughly evaluates the effectiveness of all United States foreign assistance to ensure that funds go toward activities that further U.S. foreign policy and national security interests."[661]

- In September 2018, the Administration cancelled $300 million in military aid to Pakistan because it was not meeting its counter-terrorism obligations.[662]

Indeed, Under Secretary Hale agreed that "aid has been withheld from several countries across the globe for various reasons, and, in some cases, for reasons that are still unknown just in

---

[655] Taylor Dep. Tr. at 35:8-19; *see also* J. Williams Dep. Tr. at 81:7-11 (Nov. 7, 2019) (the Vice President wanted to "hear if there was more that European countries could do to support Ukraine"); Morrison Dep. Tr. at 224:19–225:6 ("[T]he President believed that the Europeans should be contributing more in security-sector assistance.").

[656] Cooper Dep. Tr. at 14.

[657] July 25 Call Mem., *infra* Appendix A, at 2.

[658] Karen DeYoung, *U.S. Withdrawing $100 Million in Aid to Afghanistan Amid Corruption Concerns*, Wash. Post (Sept. 19, 2019), https://perma.cc/TK8K-4332.

[659] Rachel Frazin, *Trump: South Korea Should Pay 'Substantially More' for Defense Costs*, The Hill (Aug. 7. 2019), https://perma.cc/T672-JNN3.

[660] Camilo Montoya-Galvez, *U.S. Cuts Millions in Aid to Central America, Fulfilling Trump's Vow*, CBS News (June 18, 2019), https://perma.cc/2K6V-337X.

[661] Ben Gittleson & Conor Finnegan, *Trump Administration Releases Lebanon Military Aid After It Was Held Up for Months*, ABC News (Dec. 2, 2019), https://perma.cc/B4YJ-Z77C.

[662] Saphora Smith and Reuters, *Trump Admin Cancels $300m Aid to Pakistan over Terror Record*, NBC News (Sept. 2, 2018), https://perma.cc/U32X-8N69.

the past year."[663] Dr. Hill similarly explained that "there was a freeze put on all kinds of aid and assistance because it was in the process at the time of an awful lot of reviews of foreign assistance."[664] She added that, in her experience, "stops and starts [are] sometimes common . . . with foreign assistance" and that "OMB [Office of Management and Budget] holds up dollars all the time," including in the past for dollars going to Ukraine.[665] Similarly, Ambassador Volker affirmed that aid gets "held up from time-to-time for a whole assortment of reasons," and explained that "[i]t's something that had happened in [his] career in the past."[666]

4. The Aid Was Released After the President's Concerns Were Addressed.

To address President Trump's concerns about corruption and burden-sharing, a temporary pause was placed on the aid to Ukraine. Mr. Morrison testified that "OMB represented that . . . the President was concerned about corruption in Ukraine, and he wanted to make sure that Ukraine was doing enough to manage that corruption."[667] And OMB Deputy Associate Director for National Security Mark Sandy testified that he understood the pause to have been a result of the President's "concerns about the contribution from other countries to Ukraine."[668]

Over the course of the summer and early September, two series of developments helped address the President's concerns:

First, President Zelenskyy secured a majority in the Ukrainian parliament and was able to begin reforms under his anti-corruption agenda. As Mr. Morrison explained, when Zelenskyy was first elected, there was real "concern about whether [he] would be a genuine reformer" and "whether he would genuinely try to root out corruption."[669] It was also unclear whether President Zelenskyy's party would "be able to get a workable majority in the Ukrainian Parliament" to implement the corruption reforms he promised.[670] It was only later in the summer that President's Zelenskyy's party won a majority in the Rada—the Ukrainian parliament. As Mr. Morrison testified, on "the opening day of the [new] Rada," the Ukrainians worked through "an all-night session" to move forward with concrete reforms.[671] Indeed, Mr. Morrison and Ambassador Bolton were in Kyiv on August 27, and Mr. Morrison "observed that everybody on the Ukrainian side of the table was exhausted, because they had been up for days working on . . . reform legislation."[672] President Zelenskyy "named a new prosecutor general"—a reform that the NSC was "specifically interested in."[673] He also "had his party introduce a spate of legislative reforms, one of which was particularly significant," namely, "stripping Rada members of their parliamentary immunity."[674]

---

[663] *Impeachment Inquiry: Ms. Laura Cooper and Mr. David Hale Before the H.R. Permanent Select Comm. on Intelligence,* 116th Cong. 22 (Cooper-Hale Public Hearing).

[664] Hill Dep. Tr. at 225:9-12.

[665] *Id.* at 254:20-24, 352:14-20.

[666] Volker-Morrison Public Hearing, *supra* note 563, at 59–60.

[667] Morrison Dep. Tr. at 165:6-11.

[668] M. Sandy Dep. Tr. at 133:10-13 (Nov. 16, 2019).

[669] Morrison Dep. Tr. at 127:10-16.

[670] Hill Dep. Tr. at 76:6-8 ("There was, you know, speculation in all analytical circles, both in Ukraine and outside, that he might not be able to get a workable majority in the Ukrainian Parliament.").

[671] Morrison Dep. Tr. at 129:14-17.

[672] *Id.* at 129:4-8.

[673] *Id.* at 128:18-20.

[674] *Id.* at 128:20-24.

Additionally, the High Anti-Corruption Court of Ukraine commenced its work on September 5, 2019.[675]

As a result of these developments, Mr. Morrison affirmed that by Labor Day there had been "definitive developments" to "demonstrate that President Zelensky was committed to the issues he campaigned on.[676]

Second, the President heard from multiple parties about Ukraine, including trusted advisers. Senator Johnson has said that he spoke to the President on August 31 urging release of the security assistance. Senator Johnson has stated that the President told him then that, as to releasing the aid, "[w]e're reviewing it now, and you'll probably like my final decision."[677] On September 3, 2019, Senators Johnson and Portman, along with other members of the Senate's bipartisan Ukraine Caucus, wrote to the President concerning the status of the aid,[678] and on September 5 the Chairman and Ranking Member of the House Foreign Affairs Committee followed suit with another letter.[679]

Most significantly, Mr. Morrison testified that the Vice President advised the President that the relationship with Zelenskyy "is one that he could trust."[680] The Vice President had met with President Zelenskyy in Warsaw on September 1 and had heard firsthand that the new Ukrainian administration was taking concrete steps to address corruption and burden-sharing. On corruption reform, President Zelenskyy "stated his strong commitment" and shared "some of the things he had been doing," specifically what his party had done in the "2 or 3 days" since the new parliament had been seated.[681] Morrison testified that, on burden-sharing, "President Zelensky agreed with Vice President Pence that the Europeans should be doing more" and "related to Vice President Pence conversations he'd been having with European leaders about getting them to do more."[682]

Moreover, on September 11, 2019, the President heard directly from Senator Portman.[683] Mr. Morrison testified that Senator Portman made "the case . . . to the President that it was the appropriate and prudent thing to do" to lift the pause on the aid.[684] He testified that the Vice President (who had just returned from Europe on September 6) and Senator Portman thus

---

[675] *High Anti-Corruption Court Starts Work in Ukraine (Video)*, Ukrainian Independent Information Agency of News (UNIAN) (Sept. 5, 2019), https://perma.cc/2XNC-F8YF.

[676] Morrison Dep. Tr. at 129:18-24.

[677] Letter from Sen. Ron Johnson, *supra* note 568, at 6.

[678] Letter from Sen. Rob Portman et al., to Mick Mulvaney, Director, Office of Management & Budget, at 1 (Sept. 3, 2019).

[679] Letter from Eliot L. Engel, Chairman, H.R. Comm. on Foreign Affairs, and Michael T. McCaul, Ranking Member, H.R. Comm. on Foreign Affairs, to Mick Mulvaney, Director, Office of Management & Budget, and Russell Vought, Acting Director, Office of Management & Budget, at 1–2 (Sept. 5, 2019).

[680] Morrison Dep. Tr. at 209:10-210:4; *see also id.* at 210:24–211:2.

[681] *Id.* at 225:12-16; *see also* Press Release, Office of the President of Ukraine, Volodymyr Zelenskyy Discussed Military-Technical Assistance for Ukraine and Cooperation in the Energy Sphere with the U.S. Vice President (Sept. 1, 2019), https://perma.cc/4KKX-E9QL (explaining that "[t]he U.S. Vice President raised the issue of reforms and fight against corruption that will be carried out by the new government" and President Zelenskyy "noted that Ukraine was determined to transform and emphasized that over 70 draft laws had been registered on the first day of work of the new parliament, including those aimed to overcome corruption.").

[682] Morrison Dep. Tr. at 225:8-11.

[683] *Id.* at 242:12–243:7.

[684] *Id.* at 243:2-7, 244:7-12.

"convinced the President that the aid should be disbursed immediately"[685]—and the temporary pause was lifted after the meeting.[686]

C. The Evidence Refutes House Democrats' Claim that President Trump Conditioned a Meeting with President Zelenskyy on Investigations.

Lacking any evidence to show a connection between releasing the security assistance and investigations, House Democrats fall back on the alternative theory that President Trump used a bilateral meeting as leverage to pressure Ukraine to announce investigations. But no witness with any direct knowledge supported that claim either. It is undisputed that a bilateral presidential-level meeting was scheduled for September 1 in Warsaw and then took place in New York City on September 25, 2019,[687] without Ukraine saying or doing anything related to investigations.

1. A Presidential Meeting Occurred Without Precondition.

Contrary to House Democrats' claims, the evidence shows that a bilateral meeting between President Trump and President Zelenskyy was scheduled without any connection to any statement about investigations.

Mr. Morrison—whose "responsibilities" included "help[ing] arrange head of state visits to the White House or other head of state meetings"[688]—testified that he was trying to schedule a meeting without any restrictions related to investigations. He testified that he understood that arranging "the White House visit" was a "do-out" that "came from the President" on the July 25 call,[689] and he moved forward with a scheduling proposal.[690] He worked with Ambassador Taylor and the NSC's Senior Director responsible for visits to "determine dates that would be mutually agreeable to President Trump and President Zelensky."[691] But due to competing scheduling requests, "it became clear that the earliest opportunity for the two Presidents to meet would be in Warsaw" at the beginning of September.[692] In other words, Mr. Morrison made it clear that he was trying to schedule the meeting in the ordinary course. He did not say that anyone told him to delay scheduling the meeting until President Zelenskyy had made some announcement about investigations. Instead, he explained that, after the July 25 call, he understood that it was the President's direction to schedule a visit, and he proceeded to execute that direction.

Ultimately, the notion that a bilateral meeting between President Trump and President Zelenskyy was conditioned on a statement about investigations is refuted by one straightforward fact: a meeting was planned for September 1, 2019 in Warsaw without the Ukrainians saying a word about investigations. As Ambassador Volker testified, Administration officials were "working on a bilateral meeting to take place in Warsaw on the margins of the commemoration on the beginning of World War II."[693] Indeed, by mid-August, U.S. officials expected the meeting to

---

[685]   *Id.* at 243:6-7.
[686]   *Id.* at 242:22-24.
[687]   *See President Trump Meeting with Ukrainian President, supra* note 595.
[688]   Morrison Dep. Tr. at 115:10-12.
[689]   *Id.* at 106:10-15, 107:2-6.
[690]   *Id.* at 106:10–107:4, 107:10-16.
[691]   *Id.* at 106:10-15.
[692]   *Id.* at 108:20-21.
[693]   Volker Interview Tr. at 127:12-14.

occur,[694] and the Ukrainian government was making preparations.[695] As it turned out, President Trump had to stay in the U.S. because Hurricane Dorian rapidly intensified to a Category 5 hurricane, so he sent the Vice President to Warsaw in his place.[696]

Even that natural disaster did not put off the meeting between the Presidents for long. They met at the next earliest possible date—September 25, 2019, on the sidelines of the United Nations General Assembly. President Zelenskyy confirmed that there were no preconditions for this meeting.[697] Nor was there anything unusual about the meeting occurring in New York rather than Washington. As Ambassador Volker verified, "these meetings between countries sometimes take a long time to get scheduled" and "[i]t sometimes just doesn't happen."[698]

House Democrats cannot salvage their claim by arguing that the high-profile meeting in New York City did not count and that only an Oval Office meeting would do. Dr. Hill explained that what mattered was a bilateral presidential meeting, not the location of the meeting:

> [I]t wasn't always a White House meeting per se, but definitely a Presidential-level, you know, meeting with Zelensky and the President. I mean, it could've taken place in Poland, in Warsaw. It could've been, you know, a proper bilateral in some other context. But in other words, a White House-level Presidential meeting.[699]

The Ukrainians had such a meeting scheduled for September 1 in Warsaw (until Hurricane Dorian disrupted plans), and the meeting took place on September 25 in New York—all without anyone making any statement about investigations.

2. No Witness with Direct Knowledge Testified that President Trump Conditioned a Presidential Meeting on Investigations.

House Democrats' tale of a supposed quid pro quo involving a presidential meeting is further undermined by the fact that it rests entirely on mere speculation, hearsay, and innuendo. Not a single witness provided any first-hand evidence that the President ever linked a presidential meeting to announcing investigations.

Once again, House Democrats' critical witness—Sondland—actually destroys their case. He is the only witness who spoke directly to President Trump on the subject. And Sondland testified that, when he broadly asked the President what he wanted from Ukraine, the President answered unequivocally: "I want nothing. I want no quid pro quo. I just want Zelensky to do the

---

[694] Morrison Dep. Tr. at 266:8-10 ("We were expecting the President to meet with President Zelensky on 1 September. It's the middle of August; it's about 2 weeks.").

[695] *See Foreign Ministry, Presidential Office Prepares Zelensky-Trump Meeting in Warsaw*, National News Agency of Ukraine (Aug. 22, 2019), https://perma.cc/EK2G-5RSZ.

[696] Hale Dep. Tr. at 72:24–73:1; Volker Interview Tr. at 130:17-23 ("This was the President's trip to Warsaw as part of that World War II commemoration. That was when he cancelled because of the hurricane watch."); Isabel Togoh, *Hurricane Dorian: Trump Cancels Poland Trip to Focus on Storm in Last-Minute Move*, Forbes (Aug. 30, 2019), https://perma.cc/TQ83-6QKD.

[697] *See Ukraine President Downplays Trump Pressures in All-Day Media Marathon, supra* note 594.

[698] Volker Interview Tr. at 78:5-9, 78:17-25; *see also* Kent Interview Tr. at 202:14-16 ("The time on a President's schedule is always subject to competing priorities.").

[699] Hill Dep. Tr. at 145:6-12.

right thing, to do what he ran on."[700]

Sondland clearly stated that "the President never discussed" a link between investigations and a White House meeting,[701] and Sondland's mere *presumptions* about such a link are not evidence. As he put it, the most he could do is "repeat . . . what [he] heard through Ambassador Volker from Giuliani,"[702] who, he "*presumed*," spoke to the President on this issue.[703] But Ambassador Volker testified unequivocally that there was *no connection* between the meeting and investigations:

> Q. Did President Trump ever withhold a meeting with President Zelensky or delay a meeting with President Zelensky until the Ukrainians committed to investigate the allegations that you just described concerning the 2016 Presidential election?
>
> A. The answer to the question is no, if you want a yes-or-no answer. But the reason the answer is no is we did have difficulty scheduling a meeting, but there was no linkage like that.
>
> * * *
>
> Q. You said that you were not aware of any linkage between the delay in the Oval Office meeting between President Trump and President Zelensky and the Ukrainian commitment to investigate the two allegations as you described them, correct?
>
> A. Correct.[704]

Sondland confirmed the same point. When asked if "the President ever [told him] personally about any preconditions for anything," Sondland responded, "No."[705] And when asked if the President ever "told [him] about any preconditions for a White House meeting," he again responded, "[p]ersonally, no."[706] No credible testimony has been advanced supporting House Democrats' claim of a quid pro quo.

D.   House Democrats' Charges Rest on the False Premise that There Could Have Been No Legitimate Purpose To Ask President Zelenskyy About Ukrainian Involvement in the 2016 Election and the Biden-Burisma Affair.

The charges in Article I are further flawed because they rest on the transparently erroneous proposition that it would have been illegitimate for the President to mention two matters to President Zelenskyy: (i) possible Ukrainian interference in the 2016 election; and (ii) an incident in which then-Vice President Biden forced the dismissal of a Ukrainian anti-corruption prosecutor who reportedly had been investigating Burisma. House Democrats' characterizations of the President's conversation are false. Moreover, as House Democrats frame their charges, to prove

---

[700]   Sondland Public Hearing, *supra* note 614, at 74.
[701]   Sondland Interview Tr. at 216:6-7.
[702]   *Id.* at 216:4-7.
[703]   Sondland Public Hearing, *supra* note 614, at 36.
[704]   Volker Interview Tr. at 36:1-9; 40:11-16.
[705]   Sondland Public Hearing, *supra* note 614, at 70.
[706]   *Id.*

the element of "corrupt motive" at the heart of Article I, they must establish (in their own words) that the *only* reason for raising those matters would have been "to obtain an improper personal political benefit."[707] And as they cast their case, any investigation into those matters would have been "bogus" or a "sham" because, according to House Democrats, neither investigation would have been "premised on any legitimate national security or foreign policy interest."[708] That is obviously incorrect.

It would have been entirely proper for the President to ask President Zelenskyy to find out about any role that Ukraine played in the 2016 presidential election. Uncovering potential foreign interference in U.S. elections is always a legitimate goal. Similarly, it also would have been proper to ask about an incident in which Vice President Biden actually leveraged the threat of withholding one billion dollars in U.S. loan guarantees to secure the dismissal of a Ukrainian prosecutor who was reportedly investigating Burisma—at a time when his son, Hunter, was earning vast sums for sitting on Burisma's board.[709] House Democrats' own witnesses established ample justification for asking questions about the Biden-Burisma affair, as they acknowledged that Vice President Biden's conduct raises, at the very least, the appearance of a conflict of interest.[710]

1. It Was Entirely Appropriate for President Trump To Ask About Possible Ukrainian Interference in the 2016 Election.

House Democrats' theory that it would have been improper for President Trump to ask President Zelenskyy about any role that Ukraine played in interfering with the 2016 election makes no sense. Uncovering any form of foreign interference in a U.S. presidential election is squarely a matter of national interest. In this case, moreover, there is abundant information already in the public domain suggesting that Ukrainian officials systematically sought to interfere in the 2016 election to support one candidate: Hillary Clinton.

To give just a few examples, a former Democratic National Committee (DNC) consultant, Alexandra Chalupa, admitted to a reporter that Ukraine's embassy in the United States was "helpful" in her efforts to collect dirt on President Trump's then-campaign manager, Paul Manafort.[711] As *Politico* reported, "Chalupa said the [Ukrainian] embassy also worked directly with reporters researching Trump, Manafort and Russia to point them in the right directions."[712] A former political officer in that embassy also claimed the Ukrainian government coordinated directly with the DNC to assist the Clinton campaign in advance of the 2016 presidential

---

[707] H.R. Res. 755, 116th Cong. art. I.

[708] HJC Report at 4–6.

[709] *See Hunter Biden 'Was Paid $83,333 a Month by Ukrainian Gas Company to be a "Ceremonial Figure"*, The Ukrainian Week (Oct. 20, 2019), https://perma.cc/7WBU-XHCJ; Tobias Hoonhout, *Hunter Biden Served as 'Ceremonial Figure' on Burisma Board for $80,000 Per Month*, National Rev. (Oct. 18, 2019), https://perma.cc/6RAH-J5GU; *FLASHBACK, 2018: Joe Biden Brags at CFR Meeting About Withholding Aid to Ukraine to Force Firing of Prosecutor*, *supra* note 570; *Biden Faces Conflict of Interest Questions That Are Being Promoted by Trump and Allies*, *supra* note 572.

[710] *See, e.g.*, Taylor-Kent Public Hearing, *supra* note 604, at 25:3-5 (Kent: "[I]n a briefing call with the national security staff of the Office of the Vice President in February of 2015, I raised my concern that Hunter Biden's status as a board member could create the perception of a conflict of interest.").

[711] *Ukrainian Efforts to Sabotage Trump Backfire*, *supra* note 565 ("[O]fficials there [at the Ukrainian embassy] became 'helpful' in Chalupa's efforts, she said, explaining that she traded information and leads with them. 'If I asked a question, they would provide guidance, or if there was someone I needed to follow up with.'").

[712] *Id.*

election.[713] And Nellie Ohr, a former researcher for the firm that hired a foreign spy to produce the Steele Dossier, testified to Congress that Serhiy Leshchenko, then a member of Ukraine's Parliament, also provided her firm with information as part of the firm's opposition research on behalf of the DNC and the Clinton Campaign.[714] Even high-ranking Ukrainian government officials played a role. For example, Arsen Avakov, Ukraine's Minister of Internal Affairs, called then-candidate Trump "an even bigger danger to the US than terrorism."[715]

At least two news organizations conducted their own investigations and concluded Ukraine's government sought to interfere in the 2016 election. In January 2017, *Politico* concluded that "Ukrainian government officials tried to help Hillary Clinton and undermine Trump by publicly questioning his fitness for office."[716] And on the other side of the Atlantic, a separate investigation by *The Financial Times* confirmed Ukrainian election interference. The newspaper found that opposition to President Trump led "Kiev's wider political leadership to do something they would never have attempted before: intervene, however indirectly, in a US election."[717] These efforts were designed to undermine Trump's candidacy because, as one member of the Ukrainian parliament put it, the majority of Ukrainian politicians were "on Hillary Clinton's side."[718]

Even one of House Democrats' own witnesses, Dr. Hill, acknowledged that some Ukrainian officials "bet on Hillary Clinton winning the election," and so it was "quite evident" that "they were trying to curry favor with the Clinton campaign," including by "trying to collect information . . . on Mr. Manafort and on other people as well."[719]

If even a fraction of all this is true, Ukrainian interference in the 2016 election is squarely a matter of national interest. It is well settled that the United States has a "compelling interest . . . in limiting the participation of foreign citizens in activities of American democratic self-government, and in thereby preventing foreign influence over the U.S. political process."[720] Congress has forbidden foreigners' involvement in American elections.[721] And President Trump made clear more than a year ago that "the United States will not tolerate any form of foreign meddling in our elections" during his Administration.[722] Even Chairman Schiff is on record agreeing that the Ukrainian efforts to aid the Clinton campaign described above would be

---

[713] Natasha Bertrand & Kyle Cheney, *'I'm On A Mission To Testify,'*: *Dem Ukraine Activist Eager for Impeachment Cameo*, Politico (Nov. 12, 2019), https://perma.cc/7RJR-6YQQ.

[714] N. Ohr. Interview Tr., 115th Cong., 113–15 (Oct. 19, 2018), https://perma.cc/E3YE-QKYJ.

[715] *Ukrainian Efforts to Sabotage Trump Backfire*, *supra* note 565.

[716] *Id.*

[717] *Ukraine's Leaders Campaign Against 'Pro-Putin' Trump*, *supra* note 565 ("Hillary Clinton, the Democratic nominee, is backed by the pro-western government that took power after Mr. Yanukovich was ousted by street protests in 2014. . . . If the Republican candidate [Donald Trump] loses in November, some observers suggest Kiev's actions may have played at least a small role.").

[718] *Id.* (internal quotation marks omitted).

[719] Hill-Holmes Public Hearing, *supra* note 636, at 112:2-9.

[720] *United States v. Concord Mgmt. & Consulting LLC*, 347 F. Supp. 3d 38, 56 n.9 (D.D.C. 2018) (ellipsis in original) (quoting *Bluman v. FEC*, 800 F. Supp. 2d 281, 288 (D.D.C. 2011)).

[721] *See* 52 U.S.C. § 30121 (2018).

[722] President Donald J. Trump, Statement on Signing an Executive Order on Imposing Certain Sanctions in the Event of Foreign Interference in a United States Election, 2018 Daily Comp. Pres. Doc. 592 (Sept. 12, 2018), https://perma.cc/BEQ3-T3T3.

"problematic," if true.[723]

A request for Ukraine's assistance in this case also would have been particularly appropriate because the Department of Justice had already opened a probe on a similar subject matter to examine the origins of foreign interference in the 2016 election that led to the false Russian-collusion allegations against the Trump Campaign. In May of last year, Attorney General Barr publicly announced that he had appointed U.S. Attorney John Durham to lead a review of the origins and conduct of the Department of Justice's Russia investigation and targeting of members of the Trump campaign, including any potential wrongdoing.[724] As of October, it was publicly revealed that aspects of the probe had shifted to a criminal investigation.[725] As the White House explained when the President announced measures to ensure cooperation across the federal government with Mr. Durham's probe, his investigation will "ensure that all Americans learn the truth about the events that occurred, and the actions that were taken, during the last Presidential election and will restore confidence in our public institutions."[726]

Asking for foreign assistance is also routine. Such requests for cooperation are common and take many different forms, both formal and informal.[727] Requests can be made pursuant to a Mutual Legal Assistance Treaty, and the U.S. has such a treaty with Ukraine that specifically authorizes requests for cooperation.[728] There can also be informal requests for assistance.[729] Because the President is the Chief Executive and chief law enforcement officer of the federal government—as well as the "sole organ of the federal government in the field of international relations"[730]—requesting foreign assistance is well within his ordinary role.

Given the self-evident national interest at stake in identifying any Ukrainian role in the 2016 election, House Democrats resort to distorting the President's words. They strain to recast his request to uncover historical truth about the *last* election as if it were something relevant only for the President's personal political interest in the *next* election. Putting words in the President's mouth, House Democrats pretend that, because the President mentioned a hacked DNC server, he must have been pursuing a claim that Ukraine "rather than Russia" had interfered in the 2016 election[731]—and that assertion, they claim, was relevant solely for boosting President Trump's 2020 presidential campaign. But that convoluted chain of reasoning is hopelessly flawed.

---

[723] Tim Hains, *Rep. Adam Schiff: Democrats Meeting Ukrainians "Different Degree Of Involvement" Than Trump-Russia*, Real Clear Politics (July 16, 2017), https://perma.cc/D4HC-3ETE.

[724] Adam Goldman et al., *Barr Assigns U.S. Attorney in Connecticut to Review Origins of Russia Inquiry*, N.Y. Times (May 13, 2019), https://perma.cc/VS3E-DWT3. The Department of Justice has acknowledged that Mr. Durham's investigation is "broad in scope and multifaceted" and is "intended to illuminate open questions regarding the activities of U.S. and foreign intelligence services as well as non-governmental organizations and individuals." *See* Letter from Stephen Boyd, Assistant Attorney General, Dep't of Justice, to Jerrold Nadler, Chairman, House Judiciary Comm. (June 10, 2019).

[725] *See* Katie Benner & Adam Goldman, *Justice Dept. Is Said to Open Criminal Inquiry Into Its Own Russia Investigation*, N.Y. Times (Oct. 24, 2019), https://perma.cc/ZR3G-SWHE.

[726] Press Release, The White House, Statement from the Press Secretary (May 23, 2019), https://perma.cc/S9LT-LPCM.

[727] *See* U.S. Dep't of Justice, Criminal Resource Manual § 274.

[728] *See* Treaty on Mutual Legal Assistance in Criminal Matters, U.S.-Ukr., July 22, 1998, T.I.A.S. No. 12978.

[729] *See* U.S. Dep't of Justice, Criminal Resource Manual § 278.

[730] *United States v. Curtiss-Wright Export Corp.*, 299 U.S. 304, 320 (1936).

[731] H.R. Res. 755 art. I.

To start, simply asking about any Ukrainian involvement in the 2016 election—including with respect to hacking a DNC server—does not imply that Russia did *not* attempt to interfere with the 2016 election. It is entirely possible that foreign nationals from more than one country sought to interfere in our election by different means (or coordinated means), and for different reasons. Uncovering all the facts about any interference benefits the United States by laying bare all foreign attempts to meddle in our elections. And if the facts uncovered end up having any influence on the 2020 election, that would not be *improper*. House Democrats cannot place an inquiry into historical facts off limits based on fears that the facts might harm their interests in the next election.

In addition, House Democrats have simply misrepresented President Trump's words. The President did not ask narrowly about a DNC server alone, but rather raised a whole collection of issues related to the 2016 election. President Trump introduced the topic by noting that "our country has been through a lot,"[732] which referred to the entire Mueller investigation and false allegations about the Trump Campaign colluding with Russia. He then broadly expressed interest in "find[ing] out what happened with this whole situation" with Ukraine.[733] After mentioning a DNC server, the President made clear that he was casting a wider net as he said that "[t]here are a lot of things that went on" and again indicated that he was interested in "the whole situation."[734] He then noted his concern that President Zelenskyy was "surrounding [him]self with some of the same people."[735] President Zelenskyy clearly understood this to be a reference to Ukrainian officials who had sought to undermine then-candidate Trump during the campaign, as he responded by immediately noting that he "just recalled our ambassador from [the] United States."[736] That ambassador, of course, had penned a harsh, undiplomatic op-ed criticizing then-candidate Trump, and it had been widely reported that a DNC operative met with Ukrainian embassy officials during the campaign to dig up information detrimental to President Trump's campaign.[737]

Notably, Democrats have not always believed that asking Ukraine for assistance in uncovering foreign election interference constituted a threat to the Republic. To the contrary, in 2018, three Democratic Senators—Senators Menendez, Leahy, and Durbin—asked Ukraine to cooperate with the Mueller investigation and "strongly encourage[d]" then-Prosecutor General Yuriy Lutsenko to "halt any efforts to impede cooperation."[738] Not a single Democrat in either house has called for sanctions against them. Nothing that President Trump said went further than the senators' request, and efforts to claim that it was somehow improper are rank hypocrisy.

2. It Would Have Been Appropriate for President Trump To Ask President Zelenskyy About the Biden-Burisma Affair.

House Democrats' theory that there could not have been any legitimate basis for a President

---

[732] July 25 Call Mem., *infra* Appendix A, at 3.

[733] *Id.*

[734] *Id.*

[735] *Id.*

[736] *Id.*

[737] Amb. Valeriy Chaly, *Ukraine's Ambassador: Trump's Comments Send Wrong Message to World*, The Hill (Aug. 4, 2016), https://perma.cc/872A-Z28Y; *Ukrainian Efforts to Sabotage Trump Backfire*, *supra* note 565.

[738] Letter from Sen. Robert Menendez, et al. to Yuriy Lutsenko, Prosecutor General, Office of the Prosecutor General of Ukraine (May 4, 2019), https://perma.cc/9EH2-LDFG.

of the United States to raise the Biden-Burisma affair with President Zelenskyy is also wrong. The following facts have been publicly reported:

- Burisma is a Ukrainian energy company with a reputation for corruption. Lt. Col. Vindman called it a "corrupt entity."[739] It was founded by a corrupt oligarch, Mykola Zlochevsky, who has been under several investigations for money laundering.[740]

- Deputy Assistant Secretary of State Kent testified that Burisma's reputation was so poor that he dissuaded the United States Agency for International Development (USAID) from co-sponsoring an event with Burisma. He testified that he did not think co-sponsorship with a company of Burisma's reputation was "appropriate for the U.S. Government."[741]

- In April 2014, Hunter Biden was recruited to sit on Burisma's board.[742] At that time, his father had just been made the "public face of the [Obama] administration's handling of Ukraine,"[743] and Britain's Serious Fraud Office (SFO) had just recently frozen $23 million in accounts linked to Zlochevsky as part of a money-laundering investigation.[744] Zlochesvsky fled Ukraine sometime in 2014.[745]

- Hunter Biden had no known qualifications for serving on Burisma's board of directors, and just two months before joining the board, he had been discharged from the Navy Reserve for testing positive for cocaine on a drug test.[746] He himself admitted in a televised interview that he would not have gotten the board position "if [his] last name wasn't Biden."[747]

- Nevertheless, Hunter Biden was paid more than board members at energy giants like ConocoPhillips.[748]

---

[739] Vindman Dep. Tr. at 320; *see also* Volker Interview Tr. at 106:9-11 (Burisma "had a very bad reputation as a company for corruption and money laundering"); Kent Interview Tr. at 88:7 ("Burisma had a poor reputation.").

[740] Oliver Bullough, *The Money Machine: How a High-Profile Corruption Investigation Fell Apart*, The Guardian (Apr. 12, 2017), https://perma.cc/XTF6-DGJ3.

[741] Kent Interview Tr. at 88:8-9.

[742] Press Release, Burisma Holdings, *Hunter Biden Joins the Team of Burisma Holdings* (May 12, 2014), https://perma.cc/U9YS-JL5G; Adam Entous, *Will Hunter Biden Jeopardize His Father's Campaign?*, The New Yorker (July 1, 2019), https://perma.cc/UJ8G-GRWT ("Hunter joined . . . the Burisma board in April, 2014.").

[743] Susan Crabtree, *Joe Biden Emerges as Obama's Trusty Sidekick*, Wash. Examiner (Apr. 25, 2014), https://perma.cc/KVQ6-V2NF.

[744] Approved Judgement of the Central Criminal Court, Serious Fraud Office v. Mykola Zlochevskyi, ¶¶ 1, 7 (Jan. 21, 2015), https://www.justsecurity.org/wp-content/uploads/2019/09/Zlochevsky-SFO-v-MZ-Final-Judgment-Revised.doc.

[745] *Biden Faces Conflict of Interest Questions That Are Being Promoted by Trump and Allies, supra* note 572.

[746] *See The Money Machine: How a High-Profile Corruption Investigation Fell Apart, supra* note 740 ("The White House insisted the position was a private matter for Hunter Biden, and unrelated to his father's job, but that is not how anyone I spoke to in Ukraine interpreted it. Hunter Biden is an undistinguished corporate lawyer, with no previous Ukraine experience."); *Will Hunter Biden Jeopardize His Father's Campaign?, supra* note 742.

[747] Victoria Thompson, et al., *Exclusive: 'I'm Here': Hunter Biden Hits Back at Trump Taunt in Exclusive ABC News Interview*, ABC News (Oct. 15, 2019), https://abcnews.go.com/Politics/exclusive-hiding-plain-sight-hunter-biden-defends-foreign/story?id=66275416.

[748] *Biden Faces Conflict of Interest Questions That Are Being Promoted by Trump and Allies, supra* note 572; Polina Ivanova et al., *What Hunter Biden Did on the Board of Ukrainian Energy Company Burisma*, Reuters (Oct. 18, 2019),

- Multiple witnesses said it appeared that Burisma hired Hunter Biden for improper reasons.[749]

- Hunter's role on the board raised red flags in several quarters. Chris Heinz, the step-son of then-Secretary of State John Kerry, severed his business relationship with Hunter, citing Hunter's "lack of judgment" in joining the Burisma board as "a major catalyst."[750]

- Contemporaneous press reports openly speculated that Hunter's role with Burisma might undermine U.S. efforts—led by his father—to promote an anti-corruption message in Ukraine.[751] Indeed, *The Washington Post* reported that "[t]he appointment of the vice president's son to a Ukrainian oil board looks nepotistic at best, nefarious at worst."[752]

- Within the Obama Administration, Hunter's position caused the special envoy for energy policy, Amos Hochstein, to "raise[] the matter with Biden."[753] Deputy Assistant Secretary of State Kent testified that he, too, voiced concerns with Vice President Biden's office.[754]

- In fact, every witness who was asked agreed that Hunter's role created at least the appearance of a conflict of interest for his father.[755]

---

https://perma.cc/7PL4-JMPY. *Compare Hunter Biden Served as 'Ceremonial Figure' on Burisma Board for $80,000 Per Month*, *supra* note 709 (reporting Hunter Biden's monthly compensation to be $83,333 monthly, or nearly $1 million per year), *with* 2019 Proxy Statement, ConocoPhillips, at 30 (Apr. 1, 2019), https://perma.cc/4GP8-9ZWV (disclosing cash and stock awards provided to each active director with total compensation for the year ranging from $33,125 to $377,779).

[749] Vindman Dep. Tr. at 334–35 (explaining that "it doesn't look like [Hunter Biden] was" qualified); Volker Interview Tr. at 106:9-12 (speculating that Burisma hired Biden because of his connection to his politically connected father); *see also* Paul Sonne et al., *The Gas Tycoon and the Vice President's Son: The Story of Hunter Biden's Foray into Ukraine*, Wash. Post (Sept. 28, 2019), https://perma.cc/A8VJ-YUY4 (the Executive Director of Ukraine's Anti-Corruption Action Center asserting that Burisma added "people with these fancy names" to its board in an effort to "whitewash[]" the firm's reputation).

[750] *The Gas Tycoon and the Vice President's Son: The Story of Hunter Biden's Foray into Ukraine*, *supra* note 749.

[751] *The Money Machine: How a High-Profile Corruption Investigation Fell Apart*, *supra* note 740 ("The credibility of the United States was not helped by the news that . . . Hunter had been on the board of directors of Burisma"); The Editorial Board, *Joe Biden Lectures Ukraine*, N.Y. Times (Dec. 11, 2015), https://perma.cc/P9JH-YEBP ("Sadly, the credibility of Mr. Biden's message may be undermined by the association of his son with a Ukrainian natural-gas company, Burisma Holdings, which is owned by a former government official suspected of corrupt practices."); Paul Sonne and Laura Mills, *Ukrainians See Conflict in Biden's Anticorruption Message*, Wall St. J. (Dec. 7, 2015), https://www.wsj.com/articles/ukrainians-see-conflict-in-bidens-anticorruption-message-1449523458 ("[A]ctivists here say that [Joe Biden's anti-corruption] message is being undermined as his son receives money from a former Ukrainian official who is being investigated for graft.").

[752] *Hunter Biden's New Job at a Ukrainian Gas Company Is a Problem for U.S. Soft Power*, *supra* note 571.

[753] *Will Hunter Biden Jeopardize His Father's Campaign?*, *supra* note 742.

[754] Kent Interview Tr. at 227:1-8 ("And when I was on a call with somebody from the Vice President's staff and I cannot recall who it was . . . I raised my concerns that I had heard that Hunter Biden was on the board of a company owned by somebody that the U.S. Government had spent money trying to get tens of millions of dollars back and that could create the perception of a conflict of interest.").

[755] *Impeachment Inquiry: Amb. Marie "Masha" Yovanovitch Before the H.R. Permanent Select Comm. on Intelligence*, 116th Cong. 135–36 (Nov. 15, 2019) (Yovanovitch Public Hearing) ("I think that it could raise the appearance of a conflict of interest."); Taylor-Kent Public Hearing, *supra* note 604, at 25, 94–95 (Kent testifying that

- On February 2, 2016, the Ukrainian Prosecutor General obtained a court order to seize Zlochevsky's property.[756]

- According to press reports, Vice President Biden then spoke with Ukraine's President Poroshenko three times by telephone on February 11, 18, and 19, 2016.[757]

- Vice President Biden has openly bragged that, around that time, he threatened President Poroshenko that he would withhold one billion dollars in U.S. loan guarantees unless the Ukrainians fired the Prosecutor General who was investigating Burisma.[758]

- Deputy Assistant Secretary Kent testified that the Prosecutor General's removal "became a condition of the loan guarantee."[759]

- On March 29, 2016, Ukraine's parliament dismissed the Prosecutor General.[760] In September 2016, a Kiev court cancelled an arrest warrant for Zlochevsky.[761]

- In January 2017, Burisma announced that all cases against the company and Zlochevsky had been closed.[762]

On these facts, it would have been wholly appropriate for the President to ask President Zelenskyy about the whole Biden-Burisma affair. The Vice President of the United States, while operating under an apparent conflict of interest, had possibly used a billion dollars in U.S. loan guarantees to force the dismissal of a prosecutor who may have been pursuing a legitimate corruption investigation. In fact, on July 22, 2019—just days before the July 25 call—*The Washington Post* reported that the fired prosecutor "said he believes his ouster was because of his interest in [Burisma]" and "[h]ad he remained in his post . . . he would have questioned Hunter Biden."[763] Even if the Vice President's motives were pure, the possibility that a U.S.

"I raised my concern that Hunter Biden's status as a board member could create the perception of a conflict of interest . . . And my concern was that there was the possibility of a perception of a conflict of interest."); Williams-Vindman Public Hearing, *supra* note 589, at 129 (Vindman and Williams agreeing "that Hunter Biden, on the board of Burisma, has the potential for the appearance of a conflict of interest"); Sondland Public Hearing, *supra* note 614, at 171 ("Well, clearly it's an appearance of a conflict."); Hill-Holmes Public Hearing, *supra* note 636, at 89:20–90:3 (Hill affirming that "there are perceived conflict of interest troubles when the child of a government official is involved with something that that government official has an official policy role in"); Taylor Dep. Tr. at 90:3-5 (conceding that a reasonable person could say there are perceived conflicts of interest in Hunter Biden's position on Burisma's board).

[756] Letter from Lindsey O. Graham, Chairman, S. Comm. on Judiciary, to Michael R. Pompeo, Secretary of State, at 1 (Nov. 21, 2019); *see also* Interfax-Ukraine, *Court Seizes Property of Ex-minister Zlochevsky in Ukraine – PGO*, Kyiv Post (Feb. 4, 2016), https://perma.cc/P8RA-TKR6.

[757] John Solomon, *The Ukraine Scandal Timeline Democrats and Their Media Allies Don't Want America to See*, John Solomon Reports (Nov. 20, 2019), https://perma.cc/FC8V-P2AG.

[758] *Foreign Affairs Issue Launch with Former Vice President Joe Biden*, Council on Foreign Relations (Jan. 23, 2018), https://www.cfr.org/event/foreign-affairs-issue-launch-former-vice-president-joe-biden ("[Y]ou're not getting the billion . . . I looked at them and said: I'm leaving in six hours. If the prosecutor is not fired, you're not getting the money.").

[759] Kent Interview Tr. at 94:21-24.

[760] Andrew E. Kramer, *Ukraine Ousts Viktor Shokin, Top Prosecutor, and Political Stability Hangs in the Balance*, N.Y. Times (Mar. 29, 2016), https://perma.cc/J2XH-JUWH.

[761] *The Money Machine: How a High-Profile Corruption Investigation Fell Apart*, *supra* note 740.

[762] *Attorney John Buretta: In the Case of Burisma and Zlochevskiy I Met with Prosecutor General Yury Lutsenko*, Burisma (Feb. 1, 2017), https://burisma-group.com/eng/media/attorney-john-buretta-in-the-case-of-burisma-and-zlochevskiy-i-met-with-prosecutor-general-yury-lutsenko/.

[763] *As Vice President, Biden Said Ukraine Should Increase Gas Production. Then His Son Got a Job with a Ukrainian*

official used his position to derail a meritorious investigation made the Biden-Burisma affair a legitimate subject to raise. Indeed, any President would have wanted to make clear **both** that the United States was not placing any inquiry into the incident off limits **and** that, in the future, there would be no efforts by U.S. officials do something as "horrible" as strong-arming Ukraine into dropping corruption investigations while operating under an obvious conflict of interest.[764]

As the transcript shows, President Zelenskyy recognized precisely the point. He responded to President Trump by noting that "[t]he issue of the investigation of the case is actually the issue of making sure to ***restore the honesty***[.]"[765]

It is absurd for House Democrats to argue that any reference to the Biden-Burisma affair had no purpose other than damaging the President's potential political opponent. The two participants on the call—the leaders of two sovereign nations—clearly understood the discussion to advance the U.S. foreign policy interest in ensuring that Ukraine's new President felt free, in President Zelenskyy's words, to "restore the honesty" to corruption investigations.[766]

Moreover, House Democrats' accusations rest on the false and dangerous premise that Vice President Biden somehow immunized his conduct (and his son's) from any scrutiny by declaring his run for the presidency. There is no such rule of law. It certainly was not a rule applied when President Trump was a candidate. His political opponents called for investigations against him and his children almost daily.[767] Nothing in the law requires the government to turn a blind eye to potential wrongdoing based on a person's status as a candidate for President of the United States. If anything, the possibility that Vice President Biden may ascend to the highest office in the country provides a compelling reason for ensuring that, when he forced Ukraine to fire its Prosecutor General, his family was not corruptly benefitting from his actions.

Importantly, mentioning the whole Biden-Burisma affair would have been entirely justified as long as there was a reasonable basis to think that ***looking into*** the matter would advance the public interest. To defend merely ***asking a question***, the President would not bear any burden of showing that Vice President Biden (or his son) actually committed any wrongdoing.

By contrast, under their own theory of the case, for the House Managers to carry their burden of proving that merely raising the matter was "illegitimate," they would have to prove that raising the issue could have no legitimate purpose whatsoever. Their theory is obviously false. And especially on this record, the House Managers cannot possibly carry that burden, because no such definitive proof exists. Nobody, not even House Democrats' own witnesses, could testify that the Bidens' conduct did not at least facially raise an appearance of a conflict of interest. And while House Democrats repeatedly insist that any suggestions that Vice President Biden or his son

---

Gas Company, *supra* note 573 ("In an email interview with The Post, Shokin [the fired prosecutor] said he believes his ouster was because of his interest in [Burisma]. . . . Had he remained in his post, Shokin said, he would have questioned Hunter Biden.").

[764] July 25 Call Mem., *infra* Appendix A, at 4.

[765] *Id.* (emphasis added).

[766] *Id.*

[767] *See, e.g.*, Louis Nelson, *Sen. Boxer Calls for Probe Into Trump Model Management*, Politico (Sept. 7, 2016), https://perma.cc/8827-CT24; Josh Rogin, *Democrats Ask the FBI to Investigate Trump Advisers' Russia Ties*, Wash. Post (Aug. 30, 2016), https://perma.cc/7HAE-Y2NN.

did anything wrong are "debunked conspiracy theories" and "without merit,"[768] they lack any *evidence* to support those bald assertions, because they have steadfastly cut off any real inquiry into the Bidens' conduct. For example, they have refused to call Hunter Biden to testify.[769] Instead, they have been adamant that Americans must simply accept the diktat that the Bidens' conduct could not possibly have been part of a course of conduct in which the Office of the Vice President was misused to protect the financial interests of a family member.

The Senate cannot accept House Democrats' mere say-so as proof. Especially in the context of this wholly partisan impeachment, House Democrats' assurance of, "trust us, there's nothing to see here," is not a permissible foundation for building a case to remove a duly elected President from office—especially given Chairman Schiff's track record for making false claims in order to damage the President.[770]

IV. The Articles Are Structurally Deficient and Can Only Result in Acquittal.

The Articles also suffer from a fatal structural defect. Put simply, the articles are impermissibly duplicitous—that is, each article charges multiple different acts as possible grounds for sustaining a conviction.[771] The problem with an article offering such a menu of options is that the Constitution requires two-thirds of Senators present to agree *on the specific basis for conviction*. A vote on a duplicitous article, however, could never provide certainty that a two-thirds majority had actually agreed upon a ground for conviction. Instead, such a vote could be the product of an amalgamation of votes resting on several different theories, no single one of which would have garnered two-thirds support if it had been presented separately. Accordingly, duplicitous articles like those exhibited here are facially unconstitutional.

A. The Constitution Requires Two-Thirds of Senators To Agree on the Specific Act that Is the Basis for Conviction and Thus Prohibits Duplicitous Articles.

In impeachment trials, the Constitution mandates that "no Person shall be convicted without the Concurrence of two thirds of the Members present."[772] That provision requires two-thirds agreement on the specific act that warrants conviction. That is why the Senate has repeatedly made clear in prior impeachments that acquittal is required when duplicitous articles are presented.

In the Clinton impeachment,[773] for example, Senator Carl Levin explained his vote to

---

[768] HPSCI Report at 29–30, 38.

[769] *See* Letter from Devin Nunes, Ranking Member, H.R. Permanent Select Comm. on Intelligence, to Adam Schiff, Chairman, House Permanent Select Comm. on Intelligence (Nov. 9, 2019); Letter from Doug Collins, Ranking Member, H.R. Comm. on Judiciary, to Jerrold Nadler, Chairman, H.R. Comm. on Judiciary (Dec. 6, 2019).

[770] *See, e.g.*, Madeline Conway, *Schiff: There is Now 'More Than Circumstantial Evidence' of Trump-Russia Collusion*, Politico (Mar. 22, 2017), https://perma.cc/U9R4-MQVS.

[771] "'Duplicity' is the joining of two or more distinct and separate offenses in a single count"; "'[m]ultiplicity' is charging a single offense in several counts." 1A Charles Alan Wright et al., *Federal Practice and Procedure* § 142 (4th ed. 2019); *see, e.g., United States v. Root*, 585 F.3d 145, 150 (3d Cir. 2009); *United States v. Chrane*, 529 F.2d 1236, 1237 n.3 (5th Cir. 1976).

[772] U.S. Const. art. I, § 3, cl. 6.

[773] President Clinton was charged in one article of providing perjurious, false and misleading testimony on any "one or more" of four topics and in another article of obstruction through "one or more" of seven discrete "acts" that involved different behavior in different months with different persons. H.R. Res. 611, 105th Cong. (Dec. 19, 1998); *see Proceedings of the U.S. Senate in the Impeachment Trial of President William Jefferson Clinton*, 106th Cong., vol. I at 472–75 (1999) (*Clinton Senate Trial*) (Trial Mem. of President Clinton).

acquit by pointing out that the House had "made a significant and irreparable mistake in the actual drafting of the articles."[774] Because each article alleged multiple acts of wrongdoing, it would be "impossible" ever to determine "whether a two-thirds majority of the Senate actually agreed on a particular allegation."[775] Senator Charles Robb echoed those concerns, explaining that "the unconstitutional bundling of charges" in these articles "violates this constitutional requirement" of two-thirds agreement to convict.[776] As he pointed out, because Article II, in particular, "contain[ed] 7 subparts each alleging a separate act of obstruction of justice, the bundling of these allegations would allow removal of the President if only 10 Senators agreed on each of the 7 separate subparts."[777] Senator Chris Dodd agreed, explaining that "[t]his smorgasbord approach to the allegations" was a threshold legal flaw that even called for dismissal outright and pointed to the "deeply troubling prospect" of "convict[ing] and remov[ing] without two-thirds of the Senate agreeing on precisely what [the President] did wrong."[778]

The Senate similarly rejected a duplicitous article against President Andrew Johnson. That article alleged that Johnson had declared in a speech that the Thirty-Ninth Congress was not lawful and that he committed three different acts in pursuit of that declaration.[779] In opposing the article, Senator John Henderson emphasized "the great difficulty" presented by the omnibus article in ascertaining "what it really charges."[780] Senator Garrett Davis similarly complained that the allegations were apparently "drawn with studied looseness, duplicity, and vagueness, as with the purpose to mislead" and should have "been separately" and "distinctly stated."[781]

The Senate has also rejected unconstitutionally duplicitous articles of impeachment against judges. In the impeachment of Judge Nixon, for example, Senator Frank Murkowski rejected the "the omnibus nature of article III," which charged the judge with making multiple different false statements, and he "agree[d] with the argument that the article could easily be used to convict Judge Nixon by less than the super majority vote required by the Constitution."[782] Senator Herbert Kohl explained why this defect was fatal: "The House is telling us that it's OK to convict Judge Nixon on [the article] even if we have different visions of what he did wrong. But that's not fair to Judge Nixon, to the Senate, or to the American people."[783]

---

[774] *Id.*, vol. IV at 2745 (statement of Sen. Carl Levin).

[775] *Id.*

[776] *Id.* at 2655 (statement of Sen. Charles Robb).

[777] *Id.*

[778] *Id.*, vol. II at 1875–76 (statement of Sen. Chris Dodd).

[779] *Proceedings in the Trial of Andrew Johnson, President of the United States, Before the U.S. Senate, on Articles of Impeachment*, 40th Cong. 6 (1868).

[780] *Id.* at 1073–75 (statement of Sen. John Henderson).

[781] *Id.* at 912 (statement of Sen. Garrett Davis).

[782] *Proceedings of the U.S. Senate in the Impeachment Trial of Walter L. Nixon, Jr., a Judge of the U.S. District Court for the Southern District of Mississippi*, 101st Cong., 1st Sess. 464 (1989) (*Judge Nixon Senate Trial*) (statement of Sen. Frank Murkowski); H.R. Rep. No. 101-36, 101st Cong. 656 (1989).

[783] *Judge Nixon Senate Trial, supra* note 782, at 449 (statement of Sen. Herbert Kohl). The Senate similarly refused to convict Judge Louderback on an omnibus article. In that case, Senator Josiah Bailey asserted that the article "ought not to have been considered" at all. *Proceedings of the U.S. Senate in the Trial of Impeachment of Harold Louderback, U.S. District Judge for the Northern District of California*, 73d Cong., 839–40 (1933) (statement of Sen. Josiah Bailey).
Although the Senate has convicted a few lower court judges on duplicitous articles, those convictions provide no precedent to follow here. *First*, no duplicity objection appears to have been timely raised in those cases before the votes on conviction, and thus the Senate never squarely faced and decided the issue. *See, e.g.*, 80 Cong. Rec. 5606

B.   The Articles Are Unconstitutionally Duplicitous.

Here, each Article is impermissibly duplicitous. Each Article presents a smorgasbord of multiple, independent acts as possible bases for conviction. Under the umbrella charge of "abuse of power," Article I offers Senators a menu of at least four different bases for conviction: (1) "corruptly" requesting that Ukraine announce an investigation into the Biden-Burisma affair; (2) "corruptly" requesting that Ukraine announce an investigation into alleged Ukrainian interference in the 2016 election; (3) "corrupt[ly]" conditioning the release of Ukraine's security assistance on these investigations; and (4) "corrupt[ly]" conditioning a White House meeting on these investigations.[784] Article II similarly invites Senators to pick and choose among at least 10 different bases for obstruction including: (1) directing the White House and agencies, "without lawful cause or excuse," not to produce documents in response to a congressional subpoena; or (2) directing one or more of nine different individuals, "without lawful cause or excuse," not to testify in response to a congressional subpoena.[785]

As a result, the Articles invite the danger of an unconstitutional conviction if less than two-thirds of Senators agree that any particular act was an abuse of power or obstruction. With at least four independent bases alleged for abuse of power, Article I invites conviction if as few as 18 Senators agree that any one alleged act occurred and constituted an abuse of power.

The deficiency in the articles cannot be remedied by dividing the articles, because that is prohibited.[786] The only constitutional option is to reject the articles and acquit the President.

CONCLUSION

The Articles of Impeachment presented by House Democrats are constitutionally deficient on their face. The theories underpinning them would do lasting damage to the separation of powers under the Constitution and to our structure of government. The Articles are also the product of an unprecedented and unconstitutional process that denied the President every basic right guaranteed by the Due Process Clause and fundamental principles of fairness. These Articles reflect nothing more than the "persecution of an intemperate or designing majority in the House of Representatives"[787] that the Framers warned against. The Senate should reject the Articles of Impeachment and acquit the President immediately.

(1936) (parliamentary inquiry based on duplicity raised only by a Senator after Judge Ritter was convicted).

Second, far from being examples to follow, these judges' convictions only illustrate the constitutional danger of umbrella charges, which allow the form of the articles chosen by the House, rather than actual guilt or innocence, to determine conviction. Judge Ritter, for example, was charged with discrete impeachable acts in separate articles, with a catch-all article combining all of the prior articles tacked on. He was acquitted on each separate article, but convicted on the catch-all article that amounted to a charge of "general misbehavior." *Id.* at 5202–06.

Third, that the Senate may have convicted a few lower court judges on duplicitous articles is hardly precedent to be followed in a presidential impeachment. *See supra* Standards Part B.3.

[784]   H.R. Res. 755 art. I.

[785]   H.R. Res. 755 art. II.

[786]   *Rules of Procedure and Practice in the Senate when Sitting on Impeachment Trials*, Rule XXIII ("An article of impeachment shall not be divisible for the purpose of voting thereon at any time during the trial."). The committee report accompanying this rule made clear that the "more familiar" practice was to "embod[y] an impeachable offense in an individual article" rather than relying on broad, potentially duplicitous articles. *Amending the Rules of Procedure and Practice in the Senate When Sitting on Impeachment Trials*, Report of the Comm. on Rules and Admin., S. Rep. No. 99-401, 99th Cong., 8 (1986).

[787]   The Federalist No. 65, at 400 (Alexander Hamilton) (Clinton Rossiter ed., 1961).

Respectfully submitted,

/s/ Jay Alan Sekulow

Jay Alan Sekulow
Counsel to President Donald J. Trump
Washington, D.C.

/s/ Pat A. Cipollone

Pat A. Cipollone
Counsel to the President
The White House

January 20, 2020

APPENDIX A:

MEMORANDUM OF JULY 25, 2019 TELEPHONE CONVERSATION BETWEEN PRESIDENT TRUMP AND PRESIDENT ZELENSKYY

Declassified by order of the President

September 24, 2019

EYES ONLY

DO NOT COPY

MEMORANDUM OF TELEPHONE CONVERSATION

SUBJECT: (C) Telephone Conversation with President
                Zelenskyy of Ukraine

PARTICIPANTS: President Zelenskyy of Ukraine

                Notetakers: The White House Situation Room

DATE, TIME   July 25, 2019, 9:03 - 9:33 a.m. EDT
AND PLACE: Residence

(S/NF) The President: Congratulations on a great victory. We all
watched from the United States and you did a terrific job. The
way you came from behind, somebody who wasn't given much of a
chance, and you ended up winning easily. It's a fantastic
achievement. Congratulations.

(S/NF) President Zelenskyy: You are absolutely right Mr.
President. We did win big and we worked hard for this. We worked
a lot but I would like to confess to you that I had an
opportunity to learn from you. We used quite a few of your
skills and knowledge and were able to use it as an example for
our elections and yes it is true that these were unique
elections. We were in a unique situation that we were able to

CAUTION: A Memorandum of a Telephone Conversation (TELCON) is not a verbatim transcript of a
discussion. The text in this document records the notes and recollections of Situation Room Duty
Officers and NSC policy staff assigned to listen and memorialize the conversation in written form
as the conversation takes place. A number of factors can affect the accuracy of the record,
including poor telecommunications connections and variations in accent and/or interpretation.
The word "inaudible" is used to indicate portions of a conversation that the notetaker was unable
to hear.

Classified By: 2354726
Derived From: NSC SCG
Declassify On: 20441231

achieve a unique success. I'm able to tell you the following; the first time, you called me to congratulate me when I won my presidential election, and the second time you are now calling me when my party won the parliamentary election. I think I should run more often so you can call me more often and we can talk over the phone more often.

(S/NF) The President: [laughter] That's a very good idea. I think your country is very happy about that.

(S/NF) President Zelenskyy: Well yes, to tell you the truth, we are trying to work hard because we wanted to drain the swamp here in our country. We brought in many many new people. Not the old politicians, not the typical politicians, because we want to have a new format and a new type of government. You are a great teacher for us and in that.

(S/NF) The President: Well it's very nice of you to say that. I will say that we do a lot for Ukraine. We spend a lot of effort and a lot of time. Much more than the European countries are doing and they should be helping you more than they are. Germany does almost nothing for you. All they do is talk and I think it's something that you should really ask them about. When I was speaking to Angela Merkel she talks Ukraine, but she doesn't do anything. A lot of the European countries are the same way so I think it's something you want to look at but the United States has been very very good to Ukraine. I wouldn't say that it's reciprocal necessarily because things are happening that are not good but the United States has been very very good to Ukraine.

(S/NF) President Zelenskyy: Yes you are absolutely right. Not only 100%, but actually 1000% and I can tell you the following; I did talk to Angela Merkel and I did meet with her. I also met and talked with Macron and I told them that they are not doing quite as much as they need to be doing on the issues with the sanctions. They are not enforcing the sanctions. They are not working as much as they should work for Ukraine. It turns out that even though logically, the European Union should be our biggest partner but technically the United States is a much bigger partner than the European Union and I'm very grateful to you for that because the United States is doing quite a lot for Ukraine. Much more than the European Union especially when we are talking about sanctions against the Russian Federation. I would also like to thank you for your great support in the area of defense. We are ready to continue to cooperate for the next steps specifically we are almost ready to buy more Javelins from the United States for defense purposes.

(S/NF) The President: I would like you to do us a favor though because our country has been through a lot and Ukraine knows a lot about it. I would like you to find out what happened with this whole situation with Ukraine, they say Crowdstrike… I guess you have one of your wealthy people… The server, they say Ukraine has it. There are a lot of things that went on, the whole situation. I think you're surrounding yourself with some of the same people. I would like to have the Attorney General call you or your people and I would like you to get to the bottom of it. As you saw yesterday, that whole nonsense ended with a very poor performance by a man named Robert Mueller, an incompetent performance, but they say a lot of it started with Ukraine. Whatever you can do, it's very important that you do it if that's possible.

(S/NF) President Zelenskyy: Yes it is very important for me and everything that you just mentioned earlier. For me as a President, it is very important and we are open for any future cooperation. We are ready to open a new page on cooperation in relations between the United States and Ukraine. For that purpose, I just recalled our ambassador from United States and he will be replaced by a very competent and very experienced ambassador who will work hard on making sure that our two nations are getting closer. I would also like and hope to see him having your trust and your confidence and have personal relations with you so we can cooperate even more so. I will personally tell you that one of my assistants spoke with Mr. Giuliani just recently and we are hoping very much that Mr. Giuliani will be able to travel to Ukraine and we will meet once he comes to Ukraine. I just wanted to assure you once again that you have nobody but friends around us. I will make sure that I surround myself with the best and most experienced people. I also wanted to tell you that we are friends. We are great friends and you Mr. President have friends in our country so we can continue our strategic partnership. I also plan to surround myself with great people and in addition to that investigation, I guarantee as the President of Ukraine that all the investigations will be done openly and candidly. That I can assure you.

(S/NF) The President: Good because I heard you had a prosecutor who was very good and he was shut down and that's really unfair. A lot of people are talking about that, the way they shut your very good prosecutor down and you had some very bad people involved. Mr. Giuliani is a highly respected man. He was the mayor of New York City, a great mayor, and I would like him to

call you. I will ask him to call you along with the Attorney
General. Rudy very much knows what's happening and he is a very
capable guy. If you could speak to him that would be great. The
former ambassador from the United States, the woman, was bad
news and the people she was dealing with in the Ukraine were bad
news so I just want to let you know that. The other thing,
There's a lot of talk about Biden's son, that Biden stopped the
prosecution and a lot of people want to find out about that so
whatever you can do with the Attorney General would be great.
Biden went around bragging that he stopped the prosecution so if
you can look into it... It sounds horrible to me.

(S/NF) President Zelenskyy: I wanted to tell you about the
prosecutor. First of all I understand and I'm knowledgeable
about the situation. Since we have won the absolute majority in
our Parliament, the next prosecutor general will be 100% my
person, my candidate, who will be approved by the parliament and
will start as a new prosecutor in September. He or she will look
into the situation, specifically to the company that you
mentioned in this issue. The issue of the investigation of the
case is actually the issue of making sure to restore the honesty
so we will take care of that and will work on the investigation
of the case. On top of that, I would kindly ask you if you have
any additional information that you can provide to us, it would
be very helpful for the investigation to make sure that we
administer justice in our country with regard to the Ambassador
to the United States from Ukraine as far as I recall her name
was Ivanovich. It was great that you were the first one who told
me that she was a bad ambassador because I agree with you 100%.
Her attitude towards me was far from the best as she admired the
previous President and she was on his side. She would not accept
me as a new President well enough.

(S/NF) The President: Well, she's going to go through some
things. I will have Mr. Giuliani give you a call and I am also
going to have Attorney General Barr call and we will get to the
bottom of it. I'm sure you will figure it out. I heard the
prosecutor was treated very badly and he was a very fair
prosecutor so good luck with everything. Your economy is going
to get better and better I predict. You have a lot of assets.
It's a great country. I have many Ukrainian friends, their
incredible people.

(S/NF) President Zelenskyy: I would like to tell you that I also
have quite a few Ukrainian friends that live in the United
States. Actually last time I traveled to the United States, I
stayed in New York near Central Park and I stayed at the Trump

Tower. I will talk to them and I hope to see them again in the future. I also wanted to thank you for your invitation to visit the United States, specifically Washington DC. On the other hand, I also want to ensure you that we will be very serious about the case and will work on the investigation. As to the economy, there is much potential for our two countries and one of the issues that is very important for Ukraine is energy independence. I believe we can be very successful and cooperating on energy independence with United States. We are already working on cooperation. We are buying American oil but I am very hopeful for a future meeting. We will have more time and more opportunities to discuss these opportunities and get to know each other better. I would like to thank you very much for your support

~~(S/NF)~~ The President: Good. Well, thank you very much and I appreciate that. I will tell Rudy and Attorney General Barr to call. Thank you. Whenever you would like to come to the White House, feel free to call. Give us a date and we'll work that out. I look forward to seeing you.

~~(S/NF)~~ President Zelenskyy: Thank you very much. I would be very happy to come and would be happy to meet with you personally and get to know you better. I am looking forward to our meeting and I also would like to invite you to visit Ukraine and come to the city of Kyiv which is a beautiful city. We have a beautiful country which would welcome you. On the other hand, I believe that on September 1 we will be in Poland and we can meet in Poland hopefully. After that, it might be a very good idea for you to travel to Ukraine. We can either take my plane and go to Ukraine or we can take your plane, which is probably much better than mine.

~~(S/NF)~~ The President: Okay, we can work that out. I look forward to seeing you in Washington and maybe in Poland because I think we are going to be there at that time.

~~(S/NF)~~ President Zelenskyy: Thank you very much Mr. President.

~~(S/NF)~~ The President: Congratulations on a fantastic job you've done. The whole world was watching. I'm not sure it was so much of an upset but congratulations.

~~(S/NF)~~ President Zelenskyy: Thank you Mr. President bye-bye.

-- End of Conversation --

APPENDIX B:

UNAUTHORIZED SUBPOENAS PURPORTEDLY ISSUED PURSUANT TO THE HOUSE'S IMPEACHMENT POWER BEFORE HOUSE RESOLUTION 660

1. Subpoena from Eliot L. Engel to Michael R. Pompeo, Secretary of State (Sept. 27, 2019)
2. Subpoena from Adam B. Schiff to Rudy Giuliani (Nov. 30, 2019)
3. Subpoena from Elijah E. Cummings to John Michael Mulvaney, Acting White House Chief of Staff (Oct. 4, 2019)
4. Subpoena from Adam B. Schiff to Mark T. Esper, Secretary of Defense (Oct. 7, 2019)
5. Subpoena from Adam B. Schiff to Russell T. Vought, Acting Director of OMB (Oct. 7, 2019)
6. Subpoena from Adam B. Schiff to Gordon Sondland, U.S. Ambassador to the European Union (Oct. 8, 2019)
7. Subpoena from Adam B. Schiff to Igor Fruman (Oct. 10, 2019)
8. Subpoena from Adam B. Schiff to Lev Parnas (Oct. 10, 2019)
9. Subpoena from Adam B. Schiff to James Richard Perry, Secretary of Energy (Oct. 10, 2019)
10. Subpoena from Adam B. Schiff to Marie Yovanovitch, former U.S. Ambassador to Ukraine (Oct. 11, 2019)
11. Subpoena from Adam B. Schiff to Fiona Hill, former Senior Director for Russian and European Affairs, National Security Council (Oct. 14, 2019)
12. Subpoena from Adam B. Schiff to George Kent, Deputy Assistant Secretary of State for European and Eurasian Affairs (Oct. 15, 2019)
13. Subpoena from Adam B. Schiff to Dr. Charles Kupperman, former Deputy National Security Advisor (Oct. 21, 2019)
14. Subpoena from Adam B. Schiff to William B. Taylor, Jr., Acting U.S. Ambassador to Ukraine (Oct. 21, 2019)
15. Subpoena from Adam B. Schiff to Laura K. Cooper, Deputy Assistant Secretary of Defense for Russia (Oct. 23, 2019)
16. Subpoena from Adam B. Schiff to Michael Duffey, Associate Director of National Security Programs, OMB (Oct. 24, 2019)
17. Subpoena from Adam B. Schiff to Russell T. Vought, Acting Director of OMB (Oct. 24, 2019)
18. Subpoena from Peter DeFazio to Emily W. Murphy, Administrator of General Services Administration (Oct. 24, 2019)
19. Subpoena from Adam B. Schiff to Ulrich Brechbuhl, Counselor to Secretary of State (Oct. 25, 2019)
20. Subpoena from Adam B. Schiff to Philip Reeker, Acting Assistant Secretary of State of European and Eurasian Affairs (Oct. 26, 2019)
21. Subpoena from Adam B. Schiff to Alexander S. Vindman, Director for European Affairs, National Security Council (Oct. 29, 2019)
22. Subpoena from Adam B. Schiff to Catherine Croft, Special Adviser for Ukraine Negotiations, Department of State (Oct. 30, 2019)
23. Subpoena from Adam B. Schiff to Christopher Anderson, former Special Advisor for Ukraine Negotiations, Department of State (Oct. 30, 2019)

APPENDIX C:

**OFFICE OF LEGAL COUNSEL, MEMORANDUM OPINION
RE: HOUSE COMMITTEES' AUTHORITY TO INVESTIGATE
FOR IMPEACHMENT (JAN. 19, 2019)**

Office of the Assistant Attorney General   *Washington, D.C. 20530*

January 19, 2020

MEMORANDUM FOR PAT A. CIPOLLONE
COUNSEL TO THE PRESIDENT

Re: House Committees' Authority to Investigate for Impeachment

On September 24, 2019, Speaker of the House Nancy Pelosi "announc[ed]" at a press conference that "the House of Representatives is moving forward with an official impeachment inquiry" into the President's actions and that she was "directing . . . six Committees to proceed with" several previously pending "investigations under that umbrella of impeachment inquiry."[1] Shortly thereafter, the House Committee on Foreign Affairs issued a subpoena directing the Secretary of State to produce a series of documents related to the recent conduct of diplomacy between the United States and Ukraine. *See* Subpoena of the Committee on Foreign Affairs (Sept. 27, 2019). In an accompanying letter, three committee chairmen stated that their committees jointly sought these documents, not in connection with legislative oversight, but "[p]ursuant to the House of Representatives' impeachment inquiry."[2] In the following days, the committees issued subpoenas to the Acting White House Chief of Staff, the Secretary of Defense, the Secretary of Energy, and several others within the Executive Branch.

Upon the issuance of these subpoenas, you asked whether these committees could compel the production of documents and testimony in furtherance of an asserted impeachment inquiry. We advised that the committees lacked such authority because, at the time the subpoenas were issued, the House had not adopted any resolution authorizing the committees to conduct an impeachment inquiry. The Constitution vests the "sole Power of Impeachment" in the House of Representatives. U.S. Const. art. I, § 2, cl. 5. For precisely that reason, the House itself must authorize an impeachment inquiry, as it has done in virtually every prior impeachment investigation in our Nation's history, including every one involving a President. A congressional committee's "right to exact testimony and to call for the production of documents" is limited by the "controlling charter" the committee has received from the House. *United States v. Rumely*, 345 U.S. 41, 44 (1953). Yet the House, by its rules, has authorized its committees to issue subpoenas only for matters within their *legislative* jurisdiction. Accordingly, no committee may undertake the momentous move from legislative oversight to impeachment without a delegation by the full House of such authority.

---

[1] Nancy Pelosi, Speaker of the House, *Press Release: Pelosi Remarks Announcing Impeachment Inquiry* (Sept. 24, 2019), www.speaker.gov/newsroom/92419-0 ("Pelosi Press Release").

[2] Letter for Michael R. Pompeo, Secretary of State, from Eliot L. Engel, Chairman, Committee on Foreign Affairs, U.S. House of Representatives, Adam Schiff, Chairman, Permanent Select Committee on Intelligence, U.S. House of Representatives, and Elijah E. Cummings, Chairman, Committee on Oversight & Reform, U.S. House of Representatives at 1 (Sept. 27, 2019) ("Three Chairmen's Letter").

We are not the first to reach this conclusion. This was the position of the House in the impeachments of Presidents Nixon and Clinton. In the case of President Nixon, following a preliminary inquiry, the House adopted a formal resolution as a "necessary step" to confer the "investigative powers" of the House "to their full extent" upon the Judiciary Committee. 120 Cong. Rec. 2350–51 (1974) (statement of Rep. Rodino); *see* H.R. Res. 803, 93d Cong. (1974). As the House Parliamentarian explained, it had been "considered necessary for the House to specifically vest the Committee on the Judiciary with the investigatory and subpena power to conduct the impeachment investigation." 3 Lewis Deschler, *Deschler's Precedents of the United States House of Representatives* ch. 14, § 15.2, at 2172 (1994) (Parliamentarian's Note).[3] The House followed the same course in the impeachment of President Clinton. After reviewing the Independent Counsel's referral, the Judiciary Committee "decided that it must receive authorization from the full House before proceeding on any further course of action." H.R. Rep. No. 105-795, at 24 (1998). The House again adopted a resolution authorizing the committee to issue compulsory process in support of an impeachment investigation. *See* H.R. Res. 581, 105th Cong. (1998). As Representative John Conyers summarized in 2016: "According to parliamentarians of the House past and present, the impeachment process does not begin until the House actually votes to authorize [a] Committee to investigate the charges."[4]

In marked contrast with these historical precedents, in the weeks after the Speaker's announcement, House committees issued subpoenas without any House vote authorizing them to exercise the House's authority under the Impeachment Clause. The three committees justified the subpoenas based upon the Rules of the House, which authorize subpoenas for matters within a committee's jurisdiction. But the Rules assign only "legislative jurisdiction[]" and "oversight responsibilities" to the committees. H.R. Rules, 116th Cong., Rule X, cl. 1 (Jan. 11, 2019) ("Committees and their legislative jurisdictions"), cl. 2 ("General oversight responsibilities"); *see also* H.R. Rule X, cls. 3(m), 11. The House's legislative power is distinct from its impeachment power. *Compare* U.S. Const. art. I, § 1, *with id.* art. I, § 2, cl. 5. Although committees had that same delegation during the Clinton impeachment and a materially similar one during the Nixon impeachment, the House determined on both occasions that the Judiciary Committee required a resolution to investigate. Speaker Pelosi purported to direct the committees to conduct an "official impeachment inquiry," but the House Rules do not give the Speaker any authority to delegate investigative power. The committees thus had no delegation authorizing them to issue subpoenas pursuant to the House's impeachment power.

In the face of objections to the validity of the committee subpoenas that were expressed by the Administration, by ranking minority members in the House, and by many Senators, among others, on October 31, 2019, the House adopted Resolution 660, which "directed" six committees "to continue their ongoing investigations" as part of the "existing House of Representatives inquiry into whether sufficient grounds exist" to impeach President Trump. H.R. Res. 660, 116th Cong. § 1 (2019). Resolution 660's direction, however, was entirely prospective. The resolution did not purport to ratify any previously issued subpoenas or even

---

[3] Although volume 3 of *Deschler's Precedents* was published in 1979, our citations of *Deschler's Precedents* use the continuously paginated version that is available at www.govinfo.gov/collection/precedents-of-the-house.

[4] *Impeachment Articles Referred on John Koskinen (Part III): Hearing Before the H. Comm. on the Judiciary*, 114th Cong. 3 (2016).

make any mention of them. Accordingly, the pre-October 31 subpoenas, which had not been authorized by the House, continued to lack compulsory force.[5]

I.

Since the start of the 116th Congress, some members of Congress have proposed that the House investigate and impeach President Trump. On January 3, 2019, the first day of the new Congress, Representative Brad Sherman introduced a resolution to impeach "Donald John Trump, President of the United States, for high crimes and misdemeanors." H.R. Res. 13, 116th Cong. (2019). The Sherman resolution called for impeachment based upon the President's firing of the Director of the Federal Bureau of Investigation, James Comey. *See id.* Consistent with settled practice, the resolution was referred to the Judiciary Committee. *See* H.R. Doc. No. 115-177, *Jefferson's Manual* § 605, at 324 (2019).

The Judiciary Committee did not act on the Sherman resolution, but it soon began an oversight investigation into related subjects that were also the focus of a Department of Justice investigation by Special Counsel Robert S. Mueller, III. On March 4, 2019, the committee served document requests on the White House and 80 other agencies, entities, and individuals, "unveil[ing] an investigation . . . into the alleged obstruction of justice, public corruption, and other abuses of power by President Trump, his associates, and members of his Administration."[6] Those document requests did not mention impeachment.

After the Special Counsel finished his investigation, the Judiciary Committee demanded his investigative files, describing its request as an exercise of legislative oversight authority. *See* Letter for William P. Barr, Attorney General, from Jerrold Nadler, Chairman, Committee on the Judiciary, U.S. House of Representatives at 3 (May 3, 2019) (asserting that "[t]he Committee has ample jurisdiction under House Rule X(*l*) to conduct oversight of the Department [of Justice], undertake necessary investigations, and consider legislation regarding the federal obstruction of justice statutes, campaign-related crimes, and special counsel investigations, among other things"). The committee's subsequent letters and public statements likewise described its inquiry as serving a "legislative purpose." *E.g.*, Letter for Pat Cipollone, White House Counsel, from Jerrold Nadler, Chairman, Committee on the Judiciary, U.S. House of Representatives at 3–6 (May 16, 2019) (describing the "legislative purpose of the Committee's investigation" (capitalization altered)).

---

[5] This opinion memorializes the advice we gave about subpoenas issued before October 31. We separately addressed some subpoenas issued after that date. *See, e.g.*, Letter for Pat A. Cipollone, Counsel to the President, from Steven A. Engel, Assistant Attorney General, Office of Legal Counsel (Nov. 7, 2019) (subpoena to Mick Mulvaney); Letter for Pat A. Cipollone, Counsel to the President, from Steven A. Engel, Assistant Attorney General, Office of Legal Counsel (Nov. 3, 2019) (subpoena to John Eisenberg); *Exclusion of Agency Counsel from Congressional Depositions in the Impeachment Context*, 43 Op. O.L.C. __ (Nov. 1, 2019).

[6] U.S. House of Representatives Committee on the Judiciary, *Press Release: House Judiciary Committee Unveils Investigation into Threats Against the Rule of Law* (Mar. 4, 2019), judiciary.house.gov/news/press-releases/ house-judiciary-committee-unveils-investigation-threats-against-rule-law; *see also* Letter for the White House, c/o Pat Cipollone, from Jerrold Nadler, Chairman, Committee on the Judiciary, U.S. House of Representatives (Mar. 4, 2019).

Over time, the Judiciary Committee expanded the description of its investigation to claim that it was considering impeachment. The committee first mentioned impeachment in a May 8, 2019 report recommending that the Attorney General be held in contempt of Congress. In a section entitled "Authority and Legislative Purpose," the committee stated that one purpose of the inquiry was to determine "whether to approve articles of impeachment with respect to the President or any other Administration official." H.R. Rep. No. 116-105, at 12, 13 (2019).[7]

The committee formally claimed to be investigating impeachment when it petitioned the U.S. District Court for the District of Columbia to release grand-jury information related to the Special Counsel's investigation. *See* Application at 1–2, *In re Application of the Comm. on the Judiciary, U.S. House of Reps.*, No. 19-gj-48 (D.D.C. July 26, 2019); *see also* Memorandum for Members of the Committee on the Judiciary from Jerrold Nadler, Chairman, *Re: Lessons from the Mueller Report, Part III: "Constitutional Processes for Addressing Presidential Misconduct"* at 3 (July 11, 2019) (advising that the Committee would seek documents and testimony "to determine whether the Committee should recommend articles of impeachment against the President or any other Article I remedies, and if so, in what form").[8] The committee advanced the same contention when asking the district court to compel testimony before the committee by former White House Counsel Donald McGahn. *See* Compl. for Declaratory and Injunctive Relief ¶ 1, *Comm. on the Judiciary, U.S. House of Reps. v. McGahn*, No. 19-cv-2379 (D.D.C. Aug. 7, 2019) (contending that the Judiciary Committee was "now determining whether to recommend articles of impeachment against the President based on the obstructive conduct described by the Special Counsel").

In connection with this litigation, Chairman Nadler described the committee as conducting "formal impeachment proceedings." David Priess & Margaret Taylor, *What if the House Held Impeachment Proceedings and Nobody Noticed?*, Lawfare (Aug. 12, 2019), www. lawfareblog.com/what-if-house-held-impeachment-proceedings-and-nobody-noticed (chronicling the evolution in Chairman Nadler's descriptions of the investigation). Those assertions coincided with media reports that Chairman Nadler had privately asked Speaker Pelosi to support the opening of an impeachment inquiry. *See, e.g.*, Andrew Desiderio, *Nadler: 'This is Formal Impeachment Proceedings*,' Politico (Aug. 8, 2019), www.politico.com/story/2019/08/ 08/nadler-this-is-formal-impeachment-proceedings-1454360 (noting that Nadler "has privately pushed Speaker Nancy Pelosi to support a formal inquiry of whether to remove the president

---

[7] On June 11, 2019, the full House adopted Resolution 430. Its first two clauses authorized the Judiciary Committee to file a lawsuit to enforce subpoenas against Attorney General William Barr and former White House Counsel Donald McGahn and purported to authorize the Bipartisan Legal Advisory Group to approve future litigation. *See* H.R. Res. 430, 116th Cong. (2019). The next clause of the resolution then stated that, "in connection with any judicial proceeding brought under the first or second resolving clauses, the chair of any standing or permanent select committee exercising authority thereunder has any and all necessary authority under Article I of the Constitution." *Id.* The resolution did not mention "impeachment" and, by its terms, authorized actions only in connection with the litigation authorized "under the first or second resolving clauses." On the same day that the House adopted Resolution 430, Speaker Pelosi stated that the House's Democratic caucus was "not even close" to an impeachment inquiry. *Rep. Nancy Pelosi (D-CA) Continues Resisting Impeachment Inquiry*, CNN (June 11, 2019), transcripts.cnn.com/TRANSCRIPTS/1906/11/cnr.04 html.

[8] While the House has delegated to the Bipartisan Legal Advisory Group the ability to "articulate[] the institutional position of" the House, it has done so only for purposes of "litigation matters." H.R. Rule II, cl. 8(b). Therefore, neither the group, nor the House counsel implementing that group's directions, could assert the House's authority in connection with an impeachment investigation, which is not a litigation matter.

4

from office"). On September 12, the Judiciary Committee approved a resolution describing its investigation as an impeachment inquiry and adopting certain procedures for the investigation. *See* Resolution for Investigative Procedures Offered by Chairman Jerrold Nadler, H. Comm. on the Judiciary, 116th Cong. (Sept. 12, 2019), docs.house.gov/meetings/JU/JU00/20190912/ 109921/BILLS-116pih-ResolutionforInvestigativeProcedures.pdf.

Speaker Pelosi did not endorse the Judiciary Committee's characterization of its investigation during the summer of 2019. But she later purported to announce a formal impeachment inquiry in connection with a separate matter arising out of a complaint filed with the Inspector General of the Intelligence Community. The complaint, cast in the form of an unsigned letter to the congressional intelligence committees, alleged that, in a July 25, 2019 telephone call, the President sought to pressure Ukrainian President Volodymyr Zelenskyy to investigate the prior activities of one of the President's potential political rivals. *See* Letter for Richard Burr, Chairman, Select Committee on Intelligence, U.S. Senate, and Adam Schiff, Chairman, Permanent Select Committee on Intelligence, U.S. House of Representatives at 2–3 (Aug. 12, 2019). After the Inspector General reported the existence of the complaint to the intelligence committees, the President declassified the official record of the July 25 telephone call and the complaint, and they were publicly released on September 25 and 26, respectively.

On September 24, the day before the release of the call record, Speaker Pelosi "announc[ed]" that "the House of Representatives is moving forward with an official impeachment inquiry" and that she was "direct[ing] . . . six [c]ommittees to proceed with their investigations under that umbrella of impeachment inquiry." Pelosi Press Release, *supra* note 1. In an October 8, 2019 court hearing, the House's General Counsel invoked the Speaker's announcement as purportedly conclusive proof that the House had opened an impeachment inquiry. Tr. of Mot. Hrg. at 23, *In re Application of the Comm. on the Judiciary* ("We are in an impeachment inquiry, an impeachment investigation, a formal impeachment investigation because the House says it is. The speaker of the House has specifically said that it is.").

On September 27, Chairman Engel of the Foreign Affairs Committee issued a subpoena to Secretary of State Pompeo "[p]ursuant to the House of Representatives' impeachment inquiry." Three Chairmen's Letter, *supra* note 2, at 1. That subpoena was the first to rely on the newly proclaimed "impeachment inquiry." A number of subpoenas followed, each of which was accompanied by a letter signed by the chairmen of three committees (Foreign Affairs, Oversight and Reform, and the Permanent Select Committee on Intelligence ("HPSCI")). Although the September 27 letter mentioned only the "impeachment inquiry" as a basis for the accompanying subpoena, subsequent letters claimed that other subpoenas were issued both "[p]ursuant to the House of Representatives' impeachment inquiry" and "in exercise of" the committees' "oversight and legislative jurisdiction."[9]

---

[9] *E.g.*, Letter for John Michael Mulvaney, Acting Chief of Staff to the President, from Elijah E. Cummings, Chairman, Committee on Oversight & Reform, U.S. House of Representatives, Adam B. Schiff, Chairman, Permanent Select Committee on Intelligence, U.S. House of Representatives, and Eliot L. Engel, Chairman, Committee on Foreign Affairs, U.S. House of Representatives at 1 (Oct. 4, 2019); Letter for Mark T. Esper, Secretary of Defense, from Adam B. Schiff, Chairman, Permanent Select Committee on Intelligence, U.S. House of Representatives, Eliot L. Engel, Chairman, Committee on Foreign Affairs, U.S. House of Representatives, and Elijah E. Cummings, Chairman, Committee on Oversight & Reform, U.S. House of Representatives at 1 (Oct. 7,

Following service of these subpoenas, you and other officials within the Executive Branch requested our advice with respect to the obligations of the subpoenas' recipients. We advised that the subpoenas were invalid because, among other reasons, the committees lacked the authority to conduct the purported inquiry and, with respect to several testimonial subpoenas, the committees impermissibly sought to exclude agency counsel from scheduled depositions. In reliance upon that advice, you and other responsible officials directed employees within their respective departments and agencies not to provide the documents and testimony requested under those subpoenas.

On October 8, 2019, you sent a letter to Speaker Pelosi and the three chairmen advising them that their purported impeachment inquiry was "constitutionally invalid" because the House had not authorized it.[10] The House Minority Leader, Kevin McCarthy, and the Ranking Member of the Judiciary Committee, Doug Collins, had already made the same objection.[11] Senator Lindsey Graham introduced a resolution in the Senate, co-sponsored by 49 other Senators, which objected to the House's impeachment process because it had not been authorized by the full House and did not provide the President with the procedural protections enjoyed in past impeachment inquiries. S. Res. 378, 116th Cong. (2019).

On October 25, 2019, the U.S. District Court for the District of Columbia granted the Judiciary Committee's request for grand-jury information from the Special Counsel's investigation, holding that the committee was conducting an impeachment inquiry that was "preliminar[y] to . . . a judicial proceeding," for purposes of the exception to grand-jury secrecy in Rule 6(e)(3)(E)(i) of the Federal Rules of Criminal Procedure. *See In re Application of the Comm. on the Judiciary, U.S. House of Reps.*, No. 19-gj-48, 2019 WL 5485221 (D.D.C. Oct. 25, 2019), *stay granted*, No. 19-5288 (D.C. Cir. Oct. 29, 2019), *argued* (D.C. Cir. Jan. 3, 2020). In so holding, the court concluded that the House need not adopt a resolution before a committee may begin an impeachment inquiry. *Id.* at *26–28. As we discuss below, the district court's analysis of this point relied on a misreading of the historical record.

Faced with continuing objections from the Administration and members of Congress to the validity of the impeachment-related subpoenas, the House decided to take a formal vote to authorize the impeachment inquiry. *See* Letter for Democratic Members of the House from Nancy Pelosi, Speaker of the House (Oct. 28, 2019). On October 31, the House adopted a resolution "direct[ing]" several committees "to continue their ongoing investigations as part of the existing House of Representatives inquiry into whether sufficient grounds exist for the House

2019); Letter for Gordon Sondland, U.S. Ambassador to the European Union, from Adam B. Schiff, Chairman, Permanent Select Committee on Intelligence, U.S. House of Representatives, Elijah E. Cummings, Chairman, Committee on Oversight & Reform, U.S. House of Representatives, and Eliot L. Engel, Chairman, Committee on Foreign Affairs, U.S. House of Representatives at 1 (Oct. 8, 2019); Letter for James Richard "Rick" Perry, Secretary of Energy, from Eliot L. Engel, Chairman, Committee on Foreign Affairs, U.S. House of Representatives, Adam B. Schiff, Chairman, Permanent Select Committee on Intelligence, U.S. House of Representatives, and Elijah E. Cummings, Chairman, Committee on Oversight & Reform, U.S. House of Representatives at 1 (Oct. 10, 2019).

[10] Letter for Nancy Pelosi, Speaker, U.S. House of Representatives, et al., from Pat A. Cipollone, Counsel to the President at 2–3 (Oct. 8, 2019).

[11] *See* Letter for Nancy Pelosi, Speaker, U.S. House of Representatives, from Kevin McCarthy, Republican Leader, U.S. House of Representatives at 1 & n.1 (Oct. 3, 2019); Mem. Amicus Curiae of Ranking Member Doug Collins in Support of Denial at 5–21, *In re Application of the Comm. on the Judiciary* (D.D.C. Oct. 3, 2019).

of Representatives to exercise its Constitutional power to impeach Donald John Trump, President of the United States of America." Resolution 660, § 1. The resolution also adopted special procedures for impeachment proceedings before HPSCI and the Judiciary Committee.

II.

The Constitution vests in the House of Representatives a share of Congress's legislative power and, separately, "the sole Power of Impeachment." U.S. Const. art. I, § 1; *id.* art. I, § 2, cl. 5. Both the legislative power and the impeachment power include an implied authority to investigate, including by means of compulsory process. But those investigative powers are not interchangeable. The House has broadly delegated to committees its power to investigate for legislative purposes, but it has held impeachment authority more closely, granting authority to conduct particular impeachment investigations only as the need has arisen. The House has followed that approach from the very first impeachment inquiry through dozens more that have followed over the past 200 years, including every inquiry involving a President.

In so doing, the House has recognized the fundamental difference between a legislative oversight investigation and an impeachment investigation. The House does more than simply pick a label when it "debate[s] and decide[s] when it wishes to shift from legislating to impeaching" and to authorize a committee to take responsibility for "the grave and weighty process of impeachment." *Trump v. Mazars USA, LLP*, 940 F.3d 710, 737, 738 (D.C. Cir. 2019), *cert. granted*, No. 19-715 (Dec. 13, 2019); *see also id.* at 757 (Rao, J., dissenting) (recognizing that "the Constitution forces the House to take accountability for its actions when investigating the President's misconduct"). Because a legislative investigation seeks "information respecting the conditions which the legislation is intended to affect or change," *McGrain v. Daugherty*, 273 U.S. 135, 175 (1927), "legislative judgments normally depend more on the predicted consequences of proposed legislative actions and their political acceptability, than on precise reconstruction of past events," *Senate Select Comm. on Presidential Campaign Activities v. Nixon*, 498 F.2d 725, 732 (D.C. Cir. 1974) (en banc). By contrast, an impeachment inquiry must evaluate whether a civil officer did, or did not, commit treason, bribery, or another high crime or misdemeanor, U.S. Const. art. II, § 4, and it is more likely than a legislative oversight investigation to call for the reconstruction of past events.

Thus, the House has traditionally marked the shift to an impeachment inquiry by adopting a resolution that authorizes a committee to investigate through court-like procedures differing significantly from those used in routine oversight. *See, e.g., Jefferson's Manual* § 606, at 324 (recognizing that, in modern practice, "the sentiment of committees has been in favor of permitting the accused to explain, present witnesses, cross-examine, and be represented by counsel" (citations omitted)); *see also* Cong. Research Serv., R45983, *Congressional Access to Information in an Impeachment Investigation* 15 (Oct. 25, 2019) ("[D]uring both the Nixon and Clinton impeachment investigations, the House Judiciary Committee adopted resolutions affording the President and his counsel the right to respond to evidence gathered by the committee, raise objections to testimony, and cross-examine witnesses[.]").[12] A House

---

[12] The House Judiciary Committee permitted President Nixon's counsel to submit and respond to evidence, to request to call witnesses, to attend hearings and examinations, to object to the examination of witnesses and the admissibility of testimony, and to question witnesses. *See* H.R. Rep. No. 93-1305, at 8–9 (1974); 3 *Deschler's*

resolution authorizing the opening of an impeachment inquiry plays a highly significant role in directing the scope and nature of the constitutional inquest that follows.

Such a resolution does not just reflect traditional practice. It is a constitutionally required step before a committee may exercise compulsory process in aid of the House's "sole Power of Impeachment." U.S. Const. art. I, § 2, cl. 5. In this Part, we explain the basis for this conclusion. First, we address the constitutional distinction between the House's power to investigate for legislative purposes and for impeachment purposes. We next explain why an impeachment inquiry must be authorized by the House itself. Finally, we review the historical record, which confirms, across dozens of examples, that the House must specifically authorize committees to conduct impeachment investigations and to issue compulsory process.

A.

The Constitution vests several different powers in the House of Representatives. As one half of Congress, the House shares with the Senate the "legislative Powers" granted in the Constitution (U.S. Const. art. I, § 1), which include the ability to pass bills (*id.* art. I, § 7, cl. 2) and to override presidential vetoes (*id.* art. I, § 7, cl. 3) in the process of enacting laws pursuant to Congress's enumerated legislative powers (*e.g.*, *id.* art. I, § 8), including the power to appropriate federal funds (*id.* art. I, § 9, cl. 7). But the House has other, non-legislative powers. It is, for instance, "the Judge of the Elections, Returns and Qualifications of its own Members." *Id.* art. I, § 5, cl. 1. And it has "the sole Power of Impeachment." *Id.* art. I, § 2, cl. 5.

The House and Senate do not act in a legislative role in connection with impeachment. The Constitution vests the House with the authority to accuse civil officers of "Treason, Bribery, or other high Crimes and Misdemeanors" that warrant removal and disqualification from office. U.S. Const. art. I, § 2, cl. 5; *id.* art. I, § 3, cl. 7; *id.* art. II, § 4. As Alexander Hamilton explained, the members of the House act as "the inquisitors for the nation." *The Federalist* No. 65, at 440 (Jacob E. Cooke ed., 1961). And Senators, in turn, act "in their judicial character as a court for the trial of impeachments." *Id.* at 439; *see also The Federalist* No. 66, at 445–46 (defending the "partial intermixture" in the impeachment context of usually separated powers as "not only proper, but necessary to the mutual defense of the several members of the government, against each other"; noting that dividing "the right of accusing" from "the right of judging" between "the two branches of the legislature . . . avoids the inconvenience of making the same persons both

---

Precedents ch. 14, § 6.5, at 2045–47. Later, President Clinton and his counsel were similarly "invited to attend all executive session and open committee hearings," at which they were permitted to "cross examine witnesses," "make objections regarding the pertinency of evidence," "suggest that the Committee receive additional evidence," and "respond to the evidence adduced by the Committee." H.R. Rep. No. 105-795, at 25–26; *see also* 18 *Deschler's Precedents* app. at 549 (2013) (noting that, during the Clinton impeachment investigation, the House made a "deliberate attempt to mirror [the] documented precedents and proceedings" of the Nixon investigation). In a departure from the Nixon and Clinton precedents, the House committees did not provide President Trump with any right to attend, participate in, or cross-examine witnesses in connection with the impeachment-related depositions conducted by the three committees before October 31. Resolution 660 similarly did not provide any such rights with respect to any of the public hearings conducted by HPSCI, limiting the President's opportunity to participate to the Judiciary Committee, which did not itself participate in developing the investigative record upon which the articles of impeachment were premised. *See* H.R. Res. 660, 116th Cong. § 4(a); 165 Cong. Rec. E1357 (daily ed. Oct. 29, 2019) ("Impeachment Inquiry Procedures in the Committee on the Judiciary").

accusers and judges"). The House's impeachment authority differs fundamentally in character from its legislative power.

With respect to both its legislative and its impeachment powers, the House has corresponding powers of investigation, which enable it to collect the information necessary for the exercise of those powers. The Supreme Court has explained that "[t]he power of inquiry— with process to enforce it—is an essential and appropriate auxiliary to the legislative function." *McGrain*, 273 U.S. at 174. Thus, in the legislative context, the House's investigative power "encompasses inquiries concerning the administration of existing laws as well as proposed or possibly needed statutes." *Watkins v. United States*, 354 U.S. 178, 187 (1957); *see also Scope of Congressional Oversight and Investigative Power with Respect to the Executive Branch*, 9 Op. O.L.C. 60, 60 (1985) ("Congress may conduct investigations in order to obtain facts pertinent to possible legislation and in order to evaluate the effectiveness of current laws."). The Court has further recognized that the House also has implied powers to investigate in support of its other powers, including its power of impeachment. *See, e.g., Kilbourn v. Thompson*, 103 U.S. 168, 190 (1880); *see also In re Request for Access to Grand Jury Materials*, 833 F.2d 1438, 1445 (11th Cir. 1987) (the House "holds investigative powers that are ancillary to its impeachment power"); *Mazars USA*, 940 F.3d at 749 (Rao, J., dissenting) ("The House . . . has a separate power to investigate pursuant to impeachment[.]").

Because the House has different investigative powers, establishing which authority has been delegated has often been necessary in the course of determining the scope of a committee's authority to compel witnesses and testimony. In addressing the scope of the House's investigative powers, all three branches of the federal government have recognized the constitutional distinction between a legislative investigation and an impeachment inquiry.

1.

We begin with the federal courts. In *Kilbourn*, the Supreme Court held that a House committee could not investigate a bankrupt company indebted to the United States because its request exceeded the scope of the legislative power. According to the Court, the committee had employed investigative power to promote the United States' interests as a creditor, rather than for any valid legislative purpose. *See* 103 U.S. at 192–95. At the same time, the Court conceded that "the whole aspect of the case would have been changed" if "any purpose had been avowed to impeach the [S]ecretary" of the Navy for mishandling the debts of the United States. *Id.* at 193. But, after reviewing the resolution authorizing the actions of the committee, the Court confirmed that the House had not authorized any impeachment inquiry. *Id.*

In a similar vein, the D.C. Circuit distinguished the needs of the House Judiciary Committee, which was conducting an impeachment inquiry into the actions of President Nixon, from those of the Senate Select Committee on Presidential Campaign Activities, whose investigation was premised upon legislative oversight. *See Senate Select Comm.*, 498 F.2d at 732. The court recognized that the impeachment investigation was rooted in "an express constitutional source" and that the House committee's investigative needs differed in kind from the Senate committee's oversight needs. *Id.* In finding that the Senate committee had not demonstrated that President Nixon's audiotapes were "critical to the performance of its legislative functions," the court recognized "a clear difference between Congress's *legislative*

9

tasks and the responsibility of a grand jury, *or any institution engaged in like functions*," such as the House Judiciary Committee, which had "begun an inquiry into presidential impeachment." *Id.* (emphases added).

More recently, the D.C. Circuit acknowledged this same distinction in *Mazars USA*. As the majority opinion explained, "the Constitution has left to Congress the judgment whether to commence the impeachment process" and to decide whether the conduct in question is "better addressed through oversight and legislation than impeachment." 940 F.3d at 739. Judge Rao's dissent also recognized the distinction between a legislative oversight investigation and an impeachment inquiry. *See id.* at 757 ("The Framers established a mechanism for Congress to hold even the highest officials accountable, but also required the House to take responsibility for invoking this power."). Judge Rao disagreed with the majority insofar as she understood Congress's impeachment power to be the sole means for investigating past misconduct by impeachable officers. But both the majority and the dissent agreed with the fundamental proposition that the Constitution distinguishes between investigations pursuant to the House's impeachment authority and those that serve its legislative authority (including oversight).

2.

The Executive Branch similarly has long distinguished between investigations for legislative and for impeachment purposes. In 1796, the House "[r]esolved" that President Washington "be requested to lay before th[e] House a copy of the instructions" given to John Jay in preparation for his negotiation of a peace settlement with Great Britain. 5 Annals of Cong. 759–62 (1796). Washington refused to comply because the Constitution contemplates that only the Senate, not the House, must consent to a treaty. *See id.* at 760–61. "It d[id] not occur" to Washington "that the inspection of the papers asked for, c[ould] be relative to any purpose under the cognizance of the House of Representatives, *except that of an impeachment*." *Id.* at 760 (emphasis added). Because the House's "resolution ha[d] not expressed" any purpose of pursuing impeachment, Washington concluded that "a just regard to the constitution . . . forb[ade] a compliance with [the House's] request" for documents. *Id.* at 760, 762.

In 1832, President Jackson drew the same line. A select committee of the House had requested that the Secretary of War "furnish[]" it "with a copy" of an unratified 1830 treaty with the Chickasaw Tribe and "the journal of the commissioners" who negotiated it. H.R. Rep. No. 22-488, at 1 (1832). The Secretary conferred with Jackson, who refused to comply with the committee's request on the same ground cited by President Washington: he "d[id] not perceive that a copy of any part of the incomplete and unratified treaty of 1830, c[ould] be 'relative to any purpose under the cognizance of the House of Representatives, except that of an impeachment, which the resolution has not expressed.'" *Id.* at 14 (reprinting Letter for Charles A. Wickliffe, Chairman, Committee on Public Lands, U.S. House of Representatives, from Lewis Cass, Secretary of War (Mar. 2, 1832)).

In 1846, another House select committee requested that President Polk account for diplomatic expenditures made in previous administrations by Secretary of State Daniel Webster. Polk refused to disclose information but "cheerfully admitted" that the House may have been entitled to such information if it had "institute[d] an [impeachment] inquiry into the matter."

Cong. Globe, 29th Cong., 1st Sess. 698 (1846).[13] Notably, he took this position even though some members of Congress had suggested that evidence about the expenditures could support an impeachment of Webster.[14] In these and other instances, the Executive Branch has consistently drawn a distinction between the power of legislative oversight and the power of impeachment. *See Mazars USA*, 940 F.3d at 761–64 (Rao, J., dissenting) (discussing examples from the Buchanan, Grant, Cleveland, Theodore Roosevelt, and Coolidge Administrations).

3.

House members, too, have consistently recognized the difference between a legislative oversight investigation and an impeachment investigation. *See* Alissa M. Dolan et al., Cong. Research Serv., RL30240, *Congressional Oversight Manual* 25 (Dec. 19, 2014) ("A committee's inquiry must have a legislative purpose *or* be conducted pursuant to *some other constitutional power* of Congress, such as the authority . . . to . . . conduct impeachment proceedings." (emphases added)); Cong. Research Serv., *Congressional Access to Information in an Impeachment Investigation* at 1 (distinguishing between "*legislative* investigation[s]" and "[m]uch more rare[]" "*impeachment* investigation[s]").

For instance, in 1793, when debating the House's jurisdiction to investigate Secretary of the Treasury Alexander Hamilton, some members argued that the House could not adopt a resolution of investigation into Hamilton's conduct without adopting the "solemnities and guards" of an impeachment inquiry. *See, e.g.*, 3 Annals of Cong. 903 (1793) (statement of Rep. Smith); *id.* at 947–48 (statement of Rep. Boudinot) (distinguishing between the House's "Legislative capacity" and its role as "the grand inquest of the Nation"); *see also Mazars USA*, 940 F.3d at 758 (Rao, J., dissenting) (discussing the episode). In 1796, when the House debated whether to request the President's instructions for negotiating the Jay Treaty, Representative Murray concluded that the House could not meddle in treatymaking, but acknowledged that "the subject would be presented under an aspect very different" if the resolution's supporters had

---

[13] In denying the congressional request before him, President Polk suggested, in the equivalent of dictum, that, during an impeachment inquiry, "all the archives and papers of the Executive departments, public or private, would be subject to the inspection and control of a committee of their body." Cong. Globe, 29th Cong., 1st Sess. 698 (1846). That statement, however, dramatically understates the degree to which executive privilege remains available during an impeachment investigation to protect confidentiality interests necessary to preserve the essential functions of the Executive Branch. *See Exclusion of Agency Counsel from Congressional Depositions in the Impeachment Context*, 43 Op. O.L.C. __, at *3 & n.1 (Nov. 1, 2019). In a prior opinion, this Office viewed Polk as acknowledging the continued availability of executive privilege, because we read Polk's preceding sentence as "indicat[ing]" that, even in the impeachment context, "the Executive branch 'would adopt all wise precautions to prevent the exposure of all such matters the publication of which might injuriously affect the public interest, except so far as this might be necessary to accomplish the great ends of public justice.'" Memorandum for Elliot Richardson, Attorney General, from Robert G. Dixon, Jr., Assistant Attorney General, Office of Legal Counsel, *Re: Presidential Immunity from Coercive Congressional Demands for Information* at 22–23 (July 24, 1973) (quoting Polk's letter).

[14] *See, e.g.*, Cong. Globe, 29th Cong., 1st Sess. 636 (1846) (statement of Rep. Ingersoll) ("Whether . . . [Webster's] offences will be deemed impeachable misdemeanors in office, conviction for which might remove him from the Senate, and disqualify him to hold any office of honor, trust, or profit, under the United States, will remain to be considered."); Todd Garvey, *The Webster and Ingersoll Investigations, in* Morton Rosenberg, The Constitution Project, *When Congress Comes Calling* 289 (2017).

"stated the object for which they called for the papers to be an impeachment." 5 Annals of Cong. 429–30 (1796).

Similarly, in 1846, a House select committee agreed with President Polk's decision not to turn over requested information regarding State Department expenditures where the House did not act "with a view to an impeachment." H.R. Rep. No. 29-684, at 4 (1846) (noting that four of the committee's five members "entirely concur with the President of the United States" in deciding not to "communicate or make [the requested documents] public, except with a view to an impeachment" and that "[n]o dissent from the views of that message was expressed by the House"); *see also Mazars USA*, 940 F.3d at 761 (Rao, J., dissenting). To take another example, in 1879, the House Judiciary Committee distinguished "[i]nvestigations looking to the impeachment of public officers" from "an ordinary investigation for legislative purposes." H.R. Rep. No. 45-141, at 2 (1879).

Most significantly, during the impeachments of Presidents Nixon and Clinton, the House Judiciary Committee determined that the House must provide express authorization before any committee may exercise compulsory powers in an impeachment investigation. *See infra* Part II.C.1. Thus, members of the House, like the other branches of government, have squarely recognized the distinction between congressional investigations for impeachment purposes and those for legislative purposes.

B.

Although the House of Representatives has "the *sole* Power of Impeachment," U.S. Const. art. I, § 2, cl. 5 (emphasis added), the associated power to conduct an investigation for impeachment purposes may, like the House's other investigative powers, be delegated. The full House may make such a delegation by adopting a resolution in exercise of its authority to determine the rules for its proceedings, *see id.* art. I, § 5, cl. 2, and each House has broad discretion in determining the conduct of its own proceedings. *See, e.g., NLRB v. Noel Canning*, 573 U.S. 513, 551–52 (2014); *United States v. Ballin*, 144 U.S. 1, 5 (1892); *see also* 1 *Deschler's Precedents* ch. 5, § 4, at 305–06. But the House must actually exercise its discretion by making that judgment in the first instance, and its resolution sets the terms of a committee's authority. *See United States v. Rumely*, 345 U.S. 41, 44 (1953). No committee may exercise the House's investigative powers in the absence of such a delegation.

As the Supreme Court has explained in the context of legislative oversight, "[t]he theory of a committee inquiry is that the committee members are serving as the representatives of the parent assembly in collecting information for a legislative purpose" and, in such circumstances, committees "are endowed with the full power of the Congress to compel testimony." *Watkins*, 354 U.S. at 200–01. The same is true for impeachment investigations.[15] Thus, Hamilton

---

[15] When the House first considered impeachment in 1796, Attorney General Charles Lee advised that, "before an impeachment is sent to the Senate, witnesses must be examined, in solemn form, respecting the charges, before a committee of the House of Representatives, to be appointed for that purpose." Letter for the House of Representatives from Charles Lee, Attorney General, *Re: Inquiry into the Official Conduct of a Judge of the Supreme Court of the Northwestern Territory* (May 9, 1796), *reprinted in* 1 Am. State Papers: Misc. 151 (Walter Lowrie & Walter S. Franklin eds., 1834). Because the charges of misconduct concerned the actions of George Turner, a territorial judge, and the witnesses were located in far-away St. Clair County (modern-day Illinois), Lee

recognized, the impeachment power involves a trust of such "delicacy and magnitude" that it "deeply concerns the political reputation and existence of every man engaged in the administration of public affairs." *The Federalist* No. 65, at 440. The Founders foresaw that an impeachment effort would "[i]n many cases . . . connect itself with the pre-existing factions" and "inlist all their animosities, partialities, influence and interest on one side, or on the other." *Id.* at 439. As a result, they placed the solemn authority to initiate an impeachment in "the representatives of the nation themselves." *Id.* at 440. In order to entrust one of its committees to investigate for purposes of impeachment, the full House must "spell out that group's jurisdiction and purpose." *Watkins*, 354 U.S. at 201. Otherwise, a House committee controlled by such a faction could launch open-ended and untethered investigations without the sanction of a majority of the House.

Because a committee may exercise the House's investigative powers only when authorized, the committee's actions must be within the scope of a resolution delegating authority from the House to the committee. As the D.C. Circuit recently explained, "it matters not whether the Constitution would give Congress authority to issue a subpoena if Congress has given the issuing committee no such authority." *Mazars USA*, 940 F.3d at 722; *see* Dolan, *Congressional Oversight Manual* at 24 ("Committees of Congress only have the power to inquire into matters within the scope of the authority delegated to them by their parent body."). In evaluating a committee's authority, the House's resolution "is the controlling charter of the committee's powers," and, therefore, the committee's "right to exact testimony and to call for the production of documents must be found in this language." *Rumely*, 345 U.S. at 44; *see also Watkins*, 354 U.S. at 201 ("Those instructions are embodied in the authorizing resolution. That document is the committee's charter."); *id.* at 206 ("Plainly [the House's] committees are restricted to the missions delegated to them . . . . No witness can be compelled to make disclosures on matters outside that area."); *Exxon Corp. v. FTC*, 589 F.2d 582, 592 (D.C. Cir. 1978) ("To issue a valid subpoena, . . . a committee or subcommittee must conform strictly to the resolution establishing its investigatory powers[.]"); *United States v. Lamont*, 18 F.R.D. 27, 32 (S.D.N.Y. 1955) (Weinfeld, J.) ("No committee of either the House or Senate, and no Senator and no Representative, is free on its or his own to conduct investigations unless authorized. Thus it must appear that Congress empowered the Committee to act, and further that at the time the witness allegedly defied its authority the Committee was acting within the power granted to it."). While a committee may study some matters without exercising the investigative powers of the House, a committee's authority to compel the production of documents and testimony depends entirely upon the jurisdiction provided by the terms of the House's delegation.

In *Watkins*, the Supreme Court relied upon those principles to set aside a conviction for contempt of Congress because of the authorizing resolution's vagueness. The uncertain scope of the House's delegation impermissibly created "a wide gulf between the responsibility for the use of investigative power and the actual exercise of that power." 354 U.S. at 205. If the House

---

suggested that the "most solemn" mode of prosecution, an impeachment trial before the Senate, would be "very inconvenient, if not entirely impracticable." *Id.* Lee informed the House that President Washington had directed the territorial governor to arrange for a criminal prosecution before the territorial court. *See id.* The House committee considering the petition about Turner agreed with Lee's suggestion and recommended that the House take no further action. *See Inquiry into the Official Conduct of a Judge of the Supreme Court of the Northwestern Territory* (Feb. 27, 1797), *reprinted in* 1 Am. State Papers: Misc. at 157.

wished to authorize the exercise of its investigative power, then it needed to take responsibility for the use of that power, because a congressional subpoena, issued with the threat of a criminal contempt citation, necessarily placed "constitutional liberties" in "danger." *Id.*

The concerns expressed by the Court in *Watkins* apply with equal, if not greater, force when considering the authority of a House committee to compel the production of documents in connection with investigating impeachment. As John Labovitz, a House impeachment attorney during the Nixon investigation, explained: "[I]mpeachment investigations, because they involve extraordinary power and (at least where the president is being investigated) may have extraordinary consequences, are not to be undertaken in the same manner as run-of-the-mill legislative investigations. The initiation of a presidential impeachment inquiry should itself require a deliberate decision by the House." John R. Labovitz, *Presidential Impeachment* 184 (1978). Because a committee possesses only the authorities that have been delegated to it, a committee may not use compulsory process to investigate impeachment without the formal authorization of the House.

C.

Historical practice confirms that the House must authorize an impeachment inquiry. *See, e.g., Zivotofsky v. Kerry*, 135 S. Ct. 2076, 2091 (2015) (recognizing that "[i]n separation-of-powers cases," the Court has placed "significant weight" on "accepted understandings and practice"); *Noel Canning*, 573 U.S. at 514 (same). The House has expressly authorized every impeachment investigation of a President, including by identifying the investigative committee and authorizing the use of compulsory process. The same thing has been true for nearly all impeachment investigations of other executive officials and judges. While committees have sometimes studied a proposed impeachment resolution or reviewed available information without conducting a formal investigation, in nearly every case in which the committee resorted to compulsory process, the House expressly authorized the impeachment investigation. That practice was foreseen as early as 1796. When Washington asked his Cabinet for opinions about how to respond to the House's request for the papers associated with the Jay Treaty, the Secretary of the Treasury, Oliver Wolcott Jr., explained that "the House of Representatives has no right to demand papers" outside its legislative function "[e]xcept when an Impeachment is proposed *& a formal enquiry instituted.*" Letter for George Washington from Oliver Wolcott Jr. (Mar. 26, 1796), *reprinted in* 19 *The Papers of George Washington: Presidential Series* 611–12 (David R. Hoth ed., 2016) (emphasis added).

From the very first impeachment, the House has recognized that a committee would require a delegation to conduct an impeachment inquiry. In 1797, when House members considered whether a letter contained evidence of criminal misconduct by Senator William Blount, they sought to confirm Blount's handwriting but concluded that the Committee of the Whole did not have the power of taking evidence. *See* 7 Annals of Cong. 456–58 (1797); 3 Asher C. Hinds, *Hinds' Precedents of the House of Representatives of the United States* § 2294, at 644–45 (1907). Thus, the committee "rose," and the House itself took testimony. 3 *Hinds' Precedents* § 2294, at 646. Two days later, the House appointed a select committee to "prepare and report articles of impeachment" and vested in that committee the "power to send for persons, papers, and records." 7 Annals of Cong. at 463–64, 466; 3 *Hinds' Precedents*

§ 2297, at 648.[16] As we discuss in this section, we have identified dozens of other instances where the House, in addition to referring proposed articles of impeachment, authorized formal impeachment investigations.

Against this weighty historical record, which involves nearly 100 authorized impeachment investigations, the outliers are few and far between.[17] In 1879, it appears that a House committee, which was expressly authorized to conduct an oversight investigation into the administration of the U.S. consulate in Shanghai, ultimately investigated and recommended that the former consul-general and former vice consul-general be impeached. In addition, between 1986 and 1989, the Judiciary Committee considered the impeachment of three federal judges who had been criminally prosecuted (two of whom had been convicted). The Judiciary Committee pursued impeachment before there had been any House vote, and issued subpoenas in two of those inquiries. Since then, however, the Judiciary Committee reaffirmed during the impeachment of President Clinton that, in order to conduct an impeachment investigation, it needed an express delegation of investigative authority from the House. And in all subsequent cases the House has hewed to the well-established practice of authorizing each impeachment investigation.

The U.S. District Court for the District of Columbia recently reviewed a handful of historical examples and concluded that House committees may conduct impeachment investigations without a vote of the full House. *See In re Application of the Comm. on the Judiciary*, 2019 WL 5485221, at *26–28. Yet, as the discussion below confirms, the district court misread the lessons of history.[18] The district court treated the House Judiciary Committee's preliminary inquiries in the Clinton and Nixon impeachments as investigations, without recognizing that, in both cases, the committee determined that a full House vote was necessary before it could issue subpoenas. The district court also treated the 1980s judicial inquiries as if they represented a rule of practice, rather than a marked deviation from the dozens of occasions where the House recognized the need to adopt a formal resolution to delegate its investigative authority. As our survey below confirms, the historical practice with respect to Presidents, other executive officers, and judges is consistent with the structure of our

---

[16] After the House impeached Senator Blount, the Senate voted to dismiss the charges on the ground that a Senator is not a civil officer subject to impeachment. *See* 3 *Hinds' Precedents* § 2318, at 678–80.

[17] A 2007 overview concluded that "[t]here have been approximately 94 identifiable impeachment-related inquiries conducted by Congress[.]" H.R. Doc. No. 109-153, at 115 (2007). Since 2007, two more judges have been impeached following authorized investigations.

[18] The district court's erroneous conclusions rested upon the arguments offered by the House Judiciary Committee, which relied principally upon the judicial outliers from the 1980s, a misunderstanding of the Nixon impeachment inquiry, and a misreading of the committee's subpoena power under the House Rules. *See* Application at 33–34, *In re Application of the Comm. on the Judiciary* (D.D.C. July 26, 2019); Reply of the Committee on the Judiciary, U.S. House of Representatives, in Support of Its Application for an Order Authorizing the Release of Certain Grand Jury Materials, at 16 n.19, *In re Application of the Comm. on the Judiciary* (D.D.C. Sept. 30, 2019). HPSCI and the Judiciary Committee later reiterated these arguments in their reports, each contending that executive branch officials had "obstructed" the House's impeachment inquiry by declining to comply with the pre-October 31 impeachment-related subpoenas. H.R. Rep. No. 116-335, at 168–72, 175–77 (2019); H.R. Rep. No. 116-346, at 10, 13–16 (2019). But those reports asserted that the pre-October 31 subpoenas were authorized because the committees misunderstood the historical practice concerning the House's impeachment inquiries (as we discuss in Part II.C) and they misread the committees' subpoena authority under the House Rules (as we discuss in Part III.A).

Constitution, which requires the House, as the "sole" holder of impeachment power, to authorize any impeachment investigation that a committee may conduct on its behalf.

1.

While many Presidents have been the subject of less-formal demands for impeachment, at least eleven have faced resolutions introduced in the House for the purpose of initiating impeachment proceedings.[19] In some cases, the House formally voted to reject opening a presidential impeachment investigation. In 1843, the House rejected a resolution calling for an investigation into the impeachment of President Tyler. *See* Cong. Globe, 27th Cong., 3d Sess. 144–46 (1843). In 1932, the House voted by a wide margin to table a similar resolution introduced against President Hoover. *See* 76 Cong. Rec. 399–402 (1932). In many other cases, the House simply referred impeachment resolutions to the Judiciary Committee, which took no further action before the end of the Congress. But, in three instances before President Trump, the House moved forward with investigating the impeachment of a President.[20] Each of those presidential impeachments advanced to the investigative stage only after the House adopted a resolution expressly authorizing a committee to conduct the investigation. In no case did the committee use compulsory process until the House had expressly authorized the impeachment investigation.

The impeachment investigation of President Andrew Johnson. On January 7, 1867, the House adopted a resolution authorizing the "Committee on the Judiciary" to "inquire into the official conduct of Andrew Johnson . . . and to report to this House whether, in their opinion," the President "has been guilty of any act, or has conspired with others to do acts, which, in contemplation of the Constitution, are high crimes or misdemeanors." Cong. Globe, 39th Cong., 2d Sess. 320–21 (1867); *see also* 3 *Hinds' Precedents* § 2400, at 824. The resolution conferred upon the committee the "power to send for persons and papers and to administer the customary oath to witnesses." Cong. Globe, 39th Cong., 2d Sess. 320 (1867). The House referred a second

---

[19] *See, e.g.*, Cong. Globe, 27th Cong., 3d Sess. 144, 146 (1843) (John Tyler); Cong. Globe, 39th Cong., 2d Sess. 320 (1867) (Andrew Johnson); 28 Cong. Rec. 5627, 5650 (1896) (Grover Cleveland); 76 Cong. Rec. 399–402 (1932) (Herbert Hoover); H.R. Res. 607, 82d Cong. (1952) (Harry Truman); H.R. Res. 625, 93d Cong. (1973) (Richard Nixon); H.R. Res. 370, 98th Cong. (1983) (Ronald Reagan); H.R. Res. 34, 102d Cong. (1991) (George H.W. Bush); H.R. Res. 525, 105th Cong. (1998) (Bill Clinton); H.R. Res. 1258, 110th Cong. (2008) (George W. Bush); H.R. Res. 13, 106th Cong. (2019) (Donald Trump).

[20] In 1860, the House authorized an investigation into the actions of President Buchanan, but that investigation was not styled as an impeachment investigation. *See* Cong. Globe, 36th Cong., 1st Sess. 997–98 (1860) (resolution establishing a committee of five members to "investigat[e] whether the President of the United States, or any other officer of the government, ha[d], by money, patronage, or other improper means, sought to influence the action of Congress" or "by combination or otherwise, . . . attempted to prevent or defeat, the execution of any law"). It appears to have been understood by the committee as an oversight investigation. *See* H.R. Rep. No. 36-648, at 1–28 (1860). Buchanan in fact objected to the House's use of its legislative jurisdiction to circumvent the protections traditionally provided in connection with impeachment. *See* Message for the U.S. House of Representatives from James Buchanan (June 22, 1860), *reprinted in* 5 *A Compilation of the Messages and Papers of the Presidents* 625 (James D. Richardson ed., 1897) (objecting that if the House suspects presidential misconduct, it should "transfer the question from [its] legislative to [its] accusatory jurisdiction, and take care that in all the preliminary judicial proceedings preparatory to the vote of articles of impeachment the accused should enjoy the benefit of cross-examining the witnesses and all the other safeguards with which the Constitution surrounds every American citizen"); *see also Mazars USA*, 940 F.3d at 762 (Rao, J., dissenting) (discussing the episode).

resolution to the Judiciary Committee on February 4, 1867. *Id.* at 991; 3 *Hinds' Precedents* § 2400, at 824.[21] Shortly before that Congress expired, the committee reported that it had seen "sufficient testimony . . . to justify and demand a further prosecution of the investigation." H.R. Rep. No. 39-31, at 2 (1867). On March 7, 1867, the House in the new Congress adopted a resolution that authorized the committee "to continue the investigation authorized" in the January 7 resolution and to "send for persons and papers" and administer oaths. Cong. Globe, 40th Cong., 1st Sess. 18, 25 (1867); 3 *Hinds' Precedents* § 2401, at 825–26. The committee recommended articles of impeachment, but the House rejected those articles on December 7, 1867. *See* Cong. Globe, 40th Cong., 2d Sess. 67–68 (1867). In early 1868, however, the House adopted resolutions authorizing another investigation, with compulsory powers, by the Committee on Reconstruction and transferred to that committee the evidence from the Judiciary Committee's earlier investigation. *See* Cong. Globe, 40th Cong., 2d Sess. 784–85, 1087 (1868); 3 *Hinds' Precedents* § 2408, at 845.

On February 21, 1868, the impeachment effort received new impetus when Johnson removed the Secretary of War without the Senate's approval, contrary to the terms of the Tenure of Office Act, which Johnson (correctly) held to be an unconstitutional limit on his authority. *See* Cong. Globe, 40th Cong., 2d Sess. 1326–27 (1868); 3 *Hinds' Precedents* § 2408–09, at 845–47; *see also Myers v. United States*, 272 U.S. 52, 176 (1926) (finding that provision of the Tenure of Office Act "was invalid"). That day, the Committee on Reconstruction reported an impeachment resolution to the House, which was debated on February 22 and passed on February 24. Cong. Globe, 40th Cong., 2d Sess. 1400 (1868); 3 *Hinds' Precedents* §§ 2409–12, at 846–51.

The impeachment investigation of President Nixon. Although many resolutions were introduced in support of President Nixon's impeachment earlier in 1973, the House's formal impeachment inquiry arose in the months following the "Saturday Night Massacre," during which President Nixon caused the termination of Special Prosecutor Archibald Cox at the cost of the resignations of his Attorney General and Deputy Attorney General. *See* Letter Directing the Acting Attorney General to Discharge the Director of the Office of Watergate Special Prosecution Force (Oct. 20, 1973), *Pub. Papers of Pres. Richard Nixon* 891 (1973). Immediately thereafter, House members introduced resolutions calling either for the President's impeachment or for the opening of an investigation.[22] The Speaker of the House referred the resolutions calling for an investigation to the Rules Committee and those calling for impeachment to the Judiciary Committee. *See* Office of Legal Counsel, U.S. Dep't of Justice, *Legal Aspects of*

---

[21] The district court's recent decision in *In re Application of the Committee on the Judiciary* misreads *Hinds' Precedents* to suggest that the House Judiciary Committee (which the court called "HJC") began investigating President Johnson's impeachment without any authorizing resolution. According to the district court, "a resolution 'authoriz[ing]' HJC 'to inquire into the official conduct of Andrew Johnson' was passed *after* HJC 'was already considering the subject.'" 2019 WL 5485221, at *27 (quoting 3 *Hinds' Precedents* § 2400, at 824). In fact, the committee was "already considering the subject" at the time of the February 4 resolution described in the quoted sentence because, as explained in the text above, the House had previously adopted a separate resolution authorizing an impeachment investigation. *See* Cong. Globe, 39th Cong., 2d Sess. 320–21 (1867); 3 *Hinds' Precedents* § 2400, at 824.

[22] *See, e.g.*, H.R. Res. 625, 631, 635, and 638, 93d Cong. (1973) (impeachment); H.R. Res. 626, 627, 628, 636, and 637, 93d Cong. (1973) (Judiciary Committee or subcommittee investigation).

Impeachment: An Overview at 40 (Feb. 1974) ("*Legal Aspects of Impeachment*"); 3 *Deschler's Precedents* ch. 14, § 5, at 2020.

Following the referrals, the Judiciary Committee "beg[a]n an inquiry into whether President Nixon ha[d] committed any offenses that could lead to impeachment," an exercise that the committee considered "preliminary." Richard L. Madden, *Democrats Agree on House Inquiry into Nixon's Acts*, N.Y. Times, Oct. 23, 1973, at 1. The committee started collecting publicly available materials, and Chairman Peter Rodino Jr. stated that he would "set up a separate committee staff to 'collate' investigative files from Senate and House committees that have examined a variety of charges against the Nixon Administration." James M. Naughton, *Rodino Vows Fair Impeachment Inquiry*, N.Y. Times, Oct. 30, 1973, at 32.

Although the committee "adopted a resolution permitting Mr. Rodino to issue subpoenas without the consent of the full committee," James M. Naughton, *House Panel Starts Inquiry on Impeachment Question*, N.Y. Times, Oct. 31, 1973, at 1, no subpoenas were ever issued under that purported authority. Instead, the committee "delayed acting" on the impeachment resolutions. James M. Naughton, *House Unit Looks to Impeachment*, N.Y. Times, Dec. 2, 1973, at 54. By late December, the committee had hired a specialized impeachment staff. *A Hard-Working Legal Adviser: John Michael Doar*, N.Y. Times, Dec. 21, 1973, at 20. The staff continued "'wading through the mass of material already made public,'" and the committee's members began considering "the areas in which the inquiry should go." Bill Kovach, *Vote on Subpoena Could Test House on Impeachment*, N.Y. Times, Jan. 8, 1974, at 14; *see also* Staff of the H. Comm. on the Judiciary, 93d Cong., Rep. on Work of the Impeachment Inquiry Staff as of February 5, 1974, at 2–3 (1974) (noting that the staff was "first collecting and sifting the evidence available in the public domain," then "marshaling and digesting the evidence available through various governmental investigations"). By January 1974, the committee's actions had consisted of digesting publicly available documents and prior impeachment precedents. That was consistent with the committee's "only mandate," which was to "study more than a dozen impeachment resolutions submitted" in 1973. James M. Naughton, *Impeachment Panel Seeks House Mandate for Inquiry*, N.Y. Times, Jan. 25, 1974, at 1.

In January, the committee determined that a formal investigation was necessary, and it requested "an official House mandate to conduct the inquiry," relying upon the "precedent in each of the earlier [impeachment] inquiries." *Id.* at 17. On January 7, Chairman Rodino "announced that the Committee's subpoena power does not extend to impeachment and that . . . the Committee would seek express authorization to subpoena persons and documents with regard to the impeachment inquiry." *Legal Aspects of Impeachment* at 43; *see also* Richard L. Lyons, *GOP Picks Jenner as Counsel*, Wash. Post, Jan. 8, 1974, at A1, A6 ("Rodino said the committee will ask the House when it reconvenes Jan. 21 to give it power to subpoena persons and documents for the inquiry. The committee's subpoena power does not now extend to impeachment proceedings, he said."). As the House Parliamentarian later explained, the Judiciary Committee's general authority to conduct investigations and issue subpoenas "did not specifically include impeachments within the jurisdiction of the Committee on the Judiciary," and it was therefore "considered necessary for the House to specifically vest the Committee on the Judiciary with the investigatory and subpena power to conduct the impeachment investigation." 3 *Deschler's Precedents* ch. 14, § 15.2, at 2172 (Parliamentarian's Note).

On February 6, 1974, the House approved Resolution 803, which "authorized and directed" the Judiciary Committee "to investigate fully and completely whether sufficient grounds exist for the House of Representatives to exercise its constitutional power to impeach Richard M. Nixon, President of the United States of America." H.R. Res. 803, 93d Cong. § 1. The resolution specifically authorized the committee "to require . . . by subpena or otherwise . . . the attendance and testimony of any person" and "the production of such things" as the committee "deem[ed] necessary" to its investigation. *Id.* § 2(a).

Speaking on the House floor, Chairman Rodino described the resolution as a "necessary step" to confer the House's investigative powers on the Judiciary Committee:

> We have reached the point when it is important that the House explicitly confirm our responsibility under the Constitution.

> We are asking the House of Representatives, by this resolution, to authorize and direct the Committee on the Judiciary to investigate the conduct of the President of the United States . . . .

> As part of that resolution, we are asking the House to give the Judiciary Committee the power of subpena in its investigations.

> *Such a resolution has always been passed by the House. . . . It is a necessary step if we are to meet our obligations.*

> . . . .

> . . . The sole power of impeachment carries with it the power to conduct a full and complete investigation of whether sufficient grounds for impeachment exist or do not exist, and *by this resolution these investigative powers are conferred to their full extent upon the Committee on the Judiciary.*

120 Cong. Rec. 2350–51 (1974) (emphases added). During the debate, others recognized that the resolution would delegate the House's investigative powers to the Judiciary Committee. *See, e.g., id.* at 2361 (statement of Rep. Rostenkowski) ("By delegating to the Judiciary Committee the powers contained in this resolution, we will be providing that committee with the resources it needs to inform the whole House of the facts of this case."); *id.* at 2362 (statement of Rep. Boland) ("House Resolution 803 is intended to delegate to the Committee on the Judiciary the full extent of the powers of this House in an impeachment proceeding[]—both as to the persons and types of things that may be subpenaed and the methods for doing so."). Only after the Judiciary Committee had received authorization from the House did it request and subpoena tape recordings and documents from President Nixon. *See* H.R. Rep. No. 93-1305, at 187 (1974).[23]

---

[23] A *New York Times* article the following day characterized House Resolution 803 as "formally ratif[ying] the impeachment inquiry begun by the committee [the prior] October." James M. Naughton, *House, 410-4, Gives Subpoena Power in Nixon Inquiry*, N.Y. Times, Feb. 7, 1974, at 1. But the resolution did not grant after-the-fact authorization for any prior action. To the contrary, the resolution "authorized and directed" a future investigation, including by providing subpoena power. In the report recommending adoption of the resolution, the committee likewise described its plans in the future tense: "It is the intention of the committee that its investigation will be conducted in all respects on a fair, impartial and bipartisan basis." H.R. Rep. No. 93-774, at 3 (1974).

The impeachment investigation of President Clinton. On September 9, 1998, Independent Counsel Kenneth W. Starr, acting under 28 U.S.C. § 595(c), advised the House of Representatives that he had uncovered substantial and credible information that he believed could constitute grounds for the impeachment of President Clinton. 18 *Deschler's Precedents* app. at 548–49 (2013). Two days later, the House adopted a resolution that referred the matter, along with Starr's report and 36 boxes of evidence, to the Judiciary Committee. H.R. Res. 525, 105th Cong. (1998). The House directed that committee to review the report and "determine whether sufficient grounds exist to recommend to the House that an impeachment inquiry be commenced." *Id.* § 1. The Rules Committee's Chairman emphasized that the House would need to adopt a subsequent resolution if it decided to authorize an impeachment inquiry: "[T]his resolution does not authorize or direct an impeachment inquiry. . . . It merely provides the appropriate parameters for the Committee on the Judiciary . . . to . . . make a recommendation to the House as to whether we should commence an impeachment inquiry." 144 Cong. Rec. 20021 (1998) (statement of Rep. Solomon).

On October 7, 1998, the Judiciary Committee did recommend that there be an investigation for purposes of impeachment. As explained in the accompanying report: "[T]he Committee decided that *it must receive authorization from the full House before proceeding* on any further course of action. Because impeachment is delegated solely to the House of Representatives by the Constitution, the full House of Representatives should be involved in critical decision making regarding various stages of impeachment." H.R. Rep. No. 105-795, at 24 (emphasis added). The committee also observed that "a resolution authorizing an impeachment inquiry into the conduct of a president is consistent with past practice," citing the resolutions for Presidents Johnson and Nixon and observing that "numerous other inquiries were authorized by the House directly, or by providing investigative authorities, such as deposition authority, to the Committee on the Judiciary." *Id.*

The next day, the House voted to authorize the Judiciary Committee to "investigate fully and completely whether sufficient grounds exist for the House of Representatives to exercise its constitutional power to impeach William Jefferson Clinton, President of the United States of America." H.R. Res. 581, 105th Cong. § 1 (1998). The resolution authorized the committee "to require . . . by subpoena or otherwise . . . the attendance and testimony of any person" and "the production of . . . things," and to require the furnishing of information "by interrogatory." *Id.* § 2(a). "On November 5, 1998," as part of its investigation, "the Committee presented President Clinton with 81 requests for admission," which the Committee explained that it "would have . . . compelled by subpoena" had President Clinton not complied. H.R. Rep. No. 105-830, at 77, 122 (1998). And the Committee then "approved the issuance of subpoenas for depositions and materials" from several witnesses. 144 Cong. Rec. D1210–11 (daily ed. Dec. 17, 1998).

In discussing the Clinton precedent, the district court in *In re Application of the Committee on the Judiciary* treated the D.C. Circuit's approval of the disclosure of Starr's report and associated grand-jury information as evidence that the Judiciary Committee may "commence an impeachment investigation" without a House vote. 2019 WL 5485221, at *27 & n.36. But the D.C. Circuit did not authorize that disclosure because of any pending House investigation. It did so because a statutory provision required an independent counsel to "advise the House of Representatives of any substantial and credible information which such independent counsel receives . . . *that may constitute grounds for an impeachment*." 28 U.S.C. § 595(c) (emphasis added). And the D.C. Circuit viewed the report as reflecting "information of the type described in 28 U.S.C. § 595(c)." *In re Madison Guar. Sav. & Loan Ass'n*, Div. No. 94-1 (D.C. Cir. Spec. Div. July 7, 1998), *reprinted in* H.R. Doc. No. 105-331, pt. 1, at 10 (1998). The order authorizing the transmission of that information *to the House* did not imply that any committee was conducting an impeachment investigation. To the contrary, after the House received the information, "no person had access to" it until after the House adopted a resolution referring the matter to the Judiciary Committee. H.R. Rep. No. 105-795, at 5. And the House then adopted a second resolution (Resolution 581) to authorize a formal investigation. In other words, the House voted to authorize the Judiciary Committee both to review the Starr evidence and to conduct an impeachment investigation. Neither the D.C. Circuit nor the Judiciary Committee suggested that any committee could have taken such action on its own.

2.

The House has historically followed these same procedures in considering impeachment resolutions against executive branch officers other than the President. In many cases, an initial resolution laying out charges of impeachment or authorizing an investigation was referred to a select or standing committee.[24] Following such a referral, the designated committee reviewed the matter and considered whether to pursue a formal impeachment inquiry—it did not treat the referral as stand-alone authorization to conduct an investigation. When a committee concluded that the charges warranted investigation, it reported to the full House, which then considered whether to adopt a resolution to authorize a formal investigation.

For example, in March 1867, the House approved a resolution directing the Committee on Public Expenditures "to inquire into the conduct of Henry A. Smythe, collector of the port of New York." Cong. Globe, 40th Cong., 1st Sess. 132 (1867); *see also id.* (noting that the resolution had been modified following debate "so as to leave out that part about bringing articles of impeachment"). Weeks later, the House voted to authorize an impeachment investigation. *Id.* at 290 (authorizing the investigating committee to "send for persons and

---

[24] As with Presidents, many of these resolutions remained with the committees until they expired at the end of the Congress. Several merely articulated allegations of impeachment. *See, e.g.*, H.R. Res. 1028, 115th Cong. (2018) (Deputy Attorney General Rod Rosenstein); H.R. Res. 417, 114th Cong. (2015) (Administrator of the Environmental Protection Agency Regina McCarthy); H.R. Res. 411, 113th Cong. (2013) (Attorney General Eric Holder); H.R. Res. 333, 110th Cong. (2007) (Vice President Richard Cheney); H.R. Res. 629, 108th Cong. (2004) (Secretary of Defense Donald Rumsfeld); H.R. Res. 805, 95th Cong. (1977) (United Nations Ambassador Andrew Young); H.R. Res. 274, 95th Cong. (1977) (Commissioner of the Federal Trade Commission Paul Dixon); H.R. Res. 881, 94th Cong. (1975) (U.S. Attorney Jonathan Goldstein and Principal Assistant U.S. Attorney Bruce Goldstein); H.R. Res. 647, 94th Cong. (1975) (Ambassador to Iran Richard Helms); H.R. Res. 547, 94th Cong. (1975) (Special Crime Strike Force Prosecutor Liam Coonan). Others called for an investigation. *See, e.g.*, H.R. Res. 589, 110th Cong. (2007) (Attorney General Alberto Gonzales); H.R. Res. 582, 105th Cong. (1998) (Independent Counsel Kenneth Starr); H.R. Res. 102, 99th Cong. (1985) (Chairman of the Board of Governors of the Federal Reserve System Paul Volcker); H.R. Res. 101, 99th Cong. (1985) (same and others); H.R. Res. 1025, 95th Cong. (1978) (Attorney General Griffin Bell); H.R. Res. 1002, 95th Cong. (1978) (same); H.R. Res. 569, 93d Cong. (1973) (Vice President Spiro Agnew); H.R. Res. 67, 76th Cong. (1939) (Secretary of Labor Frances Perkins and others); 28 Cong. Rec. 114, 126 (1895) (Ambassador to Great Britain Thomas Bayard); 16 Cong. Rec. 17–19 (1884) (U.S. Marshal Lot Wright); Cong. Globe, 40th Cong., 1st Sess. 778–79 (1867) (Minister to Great Britain Charles Francis Adams). On occasion, the House voted to table these resolutions instead of referring them to a committee. *See, e.g.*, H.R. Res. 545, 105th Cong. (1998) (resolution of impeachment for Independent Counsel Kenneth Starr); H.R. Res. 1267, 95th Cong. (1978) (resolution of impeachment for Ambassador to the United Nations Andrew Young).

papers"). The House followed this same procedure in 1916 for U.S. Attorney H. Snowden Marshall. H.R. Res. 90, 64th Cong. (1916) (initial resolution referred to the Judiciary Committee); H.R. Res. 110, 64th Cong. (1916) (resolution approving the investigation contemplated in the initial resolution). And the process repeated in 1922 for Attorney General Harry Daugherty. H.R. Res. 425, 67th Cong. (1922) (referring the initial resolution to the committee); H.R. Res. 461, 67th Cong. (1922) (resolution approving the investigation contemplated in the initial resolution).

In a few instances, the House asked committees to draft articles of impeachment without calling for any additional impeachment investigation. For example, in 1876, after uncovering "unquestioned evidence of the malfeasance in office by General William W. Belknap" (who was then Secretary of War) in the course of another investigation, the House approved a resolution charging the Committee on the Judiciary with the responsibility to "prepare and report without unnecessary delay suitable articles of impeachment." 4 Cong. Rec. 1426, 1433 (1876). When a key witness left the country, however, the committee determined that additional investigation was warranted, and it asked to be authorized "to take further proof" and "to send for persons and papers" in its search for alternative evidence. *Id.* at 1564, 1566; *see also* 3 *Hinds' Precedents* §§ 2444–45, at 902–04.

In some cases, the House declined to authorize a committee to investigate impeachment with the aid of compulsory process. In 1873, the House authorized the Judiciary Committee "to inquire whether anything" in testimony presented to a different committee implicating Vice President Schuyler Colfax "warrants articles of impeachment of any officer of the United States not a member of this House, or makes it proper that further investigation should be ordered in his case." Cong. Globe, 42d Cong., 3d Sess. 1545 (1873); *see* 3 *Hinds' Precedents* § 2510, at 1016–17. No further investigation was authorized. A similar sequence occurred in 1917 in the case of an impeachment resolution offered against members of the Federal Reserve Board. *See* 54 Cong. Rec. 3126–30 (1917) (impeachment resolution); H.R. Rep. No. 64-1628, at 1 (1917) (noting that following the referral of the impeachment resolution, the Committee had reviewed available information and determined that no further proceedings were warranted). In 1932, the House referred to the Judiciary Committee a resolution calling for the investigation of the possible impeachment of Secretary of the Treasury Andrew Mellon. H.R. Res. 92, 72d Cong. (1932); *see also* 3 *Deschler's Precedents* ch. 14, § 14.1, at 2134–39. The following month, the House approved a resolution discontinuing any investigation of the charges. 75 Cong. Rec. 3850 (1932); *see also* 3 *Deschler's Precedents* ch. 14, § 14.2, at 2139–40.

Most recently, in the 114th Congress, the House referred to the Judiciary Committee resolutions concerning the impeachment of the Commissioner of the Internal Revenue Service, John Koskinen. *See* H.R. Res. 494, 114th Cong. (2015); H.R. Res. 828, 114th Cong. (2016). Shortly after an attempt to force a floor vote on one of the resolutions, Koskinen voluntarily appeared before the committee at a hearing. *See Impeachment Articles Referred on John Koskinen (Part III): Hearing Before the H. Comm. on the Judiciary*, 114th Cong. 2 (2016). The ranking minority member, Representative John Conyers, observed that, despite the title, "this is not an impeachment hearing" because, "[a]ccording to parliamentarians of the House past and present, the impeachment process does not begin until the House actually votes to authorize this Committee to investigate the charges." *Id.* at 3; *see also id.* at 30 (similar statement by Rep. Johnson). During the hearing, Commissioner Koskinen offered to provide a list of supporting witnesses who could be cross-examined "if the Committee decided it wanted to go to a full-scale impeachment process, which I understand this is not." *Id.* at 45. Two months later, one of the impeachment resolutions was briefly addressed on the floor of the House, and again referred to the Judiciary Committee, but without providing any investigative authority. *See* 162 Cong. Rec. H7251–54 (daily ed. Dec. 6, 2016). The committee never sought to compel the appearance of Koskinen or any other witness, and the committee does not appear to have taken any further action before the Congress expired.

In his 1978 book on presidential impeachment, former House impeachment attorney John Labovitz observed that there were a "few exceptions," "mostly in the 1860s and 1870s," to the general rule that "past impeachment investigations ha[ve] been authorized by a specific resolution conferring subpoena power." Labovitz, *Presidential Impeachment* at 182 & n.18. In our review of the history, we have identified one case from that era where a House committee commenced a legislative oversight investigation and subsequently moved, without separate authorization, to consider impeachment.[25] But the overwhelming historical practice to the contrary confirms the Judiciary Committee's well-considered conclusions in 1974 and 1998 that a committee requires specific authorization from the House before it may use compulsory process to investigate for impeachment purposes.

3.

The House has followed the same practice in connection with nearly all impeachment investigations involving federal judges. Committees sometimes studied initial referrals, but they waited for authorization from the full House before conducting any formal impeachment investigation. Three cases from the late 1980s departed from that pattern, but the House has returned during the past three decades to the historical baseline, repeatedly ensuring that the Judiciary Committee had a proper delegation for each impeachment investigation.

The practice of having the House authorize each specific impeachment inquiry is reflected in the earliest impeachment investigations involving judges. In 1804, the House considered proposals to impeach two judges: Samuel Chase, an associate justice of the Supreme Court, and Richard Peters, a district judge. *See* 3 *Hinds' Precedents* § 2342, at 711–16. There was a "lengthy debate" about whether the evidence was appropriate to warrant the institution of an inquiry. *Id.* at 712. The House then adopted a resolution appointing a select committee "to inquire into the official conduct" of Chase and Peters "and to report" the committee's "opinion whether" either of the judges had "so acted, in their judicial capacity, as to require the

---

[25] In 1878, the Committee on Expenditures in the State Department, which was charged with investigative authority for "the exposing of frauds or abuses of any kind," 7 Cong. Rec. 287, 290 (1878), was referred an investigation into maladministration at the consulate in Shanghai during the terms of Consul-General George Seward and Vice Consul-General O.B. Bradford, *id.* at 504, 769. Eventually, the committee began to consider Seward's impeachment, serving him with a subpoena for testimony and documents, in response to which he asserted his privilege against self-incrimination. *See* 3 *Hinds' Precedents* § 2514, at 1023–24; H.R. Rep. No. 45-141, at 1–3 (1879). The committee recommended articles of impeachment, but the House declined to act before the end of the Congress. *See* 8 Cong. Rec. 2350–55 (1879); 3 *Hinds' Precedents* § 2514, at 1025. During this same period, the Committee on Expenditures reported proposed articles of impeachment against Bradford but recommended "that the whole subject be referred to the Committee on the Judiciary" for further consideration. H.R. Rep. No. 45-818, at 7 (1878). The House agreed to the referral, but no further action was taken. 7 Cong. Rec. at 3667.

interposition of the constitutional power of this House." 13 Annals of Cong. 850, 875–76 (1804); 3 *Hinds' Precedents* § 2342, at 715. A few days later, another resolution "authorized" the committee "to send for persons, papers, and records." 13 Annals of Cong. at 877; *see also* 3 *Hinds' Precedents* § 2342, at 715. At the conclusion of its investigation, the committee recommended that Chase, but not Peters, be impeached. 3 *Hinds' Precedents* § 2343, at 716. The House thereafter agreed to a resolution impeaching Chase. *Id.* at 717. Congress recessed before the Senate could act, but, during the next Congress, the House appointed an almost identical select committee, which was "given no power of investigation." *Id.* §§ 2343–44, at 717–18. The committee recommended revised articles of impeachment against Chase, which were again adopted by the House. *Id.* § 2344, at 718–19. In 1808, the House again separately authorized an investigation when it considered whether Peter Bruin, a Mississippi territorial judge, should be impeached for "neglect of duty and drunkenness on the bench." *Id.* § 2487, at 983–84. A member of the House objected "that it would hardly be dignified for the Congress to proceed to an impeachment" based on the territorial legislature's referral and proposed the appointment of a committee "to inquire into the propriety of impeaching." *Id.* at 984; *see* 18 Annals of Cong. 2069 (1808). The House then passed a resolution forming a committee to conduct an inquiry, which included the "power to send for persons, papers, and records" but, like most inquiries to follow, did not result in impeachment. 18 Annals of Cong. at 2189; 3 *Hinds' Precedents* § 2487, at 984.

Over the course of more than two centuries thereafter, members of the House introduced resolutions to impeach, or to investigate for potential impeachment, dozens more federal judges, and the House continued, virtually without exception, to provide an express authorization before any committee proceeded to exercise investigative powers.[26] In one 1874 case, the Judiciary Committee realized only after witnesses had traveled from Arkansas that it could not find any resolution granting it compulsory powers to investigate previously referred charges against Judge William Story. *See* 2 Cong. Rec. 1825, 3438 (1874); 3 *Hinds' Precedents* § 2513, at 1023. In order to "cure" that "defect," the committee reported a privileged resolution to the floor of the House that would grant the committee "power to send for persons and papers" as part of the

---

[26] *See, e.g.*, 3 *Hinds' Precedents* § 2489, at 986 (William Van Ness, Mathias Tallmadge, and William Stephens, 1818); *id.* § 2490, at 987 (Joseph Smith, 1825); *id.* § 2364, at 774 (James Peck, 1830); *id.* § 2492, at 990 (Alfred Conkling, 1830); *id.* § 2491, at 989 (Buckner Thurston, 1837); *id.* § 2494, at 993–94 (P.K. Lawrence, 1839); *id.* §§ 2495, 2497, 2499, at 994, 998, 1003 (John Watrous, 1852–60); *id.* § 2500, at 1005 (Thomas Irwin, 1859); *id.* § 2385, at 805 (West Humphreys, 1862); *id.* § 2503, at 1008 (anonymous justice of the Supreme Court, 1868); *id.* § 2504, at 1008–09 (Mark Delahay, 1872); *id.* § 2506, at 1011 (Edward Durell, 1873); *id.* § 2512, at 1021 (Richard Busteed, 1873); *id.* § 2516, at 1027 (Henry Blodgett, 1879); *id.* §§ 2517–18, at 1028, 1030–31 (Aleck Boarman, 1890–92); *id.* § 2519, at 1032 (J.G. Jenkins, 1894); *id.* § 2520, at 1033 (Augustus Ricks, 1895); *id.* § 2469, at 949–50 (Charles Swayne, 1903); 6 Clarence Cannon, *Cannon's Precedents of the House of Representatives of the United States* § 498, at 685 (1936) (Robert Archbald, 1912); *id.* § 526, at 746–47 (Cornelius H. Hanford, 1912); *id.* § 527, at 749 (Emory Speer, 1913); *id.* § 528, at 753 (Daniel Wright, 1914); *id.* § 529, at 756 (Alston Dayton, 1915); *id.* § 543, at 777–78 (William Baker, 1924); *id.* § 544, at 778–79 (George English, 1925); *id.* § 549, at 789–90 (Frank Cooper, 1927); *id.* § 550, at 791–92 (Francis Winslow, 1929); *id.* § 551, at 793 (Harry Anderson, 1930); *id.* § 552, at 794 (Grover Moscowitz, 1930); *id.* § 513, at 709–10 (Harold Louderback, 1932); 3 *Deschler's Precedents* ch. 14, § 14.4, at 2143 (James Lowell, 1933); *id.* § 18.1, at 2205–06 (Halsted Ritter, 1933); *id.* § 14.10, at 2148 (Albert Johnson and Albert Watson, 1944); H.R. Res. 1066, 94th Cong. (1976) (certain federal judges); H.R. Res. 966, 95th Cong. (1978) (Frank Battisti); *see also* 51 Cong. Rec. 6559–60 (1914) (noting passage of authorizing resolution for investigation of Daniel Wright); 68 Cong. Rec. 3532 (1927) (same for Frank Cooper).

impeachment investigation. 2 Cong. Rec. at 3438. The House promptly agreed to the resolution, enabling the committee to "examine" the witnesses that day. *Id.*

In other cases, however, no full investigation ever materialized. In 1803, John Pickering, a district judge, was impeached, but the House voted to impeach him without conducting any investigation at all, relying instead upon documents supplied by President Jefferson. *See* 3 *Hinds' Precedents* § 2319, at 681–82; *see also* Lynn W. Turner, *The Impeachment of John Pickering*, 54 Am. Hist. Rev. 485, 491 (1949). Sometimes, the House authorized only a preliminary inquiry to determine whether an investigation would be warranted. In 1908, for instance, the House asked the Judiciary Committee to consider proposed articles impeaching Judge Lebbeus Wilfley of the U.S. Court for China. In the ensuing hearing, the Representative who had introduced the resolution acknowledged that the committee was not "authorized to subpoena witnesses" and had been authorized to conduct only "a preliminary examination," which was "not like an investigation ordinarily held by the House," but was instead dedicated solely to determining "whether you believe it is a case that ought to be investigated at all."[27] In many other cases, it is apparent that—even when impeachment resolutions had been referred to them—committees conducted no formal investigation.[28]

In 1970, in a rhetorical departure from well-established practice, a subcommittee of the Judiciary Committee described itself as investigating the impeachment of Justice William O. Douglas based solely upon an impeachment resolution referred to the Judiciary Committee. *See* 116 Cong. Rec. 11920, 11942 (1970); 3 *Deschler's Precedents* ch. 14, §§ 14.14–14.16, at

---

[27] *Articles for the Impeachment of Lebbeus R. Wilfley, Judge of the U.S. Court for China: Hearings Before a Subcomm. of the H. Comm. on the Judiciary*, 60th Cong. 4 (1908) (statement of Rep. Waldo); *see also id.* at 45–46 (statement of Rep. Moon) ("This committee conceives to be its duty solely, under the resolution referring this matter to them, to examine the charges preferred in the petition . . . and to report thereon whether in its judgement the petitioner has made out a prima facie case; and also whether . . . Congress should adopt a resolution instructing the Judiciary Committee to proceed to an investigation of the facts of the case."); 6 *Cannon's Precedents* § 525, at 743–45 (summarizing the Wilfley case, in which the Judiciary Committee ultimately reported that no formal investigation was warranted). The case of Judge Samuel Alschuler in 1935 similarly involved only a preliminary investigation—albeit one with actual investigative powers. The House first referred to the Judiciary Committee a resolution that, if approved, would authorize an investigation of potential impeachment charges. *See* 79 Cong. Rec. 7086, 7106 (1935). Six days later, it adopted a resolution that granted the committee investigative powers in support of "the preliminary examinations deemed necessary" for the committee to make a recommendation about whether a full investigation should occur. *Id.* at 7393–94. The committee ultimately recommended against a full investigation. *See* H.R. Rep. No. 74-1802, at 2 (1935).

[28] *See, e.g.*, 18 Annals of Cong. 1885–86, 2197–98 (1808) (Harry Innes, 1808; the House passed a resolution authorizing an impeachment investigation, which concluded that the evidence accompanying the resolution did not support impeachment); 3 *Hinds' Precedents* § 2486, at 981–83 (George Turner, 1796; no apparent investigation, presumably because of the parallel criminal prosecution recommended by Attorney General Lee, as discussed above); *id.* § 2488, at 985 (Harry Toulmin, 1811; the House "declined to order a formal investigation"); 40 Annals of Cong. 463–69, 715–18 (1822–23) (Charles Tait, 1823; no apparent investigation beyond examination of documents containing charges); 3 *Hinds' Precedents* § 2493, at 991–92 (Benjamin Johnson, 1833; no apparent investigation); *id.* § 2511, at 1019–20 (Charles Sherman, 1873; the Judiciary Committee received evidence from the Ways and Means Committee, which had been investigating corruption in Congress, but the Judiciary Committee conducted no further investigation); 6 *Cannon's Precedents* § 535, at 769 (Kenesaw Mountain Landis, 1921; the Judiciary Committee reported that "charges were filed too late in the present session of the Congress" to enable investigation); 3 *Deschler's Precedents* ch. 14, § 14.6, at 2144–45 (Joseph Molyneaux, 1934; the Judiciary Committee took no action on the referral of a resolution that would have authorized an investigation).

2151–64; *see also* Labovitz, *Presidential Impeachment* at 182 n.18 (noting that "[t]he Douglas inquiry was the first impeachment investigation in twenty-five years, and deviation from the older procedural pattern was not surprising"). Yet, the subcommittee did not resort to any compulsory process during its inquiry, and it did not recommend impeachment. 3 *Deschler's Precedents* ch. 14, §§ 14.15–14.16, at 2158–63. Accordingly, the committee did not actually exercise any of the investigative powers of the House.

In the late 1980s, the House Judiciary Committee considered the impeachment of three district-court judges without any express authorization from the House: Walter Nixon, Alcee Hastings, and Harry Claiborne. *See In re Application of the Comm. on the Judiciary*, 2019 WL 5485221, at *26 (discussing these investigations). All three judges had been criminally prosecuted, and two had been convicted. *See* H.R. Rep. No. 101-36, at 12–13 (1989) (describing Nixon's prosecution and conviction); H.R. Rep. No. 100-810, at 7–8, 29–31, 38–39 (1988) (describing Hastings's indictment and trial and the subsequent decision to proceed with a judicial-misconduct proceeding in lieu of another prosecution); H.R. Rep. No. 99-688, at 9, 17–20 (1986) (describing Claiborne's prosecution and conviction). In the Claiborne inquiry, the committee does not appear to have issued any subpoenas. *See* H.R. Rep. No. 99-688, at 4 (noting that the committee sent "[i]nvitational letters to all witnesses," who apparently cooperated to the Committee's satisfaction). The committee did issue subpoenas in the Nixon and Hastings investigations, yet no witness appears to have objected on the ground that the committee lacked jurisdiction to issue the subpoenas, and at least one witness appears to have requested a subpoena.[29] In those two cases, though, the Judiciary Committee effectively compelled production without any express authorization from the House.[30]

In the years after these outliers, the Judiciary Committee returned to the practice of seeking specific authorization from the House before conducting impeachment investigations. Most notably, as discussed above, the Judiciary Committee "decided that it *must receive authorization from the full House* before proceeding" with an impeachment investigation of President Clinton. H.R. Rep. No. 105-795, at 24 (emphasis added). And the House has used the same practice with respect to federal judges.[31] Thus, in 2008, the House adopted a resolution authorizing the Judiciary Committee to investigate the impeachment of Judge G. Thomas Porteous, Jr., including the grant of subpoena authority. *See* H.R. Rep. No. 111-427, at 7 (2010);

---

[29] *See* H.R. Rep. No. 100-810, at 11 & n.14 (stating that, in the Hastings investigation, a committee subpoena had been issued for William Borders, who challenged the subpoena on First, Fourth, Fifth, and Eighth Amendment grounds); H.R. Rep. No. 100-1124, at 130 (1989) (noting the issuance of "subpoenas *duces tecum*" in the investigation of Judge Nixon); 134 Cong. Rec. 27782 (1988) (statement of Rep. Edwards) (explaining the subcommittee's need to depose some witnesses pursuant to subpoena in the Nixon investigation); *Judge Walter L. Nixon, Jr., Impeachment Inquiry: Hearing Before the Subcomm. on Civil & Constitutional Rights of the H. Comm. on the Judiciary*, 101st Cong. 530–606 (1988) (reprinting deposition of Magistrate Judge Roper).

[30] The House did pass resolutions authorizing funds for investigations with respect to the Hastings impeachment, *see* H.R. Res. 134, 100th Cong. (1987); H.R. Res. 388, 100th Cong. (1988), and resolutions authorizing the committee to permit its counsel to take affidavits and depositions in both the Nixon and Hastings impeachments, *see* H.R. Res. 562, 100th Cong. (1988) (Nixon); H.R. Res. 320, 100th Cong. (1987) (Hastings).

[31] In the post-1989 era, as before, most of the impeachment resolutions against judges that were referred to the Judiciary Committee did not result in any further investigation. *See, e.g.*, H.R. Res. 916, 109th Cong. (2006) (Manuel Real); H.R. Res. 207, 103d Cong. (1993) (Robert Collins); H.R. Res. 177, 103d Cong. (1993) (Robert Aguilar); H.R. Res. 176, 103d Cong. (1993) (Robert Collins).

H.R. Res. 1448, 110th Cong. (2008); 154 Cong. Rec. 19502 (2008). After the Congress expired, the House in the next Congress adopted a new resolution re-authorizing the inquiry, again with subpoena authority. *See* H.R. Res. 15, 111th Cong. (2009); 155 Cong. Rec. 568, 571 (2009). Several months later, another district judge, Samuel Kent, pleaded guilty to obstruction of justice and was sentenced to 35 months of incarceration. *See* H.R. Rep. 111-159, at 9–13 (2009). The House then adopted a resolution directing the Judiciary Committee to investigate impeachment, again specifically granting subpoena authority. *See id.* at 13; H.R. Res. 424, 111th Cong. (2009); 155 Cong. Rec. at 12211–13.

Thus, the House's long-standing and nearly unvarying practice with respect to judicial impeachment inquiries is consistent with the conclusion that the power to investigate in support of the House's "sole Power of Impeachment," U.S. Const. art. I, § 2, cl. 5, may not be exercised by a committee without an express delegation from the House. In the cases of Judges Nixon and Hastings, the Judiciary Committee did exercise compulsory authority despite the absence of any delegation from the House. But insofar as no party challenged the committee's authority at the time, and no court addressed the matter, these historical outliers do not undermine the broader constitutional principle. As the Supreme Court observed in *Noel Canning*, "when considered against 200 years of settled practice," a "few scattered examples" are rightly regarded "as anomalies." 573 U.S. at 538. They do not call into question the soundness of the House's otherwise consistent historical practice, much less the constitutional requirement that a committee exercise the constitutional powers of the House only with an express delegation from the House itself.

III.

Having concluded that a House committee may not conduct an impeachment investigation without a delegation of authority, we next consider whether the House provided such a delegation to the Foreign Affairs Committee or to the other committees that issued subpoenas pursuant to the asserted impeachment inquiry. During the five weeks between the Speaker's announcement on September 24 and the adoption of Resolution 660 on October 31, the committees issued numerous impeachment-related subpoenas. *See supra* note 9. We therefore provided advice during that period about whether any of the committees had authority to issue those subpoenas. Because the House had not adopted an impeachment resolution, the answer to that question turned on whether the committees could issue those subpoenas based upon any preexisting subpoena authority.

In justifying the subpoenas, the Foreign Affairs Committee and other committees pointed to the resolution adopting the Rules of the House of Representatives, which establish the committees and authorize investigations for matters within their jurisdiction. The committees claimed that Rule XI confers authority to issue subpoenas in connection with an impeachment investigation. Although the House has expanded its committees' authority in recent decades, the House Rules continue to reflect the long-established distinction between legislative and non-legislative investigative powers. Those rules confer legislative oversight jurisdiction on committees and authorize the issuance of subpoenas to that end, but they do not grant authority to investigate for impeachment purposes. While the House committees could have sought some information relating to the same subjects in the exercise of their legislative oversight authority, the subpoenas they purported to issue "pursuant to the House of Representatives' impeachment inquiry" were not in support of such oversight. We therefore conclude that they were unauthorized.

A.

The standing committees of the House trace their general subpoena powers back to the House Rules, which the 116th Congress adopted by formal resolution. *See* H.R. Res. 6, 116th Cong. (2019). The House Rules are more than 60,000 words long, but they do not include the word "impeachment." The Rules' silence on that topic is particularly notable when contrasted with the Senate, which has adopted specific "Rules of Procedure and Practice" for impeachment trials. S. Res. 479, 99th Cong. (1986).[32] The most obvious conclusion to draw from that silence is that the current House, like its predecessors, retained impeachment authority at the level of the full House, subject to potential delegations in resolutions tailored for that purpose.

Rule XI of the Rules of the House affirmatively authorizes committees to issue subpoenas, but only for matters within their legislative jurisdiction. The provision has been a part of the House Rules since 1975. *See* H.R. Res. 988, 93d Cong. § 301 (1974). Clause 2(m)(1) of Rule XI vests each committee with the authority to issue subpoenas "[f]or the purpose of carrying out any of its functions and duties under this rule and rule X (including any matters referred to it under clause 2 of rule XII)." Rule XI, cl. 2(m)(1); *see also* Rule X, cl. 11(d)(1) (making clause 2 of Rule XI applicable to HPSCI). The committees therefore have subpoena power to carry out their authorities under three rules: Rule X, Rule XI, and clause 2 of Rule XII.

Rule X does not provide any committee with jurisdiction over impeachment. Rule X establishes the "standing committees" of the House and vests them with "their legislative jurisdictions." Rule X, cl. 1. The jurisdiction of each committee varies in subject matter and scope. While the Committee on Ethics, for example, has jurisdiction over only "[t]he Code of Official Conduct" (Rule X, cl. 1(g)), the jurisdiction of the Foreign Affairs Committee spans seventeen subjects, including "[r]elations of the United States with foreign nations generally," "[i]ntervention abroad and declarations of war," and "[t]he American National Red Cross" (Rule X, cl. 1(i)(1), (9), (15)). The rule likewise spells out the jurisdiction of the Committee on Oversight and Reform (Rule X, cl. 1(n), cl. 3(i)), and the jurisdiction of the Judiciary Committee (Rule X, cl. 1(*l*)). Clause 11 of Rule X establishes HPSCI and vests it with jurisdiction over "[t]he Central Intelligence Agency, the Director of National Intelligence, and the National Intelligence Program" and over "[i]ntelligence and intelligence-related activities of all other departments and agencies." Rule X, cl. 11(a)(1), (b)(1)(A)–(B).

The text of Rule X confirms that it addresses the *legislative* jurisdiction of the standing committees. After defining each standing committee's subject-matter jurisdiction, the Rule provides that "[t]he various standing committees shall have general oversight responsibilities" to assist the House in its analysis of "the application, administration, execution, and effectiveness of Federal laws" and of the "conditions and circumstances that may indicate the necessity or

---

[32] Unlike the House, "the Senate treats its rules as remaining in effect continuously from one Congress to the next without having to be re-adopted." Richard S. Beth, Cong. Research Serv., R42929, *Procedures for Considering Changes in Senate Rules* 9 (Jan. 22, 2013). Of course, like the House, the Senate may change its rules by simple resolution.

desirability of enacting new or additional legislation," as well as to assist the House in its "formulation, consideration, and enactment of changes in Federal laws, and of such additional legislation as may be necessary or appropriate." Rule X, cl. 2(a)(1)–(2). The committees are to conduct oversight "on a continuing basis" "to determine whether laws and programs addressing subjects within the jurisdiction of a committee" are implemented as Congress intends "and whether they should be continued, curtailed, or eliminated." Rule X, cl. 2(b)(1). Those are all functions traditionally associated with legislative oversight, not the separate power of impeachment. *See supra* Part II.A. Clause 3 of Rule X further articulates "[s]pecial oversight functions" with respect to particular subjects for certain committees; for example, the Committee on Foreign Affairs "shall review and study on a continuing basis laws, programs, and Government activities relating to . . . intelligence activities relating to foreign policy," Rule X, cl. 3(f). And clause 4 addresses "[a]dditional functions of committees," including functions related to the review of appropriations and the special authorities of the Committee on Oversight and Reform, Rule X, cl. 4(a)(1), (c)(1). But none of the "[s]pecial oversight" or "[a]dditional" functions specified in clauses 3 and 4 includes any reference to the House's impeachment power.

The powers of HPSCI are addressed in clause 11 of Rule X. Unlike the standing committees, HPSCI is not given "[g]eneral oversight responsibilities" in clause 2. But clause 3 gives it the "[s]pecial oversight functions" of "review[ing] and study[ing] on a continuing basis laws, programs, and activities of the intelligence community" and of "review[ing] and study[ing] . . . the sources and methods of" specified entities that engage in intelligence activities. Rule X, cl. 3(m). And clause 11 further provides that proposed legislation about intelligence activities will be referred to HPSCI and that HPSCI shall report to the House "on the nature and extent of the intelligence and intelligence-related activities of the various departments and agencies of the United States." Rule X, cl. 11(b)(1), (c)(1); *see also* H.R. Res. 658, 95th Cong. § 1 (1977) (resolution establishing HPSCI, explaining its purpose as "provid[ing] vigilant *legislative oversight* over the intelligence and intelligence-related activities of the United States" (emphasis added)). Again, those powers sound in legislative oversight, and nothing in the Rules suggests that HPSCI has any generic delegation of the separate power of impeachment.

Consistent with the foregoing textual analysis, Rule X has been seen as conferring legislative oversight authority on the House's committees, without any suggestion that impeachment authorities are somehow included therein. The Congressional Research Service describes Rule X as "contain[ing] the legislative and oversight jurisdiction of each standing committee, several clauses on committee procedures and operations, and a clause specifically addressing the jurisdiction and operation of the Permanent Select Committee on Intelligence." Michael L. Koempel & Judy Schneider, Cong. Research Serv., R41605, *House Standing Committees' Rules on Legislative Activities: Analysis of Rules in Effect in the 114th Congress* 2 (Oct. 11, 2016); *see also* Dolan, *Congressional Oversight Manual* at 25 (distinguishing a committee inquiry with "a legislative purpose" from inquiries conducted under "some other constitutional power of Congress, such as the authority" to "conduct impeachment proceedings"). In the chapter of *Deschler's Precedents* devoted to explaining the "[i]nvestigations and [i]nquiries" by the House and its committees, the Parliamentarian repeatedly notes that impeachment investigations and other non-legislative powers are discussed elsewhere. *See* 4 *Deschler's Precedents* ch. 15, § 1, at 2283; *id.* § 14, at 2385 n.12; *id.* § 16, at 2403 & n.4.

Rule X concerns only legislative oversight, and Rule XI does not expand the committees' subpoena authority any further. That rule rests upon the jurisdiction granted in Rule X. *See* Rule XI, cl. 1(b)(1) ("Each committee may conduct at any time such investigations and studies as it considers necessary or appropriate in the exercise of its responsibilities under rule X."). Nor does Rule XII confer any additional jurisdiction. Clause 2(a) states that "[t]he Speaker shall refer each bill, resolution, or other matter that relates to a subject listed under a standing committee named in clause 1 of rule X[.]" Rule XII, cl. 2(a). The Speaker's referral authority under Rule XII is thus limited to matters within a committee's Rule X legislative jurisdiction. *See* 18 *Deschler's Precedents* app. at 578 ("All committees were empowered by actual language of the Speaker's referral to consider only 'such provisions of the measure as fall within their respective jurisdictions under Rule X.'"). Accordingly, the Speaker may not expand the jurisdiction of a committee by referring a bill or resolution falling outside the committee's Rule X authority.[33]

In reporting Resolution 660 to the House, the Rules Committee expressed the view that clause 2(m) of Rule XI gave standing committees the authority to issue subpoenas in support of impeachment inquiries. *See* H.R. Rep. No. 116-266, at 18 (2019). But the committee did not explain which terms of the rule provide such authority. To the contrary, the committee simply asserted that the rule granted such authority and that the text of Resolution 660 departed from its predecessors on account of amendments to clause 2(m) that were adopted after the "Clinton and Nixon impeachment inquiry resolutions." *Id.* Yet clause 2(m) of Rule XI was adopted two decades before the Clinton inquiry.[34] Even with that authority in place, the Judiciary Committee recognized in 1998 that it "*must* receive authorization from the full House before proceeding" to investigate President Clinton for impeachment purposes. H.R. Rep. No. 105-795, at 24 (emphasis added). And, even before Rule XI was adopted, the House had conferred on the Judiciary Committee a materially similar form of investigative authority (including subpoena power) in 1973.[35] The Judiciary Committee nevertheless recognized that those subpoena powers did not authorize it to conduct an impeachment inquiry about President Nixon. In other words, the Rules Committee's recent interpretation of clause 2(m) (which it did not explain in its report) cannot be reconciled with the Judiciary Committee's well-reasoned conclusion, in both 1974 and

---

[33] Nor do the Rules otherwise give the Speaker the authority to order an investigation or issue a subpoena in connection with impeachment. Rule I sets out the powers of the Speaker. She "shall sign . . . all writs, warrants, and subpoenas of, or issued by order of, the House." Rule I, cl. 4. But that provision applies only when the House itself issues an order. *See Jefferson's Manual* § 626, at 348.

[34] Clause 2(m) of Rule XI was initially adopted on October 8, 1974, and took effect on January 3, 1975. *See* H.R. Res. 988, 93d Cong. The rule appears to have remained materially unchanged from 1975 to the present (including during the time of the Clinton investigation). *See* H.R. Rule XI, cl. 2(m), 105th Cong. (Jan. 1, 1998) (version in effect during the Clinton investigation); *Jefferson's Manual* § 805, at 586–89 (reprinting current version and describing the provision's evolution).

[35] At the start of the 93rd Congress in 1973, the Judiciary Committee was "authorized to conduct full and complete studies and investigations and make inquiries within its jurisdiction as set forth in [the relevant provision] of the Rules of the House of Representatives" and was empowered "to hold such hearings and require, by subpena or otherwise, the attendance and testimony of such witnesses and the production of such books, records, correspondence, memorandums, papers, and documents, as it deems necessary." H.R. Res. 74, 93d Cong. §§ 1, 2(a) (1973); *see also* Cong. Research Serv., R45769, *The Impeachment Process in the House of Representatives* 4 (updated Nov. 14, 2019) (noting that, before Rule XI vested subpoena power in standing committees, the Judiciary Committee and other committees had often been given subpoena authority "through resolutions providing blanket investigatory authorities that were agreed to at the start of a Congress").

1998, that Rule XI (and its materially similar predecessor) do not confer any standing authority to conduct an impeachment investigation.

In modern practice, the Speaker has referred proposed resolutions calling for the impeachment of a civil officer to the Judiciary Committee. *See Jefferson's Manual* § 605, at 324. Consistent with this practice, the Speaker referred the Sherman resolution (H.R. Res. 13, 116th Cong.) to the Judiciary Committee, because it called for the impeachment of President Trump. Yet the referral itself did not grant authority to conduct an impeachment investigation. House committees have regularly received referrals and conducted preliminary inquiries, without compulsory process, for the purpose of determining whether to recommend that the House open a formal impeachment investigation. *See supra* Part II.C. Should a committee determine that a formal inquiry is warranted, then the committee recommends that the House adopt a resolution that authorizes such an investigation, confers subpoena power, and provides special process to the target of the investigation. The Judiciary Committee followed precisely that procedure in connection with the impeachment investigations of Presidents Nixon and Clinton, among many others. By referring an impeachment resolution to the House Judiciary Committee, the Speaker did not expand that committee's subpoena authority to cover a formal impeachment investigation. In any event, no impeachment resolution was ever referred to the Foreign Affairs Committee, HPSCI, or the Committee on Oversight and Reform. Rule XII thus could not provide any authority to those committees in support of the impeachment-related subpoenas issued before October 31.

Accordingly, when those subpoenas were issued, the House Rules did not provide authority to any of those committees to issue subpoenas in connection with potential impeachment. In reaching this conclusion, we do not question the broad authority of the House of Representatives to determine how and when to conduct its business. *See* U.S. Const. art. I, § 5, cl. 2. As the Supreme Court has recognized, "'all matters of method are open to the determination'" of the House, "as long as there is 'a reasonable relation between the mode or method of proceeding established by the rule and the result which is sought to be attained,' and the rule does not 'ignore constitutional restraints or violate fundamental rights.'" *Noel Canning*, 573 U.S. at 551 (quoting *United States v. Ballin*, 144 U.S. 1, 5 (1892)). The question, however, is not "what rules Congress may establish for its own governance," but "rather what rules the House has established and whether they have been followed." *Christoffel v. United States*, 338 U.S. 84, 88–89 (1949); *see also Yellin v. United States*, 374 U.S. 109, 121 (1963) (stating that a litigant "is at least entitled to have the Committee follow its rules and give him consideration according to the standards it has adopted in" the relevant rule); *United States v. Smith*, 286 U.S. 6, 33 (1932) ("As the construction to be given to the rules affects persons other than members of the Senate, the question presented is of necessity a judicial one."). Statements by the Speaker or by committee chairmen are not statements of the House itself. *Cf. Noel Canning*, 573 U.S. at 552–53 (relying on statements and actions of the Senate itself, as reflected in the Journal of the Senate and the Congressional Record, to determine when the Senate was "in session"). Our conclusion here turned upon nothing more, and nothing less, than the rules and resolutions that had been adopted by a majority vote of the full House.[36]

---

[36] The Judiciary Committee has also invoked House Resolution 430 as an independent source of authority for an impeachment inquiry. *See* Tr. of Mot. Hrg. at 91–92, *In re Application of the Comm. on the Judiciary; see*

The text of those provisions determined whether the House had delegated the necessary authority. *See id.* at 552 ("[O]ur deference to the Senate cannot be absolute. When the Senate is without the *capacity* to act, under its own rules, it is not in session even if it so declares."). Thus, the Supreme Court has repeatedly made clear that a target of the House's compulsory process may question whether a House resolution has actually conferred the necessary powers upon a committee, because the committee's "right to exact testimony and to call for the production of documents must be found in [the resolution's] language." *Rumely*, 345 U.S. at 44; *see also Watkins*, 354 U.S. at 201. In *Rumely*, the Court expressly rejected the argument that the House had confirmed the committee's jurisdiction by adopting a resolution that merely held the witness in contempt after the fact. As the Court explained, what was said "after the controversy had arisen regarding the scope of the resolution . . . had the usual infirmity of *post litem motam*, self-serving declarations." 345 U.S. at 48. In other words, even a vote of the full House could not "enlarge[]" a committee's authority after the fact for purposes of finding that a witness had failed to comply with the obligations imposed by the subpoena. *Id.*

Here, the House committees claiming to investigate impeachment issued subpoenas before they had received *any* actual delegation of impeachment-related authority from the House. Before October 31, the committees relied solely upon statements of the Speaker, the committee chairmen, and the Judiciary Committee, all of which merely asserted that one or more House committees had already been conducting a formal impeachment inquiry. There was, however, no House resolution actually delegating such authority to any committee, let alone one that did so with "sufficient particularity" to compel witnesses to respond. *Watkins*, 354 U.S. at 201; *cf. Gojack v. United States*, 384 U.S. 702, 716–17 (1966). At the opening of this Congress, the House had not chosen to confer investigative authority over impeachment upon any committee, and therefore, no House committee had authority to compel the production of documents or testimony in furtherance of an impeachment inquiry that it was not authorized to conduct.

B.

Lacking a delegation from the House, the committees could not compel the production of documents or the testimony of witnesses for purposes of an impeachment inquiry. Because the first impeachment-related subpoena—the September 27 subpoena from the Foreign Affairs Committee—rested entirely upon the purported impeachment inquiry, *see* Three Chairmen's Letter, *supra* note 2, at 1, it was not enforceable. *See, e.g.*, *Rumely*, 345 U.S. at 44. Perhaps recognizing this infirmity, the committee chairmen invoked not merely the impeachment inquiry in connection with subsequent impeachment-related subpoenas but also the committees' "oversight and legislative jurisdiction." *See supra* note 9 and accompanying text. That assertion of dual authorities presented the question whether the committees could leverage their oversight jurisdiction to require the production of documents and testimony that the committees avowedly

---

also Majority Staff of H. Comm. on the Judiciary, 116th Cong., *Constitutional Grounds for Presidential Impeachment* 39 (Dec. 2019). As discussed above, however, that resolution did not confer any investigative authority. Rather, it granted "any and all necessary authority under Article I" only "in connection with" certain "judicial proceeding[s]" in federal court. H.R. Res. 430, 116th Cong. (2019); *see supra* note 7. The resolution therefore had no bearing on any committee's authority to compel the production of documents or testimony in an impeachment investigation.

intended to use for an unauthorized impeachment inquiry. We advised that, under the circumstances of these subpoenas, the committees could not do so.

Any congressional inquiry "must be related to, and in furtherance of, a legitimate task of the Congress." *Watkins*, 354 U.S. at 187. The Executive Branch need not presume that such a purpose exists or accept a "makeweight" assertion of legislative jurisdiction. *Mazars USA*, 940 F.3d at 725–26, 727; *see also Shelton v. United States*, 404 F.2d 1292, 1297 (D.C. Cir. 1968) ("In deciding whether the purpose is within the legislative function, the mere assertion of a need to consider 'remedial legislation' may not alone justify an investigation accompanied with compulsory process[.]"). Indeed, "an assertion from a committee chairman may not prevent the Executive from confirming the legitimacy of an investigative request." *Congressional Committee's Request for the President's Tax Returns Under 26 U.S.C. § 6103(f)*, 43 Op. O.L.C. __, at *20 (June 13, 2019). To the contrary, "a threshold inquiry that should be made upon receipt of any congressional request for information is whether the request is supported by any legitimate legislative purpose." *Response to Congressional Requests for Information Regarding Decisions Made Under the Independent Counsel Act*, 10 Op. O.L.C. 68, 74 (1986); *see also Congressional Requests for Confidential Executive Branch Information*, 13 Op. O.L.C. 153, 159 (1989) (recognizing that the constitutionally mandated accommodation process "requires that each branch explain to the other why it believes its needs to be legitimate").

Here, the committee chairmen made clear upon issuing the subpoenas that the committees were interested in the requested materials to support an investigation into the potential impeachment of the President, not to uncover information necessary for potential legislation within their respective areas of legislative jurisdiction. In marked contrast with routine oversight, each of the subpoenas was accompanied by a letter signed by the chairs of three different committees, who transmitted a subpoena "[p]ursuant to the House of Representatives' impeachment inquiry" and recited that the documents would "be collected as part of the House's impeachment inquiry," and that they would be "shared among the Committees, as well as with the Committee on the Judiciary as appropriate." *See supra* note 9 and accompanying text. Apart from their token invocations of "oversight and legislative jurisdiction," the letters offered no hint of any legislative purpose. The committee chairmen were therefore seeking to do precisely what they said—compel the production of information to further an impeachment inquiry.

In reaching this conclusion, we do not foreclose the possibility that the Foreign Affairs Committee or the other committees could have issued similar subpoenas in the bona fide exercise of their legislative oversight jurisdiction, in which event the requests would have been evaluated consistent with the long-standing confidentiality interests of the Executive Branch. *See Watkins*, 354 U.S. at 187 (recognizing that Congress's general investigative authority "comprehends probes into departments of the Federal Government to expose corruption, inefficiency or waste"); *McGrain*, 273 U.S. at 179–80 (observing that it is not "a valid objection to the investigation that it might possibly disclose crime or wrongdoing on [the Attorney General's] part"). Should the Foreign Affairs Committee, or another committee, articulate a legitimate oversight purpose for a future information request, the Executive Branch would assess that request as part of the constitutionally required accommodation process. But the Executive Branch was not confronted with that situation. The committee chairmen unequivocally attempted to conduct an impeachment inquiry into the President's actions, without the House, which has the "sole Power of Impeachment," having authorized such an investigation. Absent such an authorization, the committee chairs' passing mention of "oversight and legislative jurisdiction" did not cure that fundamental defect.

C.

We next address whether the House ratified any of the previous committee subpoenas when it adopted Resolution 660 on October 31, 2019—after weeks of objections from the Executive Branch and many members of Congress to the committees' efforts to conduct an unauthorized impeachment inquiry. Resolution 660 provides that six committees of the House "are directed to continue their ongoing investigations as part of the existing House of Representatives inquiry into whether sufficient grounds exist for the House of Representatives to exercise its Constitutional power to impeach Donald John Trump, President of the United States of America." Resolution 660, § 1. The resolution further prescribes certain procedures by which HPSCI and the Judiciary Committee may conduct hearings in connection with the investigation defined by that resolution.

Resolution 660 does not speak at all to the committees' past actions or seek to ratify any subpoena previously issued by the House committees. *See Trump v. Mazars USA, LLP*, 941 F.3d 1180, 1182 (D.C. Cir. 2019) (Rao, J., dissenting from the denial of rehearing en banc); *see also Exclusion of Agency Counsel from Congressional Depositions in the Impeachment Context*, 43 Op. O.L.C. __, at *5 (Nov. 1, 2019). The resolution "direct[s]" HPSCI and other committees to "continue" their investigations, and the Rules Committee apparently assumed, incorrectly in our view, that earlier subpoenas were legally valid. *See* H.R. Rep. No. 116-266, at 3 ("All subpoenas to the Executive Branch remain in full force."). But the resolution's operative language does not address any previously issued subpoenas or provide the imprimatur of the House to give those subpoenas legal force.

And the House knows how to ratify existing subpoenas when it chooses to do so.[37] On July 24, 2019, the House adopted a resolution that expressly "ratif[ied] and affirm[ed] all current and future investigations, as well as *all subpoenas previously issued* or to be issued in the future," related to certain enumerated subjects within the jurisdiction of standing or select committees of the House "as established by the Constitution of the United States and rules X and XI of the Rules of the House of Representatives." H.R. Res. 507, 116th Cong. § 1 (2019) (emphasis added). There, as here, the House acted in response to questions regarding "the validity of . . . [committee] investigations and subpoenas." *Id*. pmbl. Despite that recent model, Resolution 660 contains no comparable language seeking to ratify previously issued subpoenas. The resolution directs certain committees to "continue" investigations, and it specifies procedures to govern future hearings, but nothing in the resolution looks backward to actions previously taken. Accordingly, Resolution 660 did not ratify or otherwise authorize the

---

[37] Even if the House had sought to ratify a previously issued subpoena, it could give that subpoena only prospective effect. As discussed above, the Supreme Court has recognized that the House may not cite a witness for contempt for failure to comply with a subpoena unsupported by a valid delegation of authority at the time it was issued. *See Rumely*, 345 U.S. at 48; *see also Exxon*, 589 F.2d at 592 ("To issue a valid subpoena, . . . a committee or subcommittee must conform strictly to the resolution establishing its investigatory powers[.]").

impeachment-related subpoenas issued before October 31, which therefore still had no compulsory effect on their recipients.

IV.

Finally, we address some of the consequences that followed from our conclusion that the committees' pre-October 31 impeachment-related subpoenas were unauthorized. First, because the subpoenas exceeded the committees' investigative authority and lacked compulsory effect, the committees were mistaken in contending that the recipients' "failure or refusal to comply with the subpoena [would] constitute evidence of obstruction of the House's impeachment inquiry." Three Chairmen's Letter, *supra* note 2, at 1.[38] As explained at length above, when the subpoenas were issued, there was no valid impeachment inquiry. To the extent that the committees' subpoenas sought information in support of an unauthorized impeachment inquiry, the failure to comply with those subpoenas was no more punishable than were the failures of the witnesses in *Watkins, Rumely, Kilbourn,* and *Lamont* to answer questions that were beyond the scope of those committees' authorized jurisdiction. *See Watkins,* 354 U.S. at 206, 215 (holding that conviction for contempt of Congress was invalid because, when the witness failed to answer questions, the House had not used sufficient "care . . . in authorizing the use of compulsory process" and the committee had not shown that the information was pertinent to a subject within "the mission[] delegated to" it by the House); *Rumely,* 345 U.S. at 42–43, 48 (affirming reversal of conviction for contempt of Congress because it was not clear at the time of questioning that "the committee was authorized to exact the information which the witness withheld"); *Kilbourn,* 103 U.S. at 196 (sustaining action brought by witness for false imprisonment because the committee "had no lawful authority to require Kilbourn to testify as a witness beyond what he voluntarily chose to tell"); *Lamont,* 18 F.R.D. at 37 (dismissing indictment for contempt of Congress in part because the indictment did not sufficiently allege, among other things, "that the [Permanent Subcommittee on Investigations] . . . was duly empowered by either House of Congress to conduct the particular inquiry" or "that the inquiry was within the scope of the authority granted to the [sub]committee"). That alone suffices to prevent noncompliance with the subpoenas from constituting "obstruction of the House's impeachment inquiry."

Second, we note that whether or not the impeachment inquiry was authorized, there were other, independent grounds to support directions by the Executive Branch that witnesses not appear in response to the committees' subpoenas. We recently advised you that executive privilege continues to be available during an impeachment investigation. *See Exclusion of Agency Counsel from Congressional Depositions in the Impeachment Context,* 43 Op. O.L.C. __, at *2–5. The mere existence of an impeachment investigation does not eliminate the President's need for confidentiality in connection with the performance of his duties. Just as in the context of a criminal trial, a dispute over a request for privileged information in an impeachment investigation must be resolved in a manner that "preserves the essential functions of each branch." *United States v. Nixon,* 418 U.S. 683, 707 (1974). Thus, while a committee "may be able to establish an interest justifying its requests for information, the Executive Branch also has legitimate interests in confidentiality, and the resolution of these competing interests requires a

---

[38] The letters accompanying other subpoenas, *see supra* note 9, contained similar threats that the recipients' "failure or refusal to comply with the subpoena, including at the direction or behest of the President," would constitute "evidence of obstruction of the House's impeachment inquiry."

careful balancing of each branch's need in the context of the particular information sought." *Exclusion of Agency Counsel from Congressional Depositions in the Impeachment Context*, 43 Op. O.L.C. __, at *4.

Accordingly, we recognized, in connection with HPSCI's impeachment investigation after October 31, that the committee may not compel an executive branch witness to appear for a deposition without the assistance of agency counsel, when that counsel is necessary to assist the witness in ensuring the appropriate protection of privileged information during the deposition. *See id.* at *4–5. In addition, we have concluded that the testimonial immunity of the President's senior advisers "applies in an impeachment inquiry just as it applies in a legislative oversight inquiry." Letter for Pat A. Cipollone, Counsel to the President, from Steven A. Engel, Assistant Attorney General, Office of Legal Counsel at 2 (Nov. 3, 2019).

Thus, even when the House takes the steps necessary to authorize a committee to investigate impeachment and compel the production of needed information, the Executive Branch continues to have legitimate interests to protect. The Constitution does not oblige either branch of government to surrender its legitimate prerogatives, but expects that each branch will negotiate in good faith with mutual respect for the needs of the other branch. *See United States v. Am. Tel. & Tel. Co.*, 567 F.2d 121, 127 (D.C. Cir. 1977) ("[E]ach branch should take cognizance of an implicit constitutional mandate to seek optimal accommodation through a realistic evaluation of the needs of the conflicting branches in the particular fact situation."); *see also* Memorandum for the Heads of Executive Departments and Agencies from President Ronald Reagan, *Re: Procedures Governing Responses to Congressional Requests for Information* (Nov. 4, 1982). The two branches should work to identify arrangements in the context of the particular requests of an investigating committee that accommodate both the committee's needs and the Executive Branch's interests.

For these reasons, the House cannot plausibly claim that any executive branch official engaged in "obstruction" by failing to comply with committee subpoenas, or directing subordinates not to comply, in order to protect the Executive Branch's legitimate interests in confidentiality and the separation of powers. We explained thirty-five years ago that "the Constitution does not permit Congress to make it a crime for an official to assist the President in asserting a constitutional privilege that is an integral part of the President's responsibilities under the Constitution." *Prosecution for Contempt of Congress of an Executive Branch Official Who Has Asserted a Claim of Executive Privilege*, 8 Op. O.L.C. 101, 140 (1984). Nor may Congress "utilize its inherent 'civil' contempt powers to arrest, bring to trial, and punish an executive official who assert[s] a Presidential claim of executive privilege." *Id.* at 140 n.42. We have reaffirmed those fundamental conclusions in each of the subsequent decades.[39]

_____

[39] *See, e.g., Attempted Exclusion of Agency Counsel from Congressional Depositions of Agency Employees*, 43 Op. O.L.C. __, at *14 (May 23, 2019) ("[I]t would be unconstitutional to enforce a subpoena against an agency employee who declined to appear before Congress, at the agency's direction, because the committee would not permit an agency representative to accompany him."); *Testimonial Immunity Before Congress of the Former Counsel to the President*, 43 Op. O.L.C. __, at *20 (May 20, 2019) ("The constitutional separation of powers bars Congress from exercising its inherent contempt power in the face of a presidential assertion of executive privilege."); *Whether the Department of Justice May Prosecute White House Officials for Contempt of Congress*, 32 Op. O.L.C. 65, 65–69 (2008) (concluding that the Department cannot take "prosecutorial action, with respect to

The constitutionally required accommodation process, of course, is a two-way street. In connection with this investigation, the House committees took the unprecedented steps of investigating the impeachment of a President without any authorization from the full House; without the procedural protections provided to Presidents Nixon and Clinton, *see supra* note 12; and with express threats of obstruction charges and unconstitutional demands that officials appear and provide closed-door testimony about privileged matters without the assistance of executive branch counsel. Absent any effort by the House committees to accommodate the Executive Branch's legitimate concerns with the unprecedented nature of the committees' actions, it was reasonable for executive branch officials to decline to comply with the subpoenas addressed to them.

V.

For the reasons set forth above, we conclude that the House must expressly authorize a committee to conduct an impeachment investigation and to use compulsory process in that investigation before the committee may compel the production of documents or testimony in support of the House's "sole Power of Impeachment." U.S. Const. art. I, § 2, cl. 5. The House had not authorized such an investigation in connection with the impeachment-related subpoenas issued before October 31, 2019, and the subpoenas therefore had no compulsory effect. The House's adoption of Resolution 660 did not alter the legal status of those subpoenas, because the resolution did not ratify them or otherwise address their terms.

Please let us know if we may be of further assistance.

STEVEN A. ENGEL
Assistant Attorney General

---

current or former White House officials who . . . declined to appear to testify, in response to subpoenas from a congressional committee, based on the President's assertion of executive privilege"); *Application of 28 U.S.C. § 458 to Presidential Appointments of Federal Judges*, 19 Op. O.L.C. 350, 356 (1995) ("[T]he criminal contempt of Congress statute does not apply to the President or presidential subordinates who assert executive privilege."); *see also Authority of Agency Officials to Prohibit Employees from Providing Information to Congress*, 28 Op. O.L.C. 79, 80–82 (2004) (explaining that the Executive Branch has the constitutional authority to supervise its employees' disclosure of privileged and other information to Congress).

APPENDIX D:

LETTER OPINIONS FROM THE OFFICE OF LEGAL COUNSEL TO COUNSEL TO THE PRESIDENT REGARDING ABSOLUTE IMMUNITY OF THE ACTING CHIEF OF STAFF, LEGAL ADVISOR TO THE NATIONAL SECURITY COUNSEL, AND DEPUTY NATIONAL SECURITY ADVISOR

U.S. Department of Justice

Office of Legal Counsel

Office of the Assistant Attorney General

Washington, D.C. 20530

October 25, 2019

Pat A. Cipollone
Counsel to the President
The White House
Washington, DC 20500

Dear Mr. Cipollone:

Today, the Permanent Select Committee on Intelligence of the House of Representatives issued a subpoena seeking to compel Charles Kupperman, former Assistant to the President and Deputy National Security Advisor, to testify on Monday, October 28. The Committee subpoenaed Mr. Kupperman as part of its purported impeachment inquiry into the conduct of the President. The Administration has previously explained to the Committee that the House has not authorized an impeachment inquiry, and therefore, the Committee may not compel testimony in connection with the inquiry. Setting aside the question whether the inquiry has been lawfully authorized, you have asked whether the Committee may compel Mr. Kupperman to testify even assuming an authorized subpoena. We conclude that he is absolutely immune from compelled congressional testimony in his capacity as a former senior adviser to the President.

The Committee seeks Mr. Kupperman's testimony about matters related to his official duties at the White House. We understand that Committee staff informed Mr. Kupperman's private counsel that the Committee wishes to question him about the telephone call between President Trump and the President of Ukraine that took place on July 25, 2019, during Mr. Kupperman's tenure as a presidential adviser, and related matters. *See "Urgent Concern" Determination by the Inspector General of the Intelligence Community*, 43 Op. O.L.C. __, at *1–3 (Sept. 3, 2019) (discussing the July 25 telephone call).

The Department of Justice has for decades taken the position, and this Office recently reaffirmed, that "Congress may not constitutionally compel the President's senior advisers to testify about their official duties." *Testimonial Immunity Before Congress of the Former Counsel to the President*, 43 Op. O.L.C. __, at *1 (May 20, 2019) ("*Immunity of the Former Counsel*"). This testimonial immunity is rooted in the separation of powers and derives from the President's status as the head of a separate, co-equal branch of government. *See id.* at *3–7. Because the President's closest advisers serve as his alter egos, compelling them to testify would undercut the "independence and autonomy" of the Presidency, *id.* at *4, and interfere directly with the President's ability to faithfully discharge his responsibilities. Absent immunity, "congressional committees could wield their compulsory power to attempt to supervise the President's actions, or to harass those advisers in an effort to influence their conduct, retaliate for actions the committee disliked, or embarrass and weaken the President for partisan gain." *Immunity of the Assistant to the President and Director of the Office of Political Strategy and Outreach From Congressional Subpoena*, 38 Op. O.L.C. __, at *3 (July 15, 2014).

Congressional questioning of the President's senior advisers would also undermine the independence and candor of executive branch deliberations. *See Immunity of the Former Counsel*, 43 Op. O.L.C. at *5–7. Administrations of both political parties have insisted on the immunity of senior presidential advisers, which is critical to protect the institution of the Presidency. *Assertion of Executive Privilege with Respect to Clemency Decision*, 23 Op. O.L.C. 1, 5 (1999) (A.G. Reno).

Mr. Kupperman qualifies as a senior presidential adviser entitled to immunity. The testimonial immunity applies to the President's "immediate advisers—that is, those who customarily meet with the President on a regular or frequent basis." Memorandum for John D. Ehrlichman, Assistant to the President for Domestic Affairs, from William H. Rehnquist, Assistant Attorney General, Office of Legal Counsel, *Re: Power of Congressional Committee to Compel Appearance or Testimony of "White House Staff"* at 7 (Feb. 5, 1971). Your office has informed us that Mr. Kupperman served as the sole deputy to National Security Advisor John R. Bolton, and briefly served as Acting National Security Advisor after Mr. Bolton's departure. As Deputy National Security Advisor, Mr. Kupperman generally met with the President multiple times per week to advise him on a wide range of national security matters, and he met with the President even more often during the frequent periods when Mr. Bolton was traveling. Mr. Kupperman participated in sensitive internal deliberations with the President and other senior advisers, maintained an office in the West Wing of the White House, traveled with the President on official trips abroad on multiple occasions, and regularly attended the presentation of the President's Daily Brief and meetings of the National Security Council presided over by the President.

Mr. Kupperman's immunity from compelled testimony is strengthened because his duties concerned national security. The Supreme Court held in *Harlow v. Fitzgerald*, 457 U.S. 800 (1982), that senior presidential advisers do not enjoy absolute immunity from civil liability—a holding that, as we have previously explained, does not conflict with our recognition of absolute immunity from compelled congressional testimony for such advisers, *see, e.g., Immunity of the Former Counsel*, 43 Op. O.L.C. at *13–14. Yet the *Harlow* Court recognized that "[f]or aides entrusted with discretionary authority in such sensitive areas as national security or foreign policy," even absolute immunity from suit "might well be justified to protect the unhesitating performance of functions vital to the national interest." 457 U.S. at 812; *see also id.* at 812 n.19 ("a derivative claim to Presidential immunity would be strongest in such 'central' Presidential domains as foreign policy and national security, in which the President could not discharge his singularly vital mandate without delegating functions nearly as sensitive as his own").

Immunity is also particularly justified here because the Committee apparently seeks Mr. Kupperman's testimony about the President's conduct of relations with a foreign government. The President has the constitutional responsibility to conduct diplomatic relations, *see Assertion of Executive Privilege for Documents Concerning Conduct of Foreign Affairs with Respect to Haiti*, 20 Op. O.L.C. 5, 7 (1996) (A.G. Reno), and as a result, the President has the "exclusive authority to determine the time, scope, and objectives of international negotiations." *Unconstitutional Restrictions on Activities of the Office of Science and Technology Policy in Section 1340(a) of the Department of Defense and Full-Year Continuing Appropriations Act, 2011*, 35 Op. O.L.C. __, at *4 (Sept. 19, 2011) (quotation marks omitted). Compelling testimony about these sensitive constitutional responsibilities would only deepen the very concerns—about

2

separation of powers and confidentiality—that underlie the rationale for testimonial immunity. *See New York Times Co. v. United States,* 403 U.S. 713, 728 (1971) (Stewart, J., concurring) ("[I]t is elementary that the successful conduct of international diplomacy and the maintenance of an effective national defense require both confidentiality and secrecy.").

Finally, it is inconsequential that Mr. Kupperman is now a private citizen. In *Immunity of the Former Counsel*, we reaffirmed that for purposes of testimonial immunity, there is "no material distinction" between "current and former senior advisers to the President," and therefore, an adviser's departure from the White House staff "does not alter his immunity from compelled congressional testimony on matters related to his service to the President." 43 Op. O.L.C. at *16; *see also Immunity of the Former Counsel to the President from Compelled Congressional Testimony,* 31 Op. O.L.C. 191, 192–93 (2007). It is sufficient that the Committee seeks Mr. Kupperman's testimony on matters related to his official duties at the White House.

Please let us know if we may be of further assistance.

Steven A. Engel
Assistant Attorney General

U.S. Department of Justice

Office of Legal Counsel

Office of the Assistant Attorney General

Washington, D.C. 20530

November 3, 2019

Pat A. Cipollone
Counsel to the President
The White House
Washington, DC 20500

Dear Mr. Cipollone:

On November 1, 2019, the Permanent Select Committee on Intelligence of the House of Representatives issued a subpoena seeking to compel John Eisenberg to testify at a deposition on Monday, November 4. Mr. Eisenberg serves as Assistant to the President, Deputy Counsel to the President for National Security Affairs, and Legal Advisor to the National Security Council. The Committee subpoenaed Mr. Eisenberg as part of its impeachment inquiry into the conduct of the President. *See* H.R. Res. 660, 116th Cong. (2019). You have asked whether the Committee may compel Mr. Eisenberg to testify. We conclude that he is absolutely immune from compelled congressional testimony in his capacity as a senior adviser to the President.

The Committee has made clear that it seeks to question Mr. Eisenberg about matters related to his official duties at the White House. The Committee informed him that it is investigating the President's conduct of foreign relations with Ukraine and that it believes, "[b]ased upon public reporting and evidence gathered as part of the impeachment inquiry," that Mr. Eisenberg has "information relevant to these matters." Letter for John Eisenberg from Adam B. Schiff, Chairman, House Permanent Select Committee on Intelligence, et al. at 1 (Oct. 30, 2019); *see also* Letter for John Eisenberg from Adam B. Schiff, Chairman, House Permanent Select Committee on Intelligence, et al. at 1 (Nov. 1, 2019).

The Executive Branch has taken the position for decades that "Congress may not constitutionally compel the President's senior advisers to testify about their official duties." *Testimonial Immunity Before Congress of the Former Counsel to the President*, 43 Op. O.L.C. __, at *1 (May 20, 2019) ("*Immunity of the Former Counsel*"). This testimonial immunity is rooted in the separation of powers and derives from the President's status as the head of a separate, co-equal branch of government. *See id.* at *3–7. Because the President's closest advisers serve as his alter egos, compelling them to testify would undercut the "independence and autonomy" of the Presidency, *id.* at *4, and interfere directly with the President's ability to faithfully discharge his constitutional responsibilities. Absent immunity, "congressional committees could wield their compulsory power to attempt to supervise the President's actions, or to harass those advisers in an effort to influence their conduct, retaliate for actions the committee disliked, or embarrass and weaken the President for partisan gain." *Immunity of the Assistant to the President and Director of the Office of Political Strategy and Outreach From Congressional Subpoena*, 38 Op. O.L.C. __, at *3 (July 15, 2014) ("*Immunity of the Assistant to the President*"). Congressional questioning of the President's senior advisers would also undermine the independence and candor of executive branch deliberations. *See Immunity of the Former Counsel*, 43 Op. O.L.C. at *5 7. For these reasons, the Executive Branch has long recognized the immunity of senior presidential advisers to be critical to protecting the institution of the Presidency.

This testimonial immunity applies in an impeachment inquiry just as it applies in a legislative oversight inquiry. As our Office recently advised you, executive privilege remains available when a congressional committee conducts an impeachment investigation. *See* Letter for Pat A. Cipollone, Counsel to the President, from Steven A. Engel, Assistant Attorney General, Office of Legal Counsel at 2 & n.1 (Nov. 1, 2019). The testimonial immunity of senior presidential advisers is "broader" than executive privilege and exists in part to prevent the inadvertent disclosure of privileged information, *Immunity of the Former Counsel*, 43 Op. O.L.C. at *4, *6, so it follows that testimonial immunity also continues to apply in the impeachment context. More importantly, the commencement of an impeachment inquiry only heightens the need to safeguard the separation of powers and preserve the "independence and autonomy" of the Presidency the principal concerns underlying testimonial immunity. *Id.* at *4. Even when impeachment proceedings are underway, the President must remain able to continue to discharge the duties of his office. The testimonial immunity of the President's senior advisers remains an important limitation to protect the independence and autonomy of the President himself.

We do not doubt that there may be impeachment investigations in which the House will have a legitimate need for information possessed by the President's senior advisers, but the House may have a legitimate need in a legislative oversight inquiry. In both instances, the testimonial immunity of the President's senior advisers will not prevent the House from obtaining information from other available sources. The immunity of those immediate advisers will not itself prevent the House from obtaining testimony from others in the Executive Branch, including in the White House, or from obtaining pertinent documents (although the House may still need to overcome executive privilege with respect to testimony and documents to which the privilege applies). In addition, the President may choose to authorize his senior advisers to provide testimony because "the benefit of providing such testimony as an accommodation to a committee's interests outweighs the potential for harassment and harm to Executive Branch confidentiality." *Immunity of the Assistant to the President*, 38 Op. O.L.C. at *4 n.2. Accordingly, our recognition that the immunity applies to an impeachment inquiry does not preclude the House from obtaining information from other sources.

We next consider whether Mr. Eisenberg qualifies as a senior presidential adviser. The testimonial immunity applies to the President's "immediate advisers that is, those who customarily meet with the President on a regular or frequent basis." Memorandum for John D. Ehrlichman, Assistant to the President for Domestic Affairs, from William H. Rehnquist, Assistant Attorney General, Office of Legal Counsel, *Re: Power of Congressional Committee to Compel Appearance or Testimony of "White House Staff"* at 7 (Feb. 5, 1971). We believe that Mr. Eisenberg meets that definition. Mr. Eisenberg has served as an adviser to the President on sensitive legal and national security matters since the first day of the Administration, and his direct relationship with the President has grown over time. Your office has informed us that he regularly meets with the President multiple times each week, frequently in very small groups, and often communicates with the President multiple times per day. He is one of a small number of advisers who are authorized to contact the President directly, and the President directly seeks his advice. Mr. Eisenberg is therefore the kind of immediate presidential adviser that the Executive Branch has historically considered immune from compelled congressional testimony.

Mr. Eisenberg's eligibility for immunity is particularly justified because his duties concern national security. The Supreme Court held in *Harlow v. Fitzgerald*, 457 U.S. 800 (1982), that senior presidential advisers do not enjoy absolute immunity from civil liability—a holding that, as we have previously explained, does not conflict with our recognition of absolute immunity from compelled congressional testimony for such advisers, *see Immunity of the Assistant to the President*, 38 Op. O.L.C. at *5–9. Yet the *Harlow* Court recognized that "[f]or aides entrusted with discretionary authority in such sensitive areas as national security or foreign policy," even absolute immunity from suit "might well be justified to protect the unhesitating performance of functions vital to the national interest." 457 U.S. at 812; *see also id.* at 812 n.19 ("a derivative claim to Presidential immunity would be strongest in such 'central' Presidential domains as foreign policy and national security, in which the President could not discharge his singularly vital mandate without delegating functions nearly as sensitive as his own").

Moreover, the Committee seeks Mr. Eisenberg's testimony about the President's conduct of relations with a foreign government. The President has the constitutional responsibility to conduct diplomatic relations, *see Assertion of Executive Privilege for Documents Concerning Conduct of Foreign Affairs with Respect to Haiti*, 20 Op. O.L.C. 5, 7 (1996) (A.G. Reno), and as a result, the President has the "exclusive authority to determine the time, scope, and objectives of international negotiations." *Unconstitutional Restrictions on Activities of the Office of Science and Technology Policy in Section 1340(a) of the Department of Defense and Full-Year Continuing Appropriations Act, 2011*, 35 Op. O.L.C. __, at *4 (Sept. 19, 2011) (quotation marks omitted). Compelling testimony about these sensitive constitutional responsibilities would only deepen the very concerns—about separation of powers and confidentiality—that underlie the rationale for testimonial immunity. *See New York Times Co. v. United States*, 403 U.S. 713, 728 (1971) (Stewart, J., concurring) ("[I]t is elementary that the successful conduct of international diplomacy and the maintenance of an effective national defense require both confidentiality and secrecy.").

Please let us know if we may be of further assistance.

Steven A. Engel
Assistant Attorney General

U.S. Department of Justice

Office of Legal Counsel

Office of the Assistant Attorney General   *Washington, D.C. 20530*

November 7, 2019

Pat A. Cipollone
Counsel to the President
The White House
Washington, DC 20500

Dear Mr. Cipollone:

On November 7, 2019, the Permanent Select Committee on Intelligence of the House of Representatives issued a subpoena seeking to compel Mick Mulvaney, Assistant to the President and Acting White House Chief of Staff, to testify at a deposition on Friday, November 8. The Committee subpoenaed Mr. Mulvaney as part of its impeachment inquiry into the conduct of the President. *See* H.R. Res. 660, 116th Cong. (2019). You have asked whether the Committee may compel him to testify. We conclude that Mr. Mulvaney is absolutely immune from compelled congressional testimony in his capacity as a senior adviser to the President.

The Executive Branch has taken the position for decades that "Congress may not constitutionally compel the President's senior advisers to testify about their official duties." *Testimonial Immunity Before Congress of the Former Counsel to the President*, 43 Op. O.L.C. __, at *1 (May 20, 2019). The immunity applies to those "immediate advisers . . . who customarily meet with the President on a regular or frequent basis." Memorandum for John D. Ehrlichman, Assistant to the President for Domestic Affairs, from William H. Rehnquist, Assistant Attorney General, Office of Legal Counsel, *Re: Power of Congressional Committee to Compel Appearance or Testimony of "White House Staff"* at 7 (Feb. 5, 1971) ("Rehnquist Memorandum"). We recently advised you that this immunity applies in an impeachment inquiry just as in a legislative oversight inquiry. *See* Letter for Pat A. Cipollone, Counsel to the President, from Steven A. Engel, Assistant Attorney General, Office of Legal Counsel at 2 (Nov. 3, 2019). "Even when impeachment proceedings are underway," we explained, "the President must remain able to continue to discharge the duties of his office. The testimonial immunity of the President's senior advisers remains an important limitation to protect the independence and autonomy of the President himself." *Id.*

This immunity applies in connection with the Committee's subpoena for Mr. Mulvaney's testimony. The Committee intends to question Mr. Mulvaney about matters related to his official duties at the White House—specifically the President's conduct of foreign relations with Ukraine. *See* Letter for Mick Mulvaney from Adam B. Schiff, Chairman, House Permanent Select Committee on Intelligence, et al. (Nov. 5, 2019). And Mr. Mulvaney, as Acting Chief of Staff, is a "top presidential adviser[]," *In re Sealed Case*, 121 F.3d 729, 757 (D.C. Cir. 1997), who works closely with the President in supervising the staff within the Executive Office of the President and managing the advice the President receives. *See* David B. Cohen & Charles E. Walcott, White House Transition Project, Report 2017-21, *The Office of Chief of Staff* 15–26

(2017). Mr. Mulvaney meets with and advises the President on a daily basis about the most sensitive issues confronting the government. Thus, he readily qualifies as an "immediate adviser[]" who may not be compelled to testify before Congress. Rehnquist Memorandum at 7.

This conclusion also follows from this Office's prior recognition that certain *Deputy* White House Chiefs of Staff were immune from compelled congressional testimony. *See* Letter for Pat A. Cipollone, Counsel to the President, from Steven A. Engel, Assistant Attorney General, Office of Legal Counsel (Sept. 16, 2019) (former Deputy Chief of Staff for Policy Implementation Rick Dearborn); Letter for Fred F. Fielding, Counsel to the President, from Steven G. Bradbury, Principal Deputy Assistant Attorney General, Office of Legal Counsel (Aug. 1, 2007) (Deputy White House Chief of Staff Karl Rove). In addition, as we have noted with respect to other recently issued subpoenas, testimonial immunity is particularly justified because the Committee seeks Mr. Mulvaney's testimony about the President's conduct of relations with a foreign government. *See, e.g.,* Letter for Pat A. Cipollone, Counsel to the President, from Steven A. Engel, Assistant Attorney General, Office of Legal Counsel at 2–3 (Oct. 25, 2019); *see also Harlow v. Fitzgerald*, 457 U.S. 800, 812 n.19 (1982) ("[A] derivative claim to Presidential immunity would be strongest in such 'central' Presidential domains as foreign policy and national security, in which the President could not discharge his singularly vital mandate without delegating functions nearly as sensitive as his own.").

Please let us know if we may be of further assistance.

Steven A. Engel
Assistant Attorney General